G000161461

Hospitality, Tourism an
Management: Issu
Strategy and Culture

A selection of related titles published by Cassell

Marketing in Hospitality and Tourism
Teare, Mazanec, Crawford-Welch and Calver

Managing Projects in Hospitality Organizations
Teare, Adams and Messenger

Hotel and Food Service Marketing
Francis Buttle

Management of Foodservice Operations
Peter Jones with Paul Merricks

Principles of Hotel Front Office Operations
Baker, Bradley and Huyton

Achieving Quality Performance
Teare, Atkinson and Westwood

The Franchise Paradox
Stuart Price

The International Hospitality Business
Kotas, Teare, Logie, Jayawardena and Bowen

Small Business Management
Boer, Thomas and Webster

An up-to-date catalogue of the full range of Hospitality and Tourism titles is available from the publisher.

HOSPITALITY, TOURISM AND LEISURE MANAGEMENT: ISSUES IN STRATEGY AND CULTURE

Edited by

MALCOLM FOLEY
J. JOHN LENNON
GILLIAN A. MAXWELL

CASSELL

Cassell

Wellington House
125 Strand
London WC2R 0BB

PO Box 605
Herndon
VA 20172

© the editors and contributors 1997

All rights reserved. No part of this publication may be reproduced or transmitted in any form or by any means, electronic or mechanical, including photocopying, recording or any information storage or retrieval system, without permission in writing from the publishers or their appointed agents.

First published in 1997

British Library Cataloguing-in-Publication Data
A catalogue record for this book is available from the British Library.

ISBN   0-304-33237-2 (hardback)
          0-304-33239-9 (paperback)

Typeset by: B.G. Partners, Polegate, East Sussex
Printed and bound in Great Britain by Bookcraft (Bath) Ltd.

Contents

Contributors

EDITORS

Malcolm Foley is a reader in the Department of Hospitality, Tourism and Leisure Management, Glasgow Caledonian University, Scotland, UK. His career in education, research and consultancy for the leisure/tourism industries spans 20 years which have included connections with public, commercial and voluntary sector agencies. His current research interests are in marketing and consumerism in leisure/tourism, public sector policies for leisure/tourism, the relationships between the retail and leisure sectors and voluntarism in leisure/tourism labour markets.

J. John Lennon is Senior Lecturer in Hospitality Management, Department of Hospitality, Tourism and Leisure Management, Glasgow Caledonian University, Scotland, UK. He has particular responsibility for consultancy spanning hospitality, tourism and leisure spheres. His specialist consultancy is in tourism development in Eastern and Central Europe and attraction management. His main research interests are in dark tourism, retailing and tourism, and the privatization of the tourism industry in Eastern/ Central Europe.

Gillian A. Maxwell is Senior Lecturer (Human Resource Management), Department of Hospitality, Tourism and Leisure Management, Glasgow Caledonian University, Scotland, UK. She researches principally in the contexts of the UK hospitality and retail industries on issues related to the organizational contribution of employee management. Her published works include issues such as quality management, employee motivation and relationship marketing.

AUTHORS

Gillian Broome lectures in Ethics at Ecolé Supérieure De Commerce De La Rochelle, La Rochelle Cedex, France. She is currently researching into the stereo-typing of sex roles in television advertising, comparing the UK with France.

Richard Brush is based at Johnson and Wales University, Rhode Island, USA, where he holds a Professor's chair.

Chris Bull is Principal Lecturer and Director of the Centre for Tourism and Leisure Studies at Canterbury Christ Church College, England, UK. He is currently researching in the area of countryside recreation and rural tourism, and the role of voluntary groups in countryside management. In the last few years he has also undertaken various social surveys concerned with public attitudes to community forests.

Paul Goodale is a member of the management team of the Hyatt Carlton Tower Hotel, London, England, UK. He combines this role with research into organizational culture.

Jay Kandampully PhD is a senior lecturer in Services and Hotel Management at the Department of Economics and Marketing, Lincoln University, New Zealand. His particular research interests are service quality management, services marketing, total quality management, service innovation, service orientation and hotel and tourism management.

David Litteljohn is a Professor at the Department of Hospitality, Tourism and Leisure Management, Glasgow Caledonian University, Scotland, UK. His research specializes in international aspects of hospitality and tourism in relation to industry structure and competition.

Rosemary Lucas is Senior Lecturer at the Department of Hotel, Catering and Tourism Management, The Manchester Metropolitan University, England, UK. She specializes in research and consultancy in human resources management and industrial/employee relations. In particular, she focuses on employment policies and practices, the management of the employment relationship and labour market issues in hospitality, tourism and retailing. Her current projects include the employment of student labour, pay policy on minimum wages, individual employment rights and the nature of industrial relations.

L. Rory MacLellan is a lecturer in Tourism at the Scottish Hotel School, University of Strathclyde, Glasgow, Scotland, UK. His research interests include tourism and the natural environment, sustainable development and tourism, rural tourism, public policy and tourism in Scotland, public transport and tourism.

Gayle McPherson is Programme Leader of Leisure Management at the Department of Hospitality, Tourism and Leisure Management, Glasgow Caledonian University, Scotland, UK. Her research interests are changing public policies in the cultural services, especially when these are associated with a growth in income generation via retailing and other consumer services.

Dennis Nickson lectures in Hotel Management at the Scottish Hotel School, University of Strathclyde, Glasgow, Scotland, UK. His research interests are international and domestic human resource management and global strategy in the hospitality industry.

Susan M. Ogden is based at the Department of Hospitality, Tourism and Leisure Management, Glasgow Caledonian University, Scotland, UK. She has recently completed a PhD on compulsory competitive tendering in local government. Her current research interest lies in the strategic management of ancillary services with particular focus on the implications of compulsory competitive tendering in the public sector and the convergence debate in the public and private sector.

Michael Riley, PhD is a Senior Lecturer in Management Studies at the Department of Management Studies, University of Surrey, England, UK. He is a researcher and author in organizational behaviour and labour market behaviourism.

Sandra Watson, is a Senior Lecturer at the Department of Hospitality and Tourism Management, Napier University, Edinburgh, Scotland, UK. She researches principally in management development in hospitality and tourism, and in training and development evaluation. Her consultancy interests are training and skills analysis.

Roy C. Wood is Professor of Hospitality Management and Head of Department at the Scottish Hotel School, University of Strathclyde, Glasgow, Scotland, UK. His extensive research and consultancy work centre on human resource management, and he also publishes on aspects of food habits and the history of hospitality management.

Preface

The hospitality, tourism and leisure industries have become increasingly important in terms of economies and employment throughout the world. Service industries *per se* are increasingly important to developed economies and have taken their place as leading sectors in post-industrial society (Bell, 1973). Tourism is now recognized as the world's largest industry and generator of jobs (World Travel and Tourism Council, 1995). As an industry, tourism accounted for some 212 million jobs in 1995, one in nine of all full-time employment positions in the world. It is estimated that by 2005 this will have grown to 338 million, one in eight. In terms of output, the Gross Domestic Product (GDP) from tourism is currently standing at 10.9 per cent of the world GDP, estimated to rise to 11.4 per cent by 2005 (WTTC, 1995).

The strategic and economic importance of tourism and its centrality to an understanding of sustainable development practices and environmental considerations is pivotal to an understanding of strategy and culture in this area. As a key employer, both in the developing and developed world, understanding of this complex area underpins its effective management. The sophisticated techniques and practices in developed tourism industries are central to the contributions found in this book.

A central feature of post-industrial economies is the growth of leisure time as a result of the surpluses created by industrial production. This is displayed in an overall increase in disposable incomes attached to increased opportunities for leisure provided by emerging service sectors. Motivations for leisure consumption include pursuit of apparent freedom on the part of the recipients, whereas for providers in public, private and voluntary sectors, the key issues are often either profitability or the increase of health and moral well-being. Mass leisure is undoubtedly a feature of late-twentieth-century economies, but cannot be isolated or insulated from wider social, political and economic changes. Nor could hospitality, tourism or leisure industries be expected to have escaped the consideration of academics studying in the field of management and strategy. As markets have become apparently more sophisticated in leisure consumption, providers and users alike have developed concerns which transcend profitability and moral well-being and encompass ethical dilemmas inherent in consumption. Examples include sustainability, the quality of the service being delivered, together with the relationship between that and the success of the enterprise, the role of privatization and competitiveness, both in public sectors in Western Europe and their changing organizational cultures in emerging economies in Eastern Europe. In addition, the role of people in the efficient and effective delivery of these services has become a critical issue for academic study and managerial practice.

The hospitality industry has become a truly global industry. A critically important employer in many countries world-wide, it has become the subject of increasingly detailed analysis as an international/global phenomenon (for example, Teare and Olsen, 1992 and Jones and Pizam, 1992). Strategic analysis of the hospitality industry is becoming more sophisticated and recent work in this area (for example, Go and Pine, 1995) recognizes the centrality of human resources, organizational change, competition and information technology in building competitive advantage. An understanding of the hospitality industry provides a firm foundation and an illustrative example for understanding the macro-issues of leisure and tourism development. Hospitality provides, in many cases, the working example of an industry dealing with issues of sustainability, competition, quality enhancement and globalization. It provides a useful contrast to the work conducted in public sector and private sector leisure facilities, but also throws up interesting analogies in the form of work on motivation, empowerment and flexibility.

This book considers many of these dilemmas in the key critical areas dealt with by these industries. The editors take the position that any attempt to separately define or delineate these industries is doomed to failure. The issues of strategy and culture that are dealt with invariably cross industry boundaries. Issues such as management development, globalization and quality cut across concepts of leisure as well as industries such as hospitality and tourism. What is being attempted here, is a set of workable issues-based papers, that will help to inform management decision-making and develop awareness through illustration of emergent values and issues within the hospitality, tourism and leisure industries.

Key themes emerging in the strategic management of hospitality, tourism and leisure, relate to the development of the nature of these services themselves. These arise from fundamental internal and external pressures, whether these be from local Agenda 21 or the changing nature of multi-national corporations. Principal among these have been both consumer and producer sensitivity to the sustainability of the resources which support leisure and tourism. Sitting alongside these dilemmas have been the moral considerations attached to the production and consumption of leisure and tourism opportunities and the concomitant implications for management. Just as widely, but in a different context, the internationalization of markets – especially in the hospitality sector – has been a key feature of strategic growth in the area. As these themes have emerged and influenced the nature of the services under discussion, so managers and strategists have considered the appropriateness of delivery mechanisms. Principal among these have been the emergence of preoccupations with quality in service delivery, especially in aspects of human resources management and relationship marketing. However, alongside these considerations, whole economies in Eastern Europe and public sectors in Western Europe, have turned to the market as the principal rationing mechanism for leisure and tourism goods and services. As a consequence, bodies which had previously delivered services under a 'welfare' rationale, now see themselves in competition with each other and consequently seek strategies to ensure that services can be delivered with quality, but also to secure an advantage over other alternative possibilities for consumers.

Emergent Themes

Section 1 of this book opens with a consideration of work on quality aspects in the tourism and hospitality industries. Kandampully (Chapter 1) looks at the critical importance of service quality management in the tourism industry. His work focuses on perceptions of quality and aspects of measuring service performance. International examples of service delivery systems are explained and a critique is advanced of some aspects of quality management. His model of dynamic systems of service delivery provides a useful pointer for the hospitality and tourism industries into the next century. The work of Brush (Chapter 2), focusing on quality in the US hospitality sector, is pertinent since, in that country, quality has become – like in many parts of the world – a key aspect of developing and sustaining competitive advantage. Brush examines the origins of the work on quality from Deming and early applications in the Japanese context through to application in the USA, particularly in the hospitality sector. Significant areas of evaluation include the all too rarely examined cost implications of quality management systems, the importance of team building and the centrality of human resources to such forms of management. In order to illustrate the centrality of planning, evaluation and primacy of the customer, a case analysis of Ritz Carlton is utilized to illustrate an exemplar of quality in the USA hospitality industry. A final contribution on quality comes from Goodale and Wood (Chapter 3) who attempt to debunk some of the clichés of quality and 'excellence' associated with some of the more superficial work in this area. The importance of the bottom line, return on investment, equity returns and the centrality of share performance is advanced as the real reason underlying the need to develop quality systems in order to maintain leading position(s) and earnings. A practical review of luxury hotels is examined as a pertinent sector for the operation of quality management systems and the significance of understanding and developing cultures is reviewed. Goodale and Wood consider the operation of quality in terms of organizational attitudes and approach as intimated in mission statements, organization structure, use of language, forms of improvement, appraisal and staff motivation. They conclude that quality will be central to any understanding of hospitality and tourism management for the future. However, the centrality of understanding culture and exploiting techniques and practices of cultural management, though complex and intangible, are perhaps central to future organizational success.

The authors in Section 2 centre their analyses around the role of human resource management strategies in delivering organizational performance, predominantly in the hospitality industries. Nevertheless, the lessons learned in commercial hospitality operations are certainly appropriate for those working in tourism and leisure. Maxwell (Chapter 4) points to changes in organizations' environments which have precipitated human resource management responses: more sophisticated buying behaviour, shortages of skilled labour, increased use of information technology, emergence of fierce competition and the search for quality and value among consumers. These themes are repeated throughout the chapters in this section, and, indeed, elsewhere in the volume. Maxwell advocates the use of employee empowerment as a strategic response, particularly when this is integrated within the totality of organizational culture. Thus, she considers empowerment as a holistic phenomenon and provides a case study which explores this approach. Similarly, Watson (Chapter 5) argues for the analysis of management development in a holistic way. As a complex process emerging from changing business performance, recession, demographic implications of ageing populations in Western Europe together with government intervention and internationalization, she argues that many organizations feel the need to develop more flexible human resource management strategies to achieve performance. Issues of training and education, particularly in relation to new entrants to the hospitality industry, are examined as a critical feature in securing long term viability and productivity enhancement. In addition, Watson cites examples of workers (i.e. young workers and older workers), both of whom are emerging as keys to the new flexibility in hospitality industries. This flexibility is developed further by Lucas (Chapter 6) in her consideration of the use of part-time workers, especially vocational students, in the hospitality industries. In particular, she considers implications of adopting the use of part-time workers as an organizational strategy and poses the question of whether, indeed, strategy or pragmatism is the appropriate description for current hospitality industry responses.

The authors in Section 3 consider issues of strategic change, generally from the perspective of moving from an instrumental towards an entrepreneurial approach. Ogden (Chapter 7) considers the implications of moving from a public sector culture (broadly public administration) to contracting out (broadly public management) in UK hospitality and leisure services. In particular, she identifies the extent to which public services in these industries have been open to emerging competitive environments and the implications of this for organizational fabric and human resource management approaches. The latter is examined in respect of changing operational work practices, most especially in the shift from so-called 'professional' values towards more managerialist models in what is known as the 'enabling authority'. McPherson (Chapter 8) examines similar issues, although contracting out is not yet present in museums in the UK. A professional model of curatorship in British museums is slowly giving way to more entrepreneurial approaches associated with entertainment and popular culture leisure, rather than the Victorian idea of the educative element of museums as rational recreation. McPherson advocates relationship marketing as an approach which can help bridge the gap between these two sets of values. In a broader context, Riley (Chapter 9) considers the implications for service workers in Eastern European economies where significant changes in economics and politics have led to the increased consumption of tourism and hospitality. The implication for businesses in hospitality and tourism has been that expectations of those who consume the services is rather different from the norms of service delivery associated with pre-liberalization days. In particular, Riley contrasts the notions of service and servility, and cites the importance of organizational culture in supporting more entrepreneurial roles for those at the 'sharp end' of delivery.

Ethical dilemmas in hospitality, tourism and leisure practices are receiving considerably more attention in the late twentieth century than ever before. The work of the authors in Section 4 into this area, is central to an understanding of issues of taste, expediency and motivation in terms of tourism. Foley and Lennon (Chapter 10) examine the ethics and motivations of 'dark tourism'. Dark elements of popular culture provide the focus for a number of either real or created attractions. Such 'death and disaster' sites provide sensation and spectacle for visitors/tourists and remain popular as attractions despite their negative connotations. This creates ethical dilemmas for operators and managers of such sites in terms of return on investment, interpretation and associated income generation activities, as well as the problems of immediacy of interpretation at some more notorious sites. The authors attempt to detail some of the ethical dilemmas that face tourism administrators and attraction developers in this field. Broome (Chapter 11) deals with practical ethical issues faced by managers in the hospitality and tourism sector. She considers dilemmas of service and blame culture as aspects of ethical management in commercial environments. The fieldwork considers majority 'good' and teleological approaches; the author provides useful recommendations on how ethical practices can be translated to the workplace and the commercial context.

The authors in Section 5 explore the concept of sustainability from different angles. MacLellan (Chapter 12) provides a strong case for a move away from idealism in the debates about sustainability towards 'hard' strategy and policy initiatives. In particular he argues for mass alternative tourism, rejuvenation of existing resorts and further statutory, legislative powers. In addition, he suggests that the tourism industry would be more likely to adopt sustainability if there was to be an instrumental imperative attached to its adoption. Bull (Chapter 13) contends that leisure sustainability differs, at least in part, from arguments about sustainability regularly propounded in the context of tourism. He too explores the role of public policy, especially that emanating from 'New Right' thinking and analyses approaches to both pricing the outdoors and valuing the environment. In particular he sees, and quantifies, the possibilities for community involvement as a strategy for sustainability in the outdoor leisure industries.

In Section 6 the work of Nickson and Litteljohn explores aspects of internationalization and globalization. This has been an area which has received considerable attention in the hospitality, tourism and leisure areas. Work in the field tends to focus upon application of strategic theory, growth of multinationals and analysis of dominant models of performance. Nickson (Chapter 14) is particularly interesting in this respect, since he attempts to detail the rise and fall of the US model of management practice in multi-national hotels and its consequent importance in the tourism and leisure industries. The dominance of the USA as a major player in world tourism product provision is well known. This author looks at the advantages and disadvantages of standardization in managerialism and in product quality. The decline and decrease in significance of American management and American hotel internationalization is theorized. The increasing role of European and South East Asian operators bringing with them new developments in management and quality is also considered.

Litteljohn (Chapter 15) reviews the mature market conditions faced by hotel chains and considers how economies of scale will favour growth scenarios. Strategic analysis of chain development is subject to rigorous analysis and the management imperatives of hotel chains are critically evaluated. Litteljohn argues that on the one hand, chain development will shift operations delivery from a core focus to a core requirement. Included with operations, the areas of asset management, technology management and marketing management will become increasingly important in terms of planning. The chapter goes on to explore the nature of strategic decisions in this context, focusing on the different organizational arrangements that will occur in chains such as: franchise, management contract, and consortium membership. It is proposed that chains will need to consider their competitive advantages closely, and that this is likely to make chains more differentiated.

Clearly the variety and range of these contributions and their organizational contexts are indicative that in the practical context, the boundaries between hospitality, tourism and leisure are more imagined than real. Strategy by definition should be cross-sectoral and in this respect, this book should aid understanding and promote new approaches both across and within a range of fields.

M. FOLEY, J. LENNON, G. MAXWELL
Glasgow 1997

REFERENCES

Bell, D. (1973) *The Coming of Post-Industrial Society: A Venture in Social Forecasting* New York: Basic Books.

Go, F. and Pine, R. (1995) *Globalization Strategy in the Hotel Industry* London: Routledge.

Jones, P. and Pizam, A. (eds) (1992) *The International Hospitality Industry Organisational and Operational Issues* London: Pitman Publishing.

Teare, R. and Olsen, M. (1992) *International Hospitality Management – Corporate Strategy in Practice* London: Pitman Publishing.

World Travel and Tourism Council (1995) *The 1995 WTTC Report – Research Edition* Oxford: Pergamon.

SECTION ONE
QUALITY

1

Quality Service in Tourism

Jay Kandampully

The focus of this chapter is an analysis of the concepts and nature of service in the tourism industry. Key variables affecting the quality of service are discussed. To facilitate effective service quality improvement, a dynamic and systematic model – Process Flow in Dynamic Service Quality – is proposed.

INTRODUCTION

Tourism has become a major component of economic development in many countries and regions throughout the world. Forecasts of continued growth (WTO, 1990) for the tourism industry beyond the turn of this century have attracted much attention world-wide. Tourism, typically a service industry, is considered by many nations as a crucial component of economic development (Shaw and Williams, 1990). The proponents of tourism assert its potential to create and support employment and generate local income. Thus in many countries we see local and federal government agencies actively encouraging tourism-related entrepreneurial undertakings. This has resulted in an ever increasing number of individuals and organizations venturing into tourism-related services.

However, many who enter tourism-related businesses often have limited experience and understanding of the service product they undertake to offer. The tourism product is essentially both subjective and intangible in nature and hence service managers may fail to see the tourism product within the holistic perspective that they would apply to a tangible product. This can result in an inability to focus on a deep-rooted understanding of the finer components and lack of professional approach to the management of their organization.

In common with tangible products, a service product also needs to be designed with consideration to the different processes involved in its production (Kandampully, 1993b). Tourism services may be defined as an assemblage of diverse individual services. To the tourist, however, they represent an 'experience'. Hence a detailed understanding of the holistic perspective of the offering is essential to manage tourism services effectively.

From the middle of the last decade we have witnessed a gradual change in the patterns of tourism consumption world-wide. These changes have had a marked influence on tourism related sectors in the western hemisphere since the early 1990s. A massive shift in people's value structure has emerged. What we see now is a paradigm shift from the traditional sun, sea and amusement perspective of tourism, to one of knowledge seeking: cultural, environmental and educational tourism. Thus fundamental changes are occurring in the tourism market with the development of new patterns of tourism consumption (Krippendorf, 1987a,b). Additionally it is expected that the influence of technology, demographics, lifestyle patterns, etc., will dramatically alter the tourism industry by the turn of the century (Goeldner, 1992). Socio-demographic changes and high spending powers have also created a change in tourists' values (Hall and Weiler, 1992). Tourists today are highly critical of the quality of service. Prompted by the influences of a competitive marketplace, they are unwilling to compromise themselves to a mediocre service. The already turbulent tourism business now faces a powerful new wave of 'service' expectation, or more specifically an intense preoccupation with the 'quality of service'.

PREMISE OF QUALITY

Traditionally, quality which had been developed in manufacturing by engineers and statisticians focused on goods (Gummesson, 1992). Quality was introduced into services literature at the beginning of the 1980s. The main emphasis of services at that time was on marketing, or rather, marketing orientation. Additionally, traditional marketing models do not consider quality as an integral marketing component. Thus quality concepts or quality management models were not addressed in product marketing. Indeed, quality was more or less treated as a given variable (Gronroos, 1992) since it was considered a production engineer's responsibility. Interest in service quality came predominantly from services marketing research where it was recognized as distinct from that of product marketing.

Service marketers identified numerous characteristics unique to services including intangibility, inseparability of production and consumption, heterogeneity, and perishability. These unique features directed them to address the managerial challenges of services. Given the inappropriateness of adopting tangible product management concepts in services, a new concept had to be developed very much from scratch. Based on the unique characteristics and its recognition of customers' perceptions of quality in services, quality concepts were founded and developed from models of consumer behaviour.

FACTORS AFFECTING QUALITY IN A SERVICE INTERFACE

Although it is currently well accepted that service quality is crucial to the success of any service organization, there are no uniformly accepted definitions of service quality. Defining quality in services is especially difficult because of the intangible nature of the service offering. Brown *et al.* (1991) are of the view that definition of quality may vary from person to person, and from situation to situation. Furthermore, they argue that the critical time for service quality to be clearly defined, is in the one to one interactions that occur between the consumer and the provider. According to Parasuraman *et al.* (1985), service quality is an abstract and illusive construct because of three features unique to services:

- intangibility;
- heterogeneity; and
- the inseparability of production and consumption.

Kandampully (1993c) argues that, in addition, service quality is progressive in nature, rendering it difficult to conceptualize.

Intangibility

One of the unique features universally cited by authors (e.g. Bateson, 1977; Berry, 1980; Lovelock, 1981; Rathmell, 1966, 1974; Shostack, 1977) is intangibility. They suggest that most services are performances, rather than objects. Services cannot be seen, felt, tasted or touched in the same manner in which goods can be sensed. Hence most services can neither be counted, measured, inventoried, tested nor verified prior to sales to assure quality. Zeithaml (1981) is of the view that because of intangibility, the firm may find it difficult to understand how consumers perceive their services and evaluate service quality. Intangibility, according to Bateson (1979), is the critical goods–service distinction from which all other differences emerge.

Heterogeneity

Many services are labour intensive. Heterogeneity in service delivery is a major problem for labour-intensive services. Heterogeneity concerns the potential for high variability in the performance of services (Sasser, 1976). Numerous employees may be in contact with an individual customer, raising the problem of inconsistency of behaviour (Langeard *et al.*, 1981). The problems encountered by services in respect of heterogeneity are well expressed by Knisely (1979). According to him:

> In a service business, you're dealing with something that is primarily delivered by people to people. Your people are as much of your product in the customer's mind as any other attribute of that service. People's performance day in and day out fluctuates. Therefore, the level of consistency that you can count on and try to communicate to the customer is not a certain thing.

In short:

   a)   the quality of service performance varies from one service organization to another;
   b)   the quality of service performance varies from one service performer to another;
   c)   the quality of service performance varies for the same performer from one occasion to another.

Thus a uniform service quality is difficult to assure (Booms and Bitner, 1981) because there is no guarantee of consistent behaviour from the service personnel. This means that what the firm has promised to deliver may be entirely different from that which the service customer receives.

Inseparability of Production and Consumption

This involves the simultaneous production and consumption which characterizes most services (Carmen and Langeard, 1980; Gronroos, 1978; Regan, 1963; Upah, 1980). While goods are first produced, sold and then consumed; services are first sold, then produced and consumed simultaneously (Regan, 1963). Simultaneous production and consumption implies that the service customer must be present during the production of services (tourism services, aeroplane trips, entertainment performances, etc.). Inseparability 'forces the buyer into intimate contact with the production process' (Carmen and Langeard, 1980) and the service provider. This also means that there is no time lapse between production and consumption. Because of this intimacy linking production and consumption, services cannot be subjected to quality control checks prior to consumption. In other words, services cannot be withheld for quality inspection after their production. As Czepiel (1980) suggests, service providers are human, and client-provider interaction is both simultaneous and spontaneous, rendering the control of service quality a difficult and complex issue.

Kandampully (1993c) points out that to offer or to maintain superior service is often found difficult by many organizations because quality is progressive. He argues that the progressive nature of quality expectation renders superior service seemingly insurmountable to many organizations. In other words, what customers consider to be excellent today may only be adequate or even insufficient tomorrow.

NATURE OF TOURISM SERVICES

Tourism as a service can be explained as an 'experience'. An experience during which a visitor encounters and interacts at an intimate level with the service provider, other participating visitors and both the physical and natural envir onment. On a conceptual level this experience can be expressed as a 'package' or 'assemblage'. This assemblage is in fact a mixture of different tangible and intangible products and services brought together. For example, it may include:

- a pleasant flight;
- food served in the flight;
- friendly interaction with the immigration authorities at the airport;
- helpfulness of the courtesy bus driver;
- friendliness of the hotel receptionist; and
- a comfortable hotel room.

These are a few of the many aspects comprising the tourism package. In other words, a package is the sum total of the goods, services and experiences offered to the customer (Albrecht and Zemke, 1985). In services literature the concept of service package has been described by a number of authors including Eiglier and Langeard (1977a,b), Lehtinen (1983), Norman (1984) and Gronroos (1990).

Norman (1984) suggests that most service offerings or service packages consist of a 'core service' (the centrepiece of the service offering which is the primary benefit sought by the customer), and 'peripheral services' (the little things, or added bonuses, that supplement the primary benefit). Peripherals provide 'leverage' and help to accentuate the value of the total package in the customer's eyes. Thus the concept of core and peripheral service provides a framework for thinking systematically about the delivery system. Therefore in a service operation, the strategy will define the business, and the package will define the offer, thereby assisting to develop a system to deliver the service.

In most services the core service is the centrepiece of the service offering. All other services (peripherals) are created to complement the core service. Core service is the basic reason for being in business. Without the core service, a business enterprise would make no sense. Thus, the differentiation of core and peripheral services is crucial to an organization's control of its core and hence the ability to ensure that the core service consistently meets and exceeds expectation. Therefore, the effectiveness of a service firm is directly determined by the extent to which management is able to control their core service.

The core service in tourism is the holiday experience which comprises both tangible and intangible services. Customer satisfaction can be achieved only if an organization's core offering is able to meet the expectations of the customer. However, peripheral offerings serve to provide added attractions to the core service. For example, in a hotel, boarding and lodging are the core services whereas free parking, the swimming pool and the wake-up call are referred to as peripherals. They are added attractions but do not constitute the core offering.

Thus the concept of core and peripheral service is a significant factor in the effective management of tourism services. In many tourism services the core service focuses on the one to one interaction needed between the visitor and the service provider. For example, the service offered by a tour guide *is* the core service. Even in tourism services where tangible core services are apparent, the one to one interaction between the visitor and the service provider is perceived by the customer as an indispensable part of the core service, not a component of peripheral service. If we subsequently consider the food service in a restaurant, the food represents the tangible component of the core service, but the performance of the employee – 'how' the service is rendered – forms the intangible component of the core service. The author argues that it is, therefore, essential that tourism managers see the performance of the employee as a component of the core service and not as a peripheral service. Hence a conceptual merger of the performance of the employee to that of the core service is of paramount importance for the effective management of tourism quality. Service quality management literature has repeatedly illustrated that, in tourism services, positive interaction between the employee and the visitor, the so called 'moments of truth', is the factor most important in determining customer satisfaction and a subsequent indicator of the perceived quality of service. These positive interactions are so influential that they have the potency to offset an otherwise negative experience and many times are the key to the organization's success (Kandampully, 1993c).

It is thus paradoxical that we often see only lip service being paid to the performance of the employee. Acknowledging the interaction skills of employees as core service acts to elevate the importance of employees' interpersonal skills. Hence this argument calls for management's continuous focus on training frontline employees on personal interaction skills. Such training programmes should then be reinforced through regular feedback and reward systems.

Additionally, in some tourism offerings the concept of core and peripheral service may prove to be less relevant. This is so in those tourism products where the real distinction between core and peripheral services becomes less distinguishable and conspicuous. This happens where both core and peripherals are experiences comprising mainly intangible and subjective factors. Hence in cases such as adventure tourism, the services are effectively conceived as experiences by the customer. However, either as core or as peripherals the experience factor in tourism service maintains a significant consideration in customers' evaluation of the quality of service. This is an important factor to consider in the marketing and advertising of such tourism services. Often these experiences are far beyond the control of tourism producers. Nevertheless, customers' high expectations of such experiences, engendered through ambiguous marketing and advertisement information, can become the cause of customer dissatisfaction.

CONCEPTS OF SERVICE QUALITY AS APPLICABLE TO TOURISM

Service quality management is now identified in tourism as the cutting edge practice. Quality concepts in services have been based, from their onset, on the fact that it is the customers perception of quality that is important, not what designers or operations managers deem to be good or bad.

Consumer behaviour models suggest that post-purchase perception of a product is a function of the pre-purchase expectations. This notion was the foundation of the so-called confirmation–disconfirmation concept adopted by services. In services, the 'perceived quality' of a given service will be the outcome of an evaluation process where consumers compare their expectations with the service they perceive they have received (Gronroos, 1984); that is, they compare the 'perceived service' against the 'expected service'.

Thus, it has been recognized that customers evaluate service quality by comparing their experience of service performance, 'perceptions', with what they think performance should be, 'expectations' (Lewis and Booms, 1982; Gronroos, 1984; Parasuraman *et al.*, 1985; Ramm-Schmidt, 1985; Lindqvist, 1987; Berry *et al.*, 1988; Zeithaml *et al.*, 1988; Parasuraman *et al.*, 1990; Berry *et al.*, 1990).

Sasser *et al.* (1978) have identified three different dimensions of service performance: levels of material, facilities and personnel. According to them, service performance or service quality is affected by the quality of the materials which constitute part of the service offering, for example, food in a restaurant. This is true also of the quality of facilities which complement the core offering, for example, comfortable seating in an aircraft. The behaviour of the personnel will similarly influence the service quality. The important aspect of this trichotomy is the notion that service quality involves more than the outcome quality. A further development of this view was proposed by Gronroos (1982) and by Lehtinen and Lehtinen (1982).

Gronroos (1982) identifies two dimensions in service quality. He argues that service quality is a combination of 'technical quality' (what is delivered), and 'functional quality' (how it is delivered), which are quite different in nature. For example:

- food in a restaurant;
- room and bed in a hotel;
- computerized ticketing systems at a travel agent,

may all be defined as technical dimensions. On the other hand:

- the attitude of the waiter;
- a willingness to help and serve as expressed by the flight attendant; and
- the behaviour exhibited by a tour guide,

may be described as functional dimensions. He argues that 'how' the service is rendered by the firm's contact personnel – i.e., the 'functional quality' of a service – commonly assumes much more importance.

Lehtinen and Lehtinen (1982) also identified two sets of quality dimensions. According to them, 'process quality' and 'output quality' are inherent in all services and, when combined, exist as service quality. Lehtinen argues that, through the intimacy of production process with the customer, in many services, the customer experiences the production process through interaction and participation. Process quality in services is, therefore, subjective in nature and judged by the customer during service. For example, the tour guide's conversation with tourists while escorting them around, his/her technical skill in explaining historic and scientific things: both involve process quality. On the other hand 'output quality' is customers' evaluation of the service relative to its result. In services such as tourism where there are no apparent final products, it is process quality which is of vital importance to the visitor.

Parasuraman *et al.* (1985) define the quality perceived in a service to be a function of the gap between consumers' expectations of service and their perceptions of the actual service as delivered by the organization. In other words customers assess service quality by comparing the service they 'receive' (perceptions – 'what I get') with the service they 'desire' (expectations – 'what I want'). They suggest that this gap is influenced by several other discrepancies or gaps which include:

- differences in service design;
- communications;
- management; and
- service delivery.

DYNAMIC CONCEPT OF QUALITY

Our current knowledge of service quality is based on the so-called perceived service quality model. Gronroos (1992) argues that the perceived service quality model is a static model. He goes on to argue that any attempt to develop a quality improvement model based on a static model has limitations. Customers constantly change their expectations and in doing so become more and more demanding (James and Walker, 1988). Satisfaction and expectation are therefore time-specific, so that customers expect more today than in the past. If service firms are to continue to satisfy their customers, firms must clearly be capable of constant improvement. Moreover, the need for an ongoing quality upgrading process has become increasingly significant given the facts that tourism is now a world-wide industry and that technological advances and increased competition have rendered continuous innovation unavoidable. Thus Kandampully (1993c) argues that customer/market perceived quality is dynamic and, therefore, necessitates the adoption of a dynamics model. Hence for an effective management of quality in services, a dynamic model is essential. By its very design, the model will demand spontaneous and ongoing improvement.

Indeed the ongoing vitality of the service sector in the 1990s will be determined predominantly by the extent to which service organizations address these questions:

- Is it enough if we deliver good service in order to satisfy the customer? or
- Should we deliver excellent service in order to overwhelm and surprise the customer?

Brown *et al.* (1992) suggest that customer satisfaction will no longer be the key watchword but will be replaced by customer delight. Since increasing number of firms are effectively meeting customer expectation, to distinguish themselves from the competition firms will need to truly delight the customer (Kandampully, 1993a). This delight factor will require firms to understand different levels of customer/market expectations and exceed them on a regular basis.

To achieve service excellence, service organizations are thus faced, more than ever, with a need for a better understanding of the expectation and satisfaction issues of their customers, both present and potential. The dynamic service quality concept integrates Total Quality Management (TQM) philosophy with the application of process management and service design re-engineering, which are gaining increasing recognition in service quality literature. This concept of dynamic service quality suggests a practical approach which can be adopted and implemented by service organizations for a continuous step-by-step improvement of quality according to the customer/market perception and demand. A practical model to integrate the dynamic concept, consists of a spontaneous feedback system interlinking the three crucial participants of services (customers, employees and management). This approach also suggests the utilization of service quality standards (indicators) which will be subject to review and upgrading to render them consistent with customer expectation.

Services demand a dynamic and systematic approach to quality to reflect the fact that satisfaction and expectations are themselves dynamic in nature and hence not static characteristics. As customers constantly change their expectations and become more demanding, some service features which were considered a 'plus' may soon become a 'hygiene' factor as customers get used to them. Customers' expectations change over time, as discussed earlier. For example, 'Punctuality', which was Scandinavian Airline's selling point in 1982, is no longer listed in the customer's choice criteria. Today punctuality must be offered by an airline as a minimum level of quality. Bloch (1982) suggests that services must constantly improve because customers' expectations today exceed those of the past. Gronroos (1992) maintains that what service management needs is a dynamic version of the perceived service quality model. He argues that since customers' expectations change continuously, quality perception also changes continuously.

A dynamic model (Figure 1.1) for service quality improvement which embraces the key quality dimensions is given on the following page. This model is adoptable by all service sectors and pertinent to the tourism/hospitality sector in particular. In implementing this conceptual model, two dynamic management tools are used, namely:

1)   interactive feedback communication systems supported by rewards;
2)   upgrading service quality standards or indicators.

These tools are dynamic in both vision and mission. They are designed to facilitate a dynamic process where the term 'process' denotes continuity, while 'dynamic' implies spontaneity. Thus their combined effect will play a vital role in promoting continuous improvement in services.

As discussed earlier, service quality refers to customer perceived quality. It is the customer who determines and is the final judge of quality, hence it is the customer's definition (interpretation) of quality which counts. The implications for service organizations are clearly important. Most crucial is an ability to gather continuous and reliable information about customer/market perceptions and expectations. These perceptions and expectations may subsequently be utilized and translated into service quality standards or operating procedures (Kandampully, 1993b), and assist management to design or even to customize services to meet market perceptions.

For this the interactive feedback communication system through rewards – the first dynamic tool – can be used. According to Kandampully (1993a,c) an interactive feedback communication process should create a system which will marry the various interrelated functions and also the three participants of the service, namely:

• customers;
• service deliverer; and
• strategist.

This interactive feedback system should be designed to facilitate a simultaneous two-way flow of information (see Figure 1.1) which implies simultaneous qualitative and quantitative information gathering, through formal (customer satisfaction research) and informal (contact employee feedback) methods. The efficiency of this two way communication process will also be enhanced by the fact that it is dialectic, since the provider and the collector of the information are able to exchange views and ideas (Kandampully, 1993c).

Implementing this system does not necessitate structural or system changes. It can, therefore, easily be adopted for practical application into any service organization with minimal disruption to the existing system. In a survey

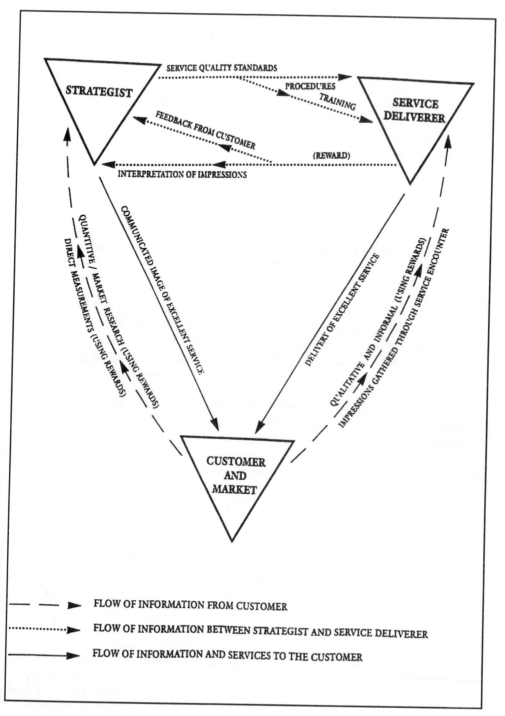

Figure 1.1: Process flow in dynamic service quality

Kandampully (1993c) conducted within the hotel industry, it was observed that tools such as:

- feedback systems;
- reward systems; and
- standards,

exist in most hotel organizations in one form or another. However, it is necessary to encompass these programmes within a planned system to ensure that they function to achieve a designated common goal.

Beyond the primary purpose of information, a dynamic system will also create a number of valuable by-products for the organization. These include:

- a better understanding between management and employees;
- improved morale among managers and employees; and
- the development of strong and positive corporate culture, engendering commitment and participation from every member of the organization towards the common goal.

The implementation of a feedback communication system at all stages via incentive/reward programmes will affect improvement of operational systems. Such operational commitment will project a quality image to both customers and employees, thereby functioning as a marketing and public relations tool directed at customers, employees and managers alike.

The second dynamic tool – the continuous upgrading of service quality standards or procedures – has two functional roles. First, service standards help to maintain consistency in the service delivery which constitutes one of the main attributes of superior service quality. Schmalensee *et al.* (1984) maintain that consistency is the ability to offer customers a consistent standard of service without undue surprises. They go on to suggest that consistency also means:

> doing what organizations say that they are going to do and doing it every time, all the time.

Empirical findings of Parasuraman, Berry and Zeithaml (1985; 1986; 1987; 1988; 1990; 1991; 1992) conclude that service reliability is at the heart of excellent service, the single most important factor and the 'core' to most customers. Consistency refers to the absence of variation in the output of the service (Chase and Bowen, 1991) or the ability to offer a consistent standard of service. In order to reduce variability or to ensure consistency, services need to be managed. Berry *et al.* (1990) suggest that service standards should be customer expectations stated in a way that renders them meaningful to employees. According to them, if well conceived, standards will guide and energize both managers and employees. Additionally, they will clarify the service task against which employees can judge their own performance and managers can judge the employee's and the organization's performance. Above all, service standards bring a customer focus into the employee's day-to-day reality of service delivery.

Second, if standards are continuously upgraded according to customer/market needs they will form the cornerstone for continuous improvement in benchmarking the firm's performance, regarding both customer requirements and the competition. Ernst & Young consulting group (1990) advise service organizations to document standards for the benefit of reference and training. According to them, standards should aim to bind everyone in the organization, to ensure that everyone works within the standards, and also that standards become the working practice. Thus standards are indeed the cornerstones to continuous improvement. The dynamic model will subsequently assist service organizations to continuously review and upgrade their existing standards in accordance with customer/market demand.

The dynamic model will assist service organizations to effectively gather feedback information from the customers on a regular and consistent basis. The resulting information can subsequently be used as the basis for consultation between management and employees, regarding the modification of service standards, and the guiding of management decisions. Such a continuous and planned review of customer desired standards will subsequently necessitate redesigning of the service process and systems.

If the information gathering and standard setting processes are interlinked, they will function as a spontaneous system, since the processes themselves are designed to initiate spontaneity. The system works in such a way that one process consecutively activates the other, creating a continuous step-by-step improvement. This concept of a dynamic quality improvement process can be incorporated into any process or sub-process of a service, whether it relates to the internal or external services of the firm. It is by incorporating quality improvement into every service feature that tourism organizations will achieve service excellence.

REFERENCES

Albrecht, K. and Zemke, R. (1985) *Service America: Doing Business in the New Economy* Dow Jones Irwin.

Bateson, J.E.G. (1977) Do We Need Services Marketing? *Marketing Consumer Services: New Insights* Report, December, No. 77–115, Cambridge, MA: Marketing Science Institute.

Bateson, J.E.G. (1979) Why We Need Service Marketing. In O.C. Ferrell, S.W.Brown and C.W. Lamb Jr (eds) *Conceptual and Theoretical Developments in Marketing* pp 131–146, Chicago: American Marketing.

Berry, L.L. (1980) Services Marketing is Different, *Business* 30, May–June, pp 24–29.

Berry, L.L., Parasuraman, A. and Zeithaml, V.A. (1988) The Service-Quality Puzzle, *Business Horizon,* September–October, Homewood, IL.

Berry, L.L., Zeithaml, V.A. and Parasuraman, A. (1990) Five Imperatives for Improving Service Quality, *Sloan Management Review*, September.

Berry, L.L. and Parasuraman, A. (1991) Competing Through Quality, *Marketing Services* Free Press.

Berry, L.L. and Parasuraman, A. (1992) Prescriptions for a Service Quality Revolution in America, *Organizational Dynamics,* Spring, pp 5–15.

Bloch, M.T. (1982) Innovations In Services Marketing. In L.L. Berry, G.L. Shostack and G.D. Upah (eds) *Emerging Perspectives on Services Marketing* AMA Services Marketing Conference Proceedings, Lexinton, Ma.

Booms, H.B. and Bitner, M.J. (1981) Marketing Strategies and Organization Structures for Service Firms. In J. Donnelly and W. George (eds) *Marketing of Services* AMA Services Marketing Conference Proceedings.

Brown, W.S., Gummesson, E., Edvardsson, B. and Gustavsson, B. (1991) *Service Quality: Multidisciplinary and Multinational Perspectives* Lexington Books, Lexington, Ma.

Brown, W.S., Bowen, D.E. and Swartz, T.A. (1992) *The Future of Quality in Services.* Paper presented at the Quality in Services Quis-3 Conference at Karlstad University Sweden.

Carmen, J.M. and Langeard, E. (1980) Growth Strategies of Service Firms, *Strategic Management Journal* 1, January–March, pp 7–22.

Chase, R.B. and Bowen, D.E. (1991) Service Quality and the Service Delivery System: A Diagnostic Framework. In W.S. Brown, E. Gummesson, B. Edvardsson, and B. Gustavsson (eds) *Service Quality: Multidisciplinary and Multinational Perspectives* pp 157–176, Lexington Books, Lexington, Ma.

Czepiel, J.A. (1980) *Managing Customer Satisfaction In Consumer Service* Research Programme, Working Paper, Cambridge, MA: Business Marketing Science Institute.

Eiglier, P. and Langeard, E. (1977a) A New Approach to Service Marketing, *Marketing Consumer Services: New Insights* Cambridge, MA: Marketing Science Institute.

Eiglier, P. and Langeard, E. (1977b) Services as Systems: Marketing Implications. In *Marketing Consumer Services: New Insights* Marketing Science Institute, Report No. 77–115, pp 83–102.

Ernst & Young (1990) *Total Quality, An Executive's Guide for the 1990s* The Ernst & Young Homewood, IL: Quality Improvement Consulting Group (ed.) Business One Irwin.

Goeldner, R.C. (1992) Trends in North American Tourism, *American Behavioral Scientist* 36(2).

Gronroos, C. (1978) A Service-Oriented Approach to Marketing of Services, *European Journal of Marketing* 12(8), pp 588–601.

Gronroos, C. (1984) *Strategic Management and Marketing in the Service Sector* Helsingfors: Swedish School of Economics.

Gronroos, C. (1990) *Service Management and Marketing, Managing the Moments of Truth in Service Competition* MA: Lexington Books.

Gronroos, C. (September 1982) *Towards A Third Phase In Service Quality Research. Challenges and Future Directions.* Report presented at the AMA Services marketing conference, Vanderbilt University, Nashville, TN.

Gummesson, E. (1992) *Service Productivity: A Blasphemous Approach.* Paper presented at the 2nd International Research Seminar, 9–12 June 1992. In Service Management, France.

Hall, C.M. and Weiler, B. (1992) What's Special about Special Interest Tourism? In B. Weiler and C.M. Hall (eds) *Special Interest Tourism* London: Belhaven Press.

James, J. and Walker, C.E. (1988) Measurement and Integration of Customer Perception into Company Performance and Quality. In M.J. Bitner and L.A. Crosby (eds) *Designing a Winning Service Strategy* AMA Services Marketing Conference Proceedings.

Kandampully, J. (1993a) *An Approach to Facilitate Dynamic Service Quality* Paper presented at the Service Industry Management Research Unit Conference 1993, University of Wales, Cardiff, UK.

Kandampully, J. (1993b) Service Quality and The Dilemma of Service Quality Standards. In R. Johnston and N.D.C. Slack (eds) *Service Superiority: The Design and Delivery of Effective Service Operations* Warwick University, UK International Operations Management Association, Warwick Business School.

Kandampully, J. (1993c) *Total Quality Management Through Continuous Improvement in Service Industries*. Unpublished doctoral thesis, University of Exeter.

Knisely, G. (1979) Greater Marketing Emphasis by Holiday Inns Breaks Mould *Advertising Age* 15, January, pp 47–51.

Krippendorf, J. (1987a) Tourism in Asia and the Pacific, *Tourism Management* June, pp 137–139.

Krippendorf, J. (1987b) *The Holiday Makers: Understanding the Impact of Leisure and Travel* Oxford: Heinemann Professional Publishing.

Langeard, E., Bateson, C., Lovelock, H. and Eiglier, P. (1981) *Services Marketing: New Insights From Consumers and Managers* Cambridge, MA: Marketing Science Institute.

Lehtinen, J.R (1983) *To Improve Service Quality by Analysing the Service Production Process*. Unpublished working paper, Helsinki: Services Management Institute.

Lehtinen, U. and Lehtinen, J.R. (1982) *Service Quality: A Study of Quality Dimensions* Unpublished working paper, Helsinki: Service Management Institute.

Lewis, R.C. and Booms, B.H. (1982) The Marketing Aspects of Service Quality In Berry *et al*. (eds) *Emerging Perspectives on Services Marketing* AMA Services Marketing Conference Proceedings.

Lindqvist, J.L. (1987) Quality and Service Value in the Consumption of Services. In *Value to Your Service* AMA 6th Annual Services Marketing Conference Proceedings.

Lovelock, C.H. (1981) Why Marketing Management Needs To Be Different for Services. In J.H. Donnelly and W.R.George (eds) *Marketing of Services* AMA Services Marketing Conference Proceedings pp 5–9, Chicago: American Marketing.

Normann, R. (1984) *Service Management: Strategy and Leadership in Service Business* New York: John Wiley and Sons.

Parasuraman, A., Zeithaml, V.A. and Berry, L.L. (1985) A Conceptual Model of Service Quality and its Implications for Future Research, *Journal of Marketing* 49, pp 41–50.

Parasuraman, A., Zeithaml, V.A. and Berry, L.L. (1986) SERVQUAL: A Multi-Item Scale for Measuring Customer Perception of Service Quality Research Report No. 86–108, Cambridge, MA: Marketing Science Institute.

Parasuraman, A. (1987) An Attributional Framework For Assessing The Perceived Value of A Service. In C. Surprenant (ed.) *Add Value To Your Service* AMA Services Marketing Conference Proceedings.

Parasuraman, A., Berry, L.L. and Zeithaml, V.A. (1990) Guidelines for Conducting Service Quality Research, *Marketing Research* December.

Ramm-Schmidt, C. (1985) Implementing A Service-Oriented Marketing Strategy. In C. Gronroos and E. Gummesson *Service Marketing – Nordic School Perspective* University of Stockholm, Sweden.

Rathmell, J.M. (1966) What is Meant by Services? *Journal of Marketing* October, pp 32–36.

Rathmell, J.M. (1974) *Marketing in the Service Sector* Cambridge, MA: Winthrop Publishers Inc.

Regan, W.J. (1963) The Service Revolution, *Journal of Marketing* July, pp 57–62.

Sasser, W.E. (1976) Match Supply and Demand in Service Industries, *Harvard Business Review* November–December, pp 133–141.

Sasser, W.E., Olsen, R.P. and Wyckoff, D.D. (1978) *Management of Service Operations Text & Cases,* Boston: Allyn and Bacon.

Schmalensee, D.H., Bernardt, K. and Gust, N. (1984) Keys to Successful Services Marketing: Customer Orientation, Creed, Consistency. In T.M. Bloch, G.D. Upah and V.A. Zeithaml (eds) *Services Marketing in a Changing Environment* AMA Services Marketing Conference Proceedings.

Shaw, G. and Williams, A.M. (1990) Tourism and Development. In D. Pinder (ed.) *Western Europe: Challenge and Change* London: Institute of British Geographers, Belhaven Press.

Shostack, G.L. (1977) Human Evidence: A New Part of the Marketing Mix, *Bank Marketing* March, pp 32–34.

Upah, G.D. (1980) Mass Marketing in Service Retailing: A Review and Synthesis of Major Methods, *Journal of Retailing* 56, pp 59–76.

World Tourism Organization (1990) *Tourism to the Year 2000: Qualitative Aspects Affecting Global Growth* Madrid: Author.

Zeithaml, V.A. (1981) How Consumer Evaluation Process Differ Between Goods and Services. In *Marketing of Services* AMA Services Marketing Conference Proceedings.

Zeithaml, V.A., Berry, L.L. and Parasuraman, A. (1988) Communication and Control Process in the Delivery of Service Quality, *Journal of Marketing* 52, pp 35–48.

2

Managing Quality Organizations in the US Hospitality Sector

Richard Brush

Quality improvement is now recognized as an essential dimension of strategic planning in US hospitality organizations. Yet quality management practices in the service industries are in the early stages of development. This chapter explains the quality drive in terms of its origins, sectoral definition, measurement and cost. A model of Total Quality Management appropriate for the hospitality sector is presented as a basis for development of quality improvement.

BACKGROUND

During the Second World War, Japanese engineers would examine captured American aeroplane engines and be appalled at how technologically superior they were to Japanese design and manufacture. They knew they were sending Japanese pilots into the sky hopelessly mismatched. If it rained in Tokyo, ten thousand phone lines might be out of order (Halberstam, 1986). In the 1950s and 1960s the phrase 'Made in Japan' was an international slogan for shoddy manufacturing and poor quality design. In 1979, Japanese car manufacturers had captured a 25 per cent share of the US auto market.

In 1982, Tom Peters and Robert Waterman published *In Search of Excellence*, a book about American management. The book proposed that there were a number of common attributes among 'excellent' American firms where excellence was defined as historical profitability and management innovation. The book was an instant best seller and unlike almost any management book before or since seemed to capture the popular imagination. What was a book on American management doing on the best seller list? Why was the American general public so eager to learn about why some firms were 'excellent' and some were not? After all, most Americans were not managers themselves and probably did not spend much time thinking about it. The answer may have a lot to do with American pride and an American sense of its 'economic place' in the world. Of the most quintessentially American business, auto manufacturing, many said that the reason that the US had lost market share was unmistakable: Japanese manufacturers made cars that people wanted, they made them better and they made them cheaper.

Many suspected that the Japanese managers were simply better managers than their American counterparts. Countless books and articles appeared about the Japanese management style, Japanese management/labour relations, Japanese manufacturer/supplier relations, and Japanese manufacturing techniques. Many of the books pointed out a central irony: that if Japan had learned to manufacture many products better than the American manufacturers it was at least in part, because they had listened to an American, W. Edwards Deming, who for years had been preaching quality control methods to American industry, to no avail. Japanese manufacturers, on the other hand, listened to Deming and they learned his central lessons: first, that contrary to popular opinion, the introduction of quality systems and procedures into manufacturing saved, rather than cost money; and second (also contrary to the popularly held beliefs of many captains of American industry), that consumers wanted quality goods and services and would pay for them.

Many American consumers by the early 1980s knew what some American manufacturers did not: that quality counted and that quality products and services – not price (Sweeney *et al.*, 1992), not gimmicks, not advertising messages – were what was driving their buy-decisions. What Peters and Waterman pointed out in *In Search of Excellence* (1982) was that only the very best American firms really understood the concepts of Quality Improvement; espoused by Deming and others, that had made much of Japanese manufacturing so successful. Americans wanted to know what had happened to the once all-powerful American industrial machine and Peters and Waterman (1982) started to reveal some of the answers.

In 1987, the US government introduced the Malcolm Baldrige National Quality Award, designed to promote and reward excellence in quality manufacturing and service. In 1991, the Ritz-Carlton Hotel Company won the Baldrige award.

WHAT IS QUALITY?

By the 1970s and early 1980s the better American manufacturing companies were becoming believers in something called Total Quality Management (TQM) or Quality Improvement (QI).[1] But service companies, including in the hospitality industry, were lagging behind (Stephenson, 1993). Before the service industries could begin to develop quality improvement programmes, they needed to address several questions.

First, how should quality be defined in the service sector? In manufacturing the definition of quality is fairly simple: it is the absence of defects. Second, how was quality to be measured? Again, in the industrial sector measurement is straightforward: as products rolled off the assembly line a certain number of items would be identified, either by machine or human inspection, as faulty or defective. That number was then divided by the total number of manufactured items giving a percentage of defects. The lower the percentage the higher the quality. Finally, how to measure the cost of quality. Again, the solution was not as clear in the service industries as it was in manufacturing.

A Definition of Service Quality

Defining service quality is problematic. An understanding of the differences between manufacturing and services (such as perishability and intangibility of product, simultaneous production and consumption of 'product' and the changing needs and expectations of providers and users) makes explicit these problems. Slowly, however, a good, simple working definition of service quality began to appear, first in academia and then in industry. Quality is conformance to standards.[2] But defining quality as 'conformance to standards' was not enough; this definition required further amplification. The standards must be largely market-driven and they must be honest and ethical in nature.

The former president of the American Hotel & Motel Association (AH&MA), Douglas Fontaine, makes the point about standards being tied to market or customer expectations when he states:

> People tend to think that the more expensive something is, the better the quality. If this were the case, it would be impossible to run a quality hotel or restaurant that charged average rates or catered to the average guest. French gourmet restaurants are wonderful; those who can afford them appreciate the excellent service, outstanding presentation, and exquisite food. The American hamburger, however, properly prepared and presented, can be just as pleasant a dining experience – but the quality must be there! (Hall, 1990).

Paul Kirwin, vice president for the Carlson Hospitality Group's Country Hospitality Corporation:

> recommend[s] to our franchisees that they allocate funds for customer-service expenses as part of their marketing department. (Kirwin, 1991).

so that they do not miss the point that marketing and quality customer service are one and the same.

Hall (1990) makes a point about ethics. He suggests that before a standard can be accepted it must be grounded in generally recognized community moves. He defines a standard as 'right' if it meets the following tests:

1) Is the standard fair?
2) Is the standard legal?
3) Does the standard hurt anyone?
4) Have we been honest with those affected by the standard?
5) Can we personally live with a clear conscience with the standard or the action taken?
6) Would I publicize my decision?
7) What if everyone did it?

Finally, implicit in this definition of quality is the notion that in order for quality to exist the standards must be met consistently. Conformance to standards does not mean conformity only some or even most of the time. 100 per cent conformance should be the goal of every organization dedicated to improving quality.

Measuring Quality

The 'conformance to standards' definition is helpful because it gives management something to measure against – the 'standard'. One of Deming's important principles was that unless there were measurements of quality, one could never be sure that quality was, in fact, improving. Hall (1990) makes the point regarding measurements in the service industry. He notes that there are really three classes of standards and each requires different techniques for measurement. Class A standards are 'finite' in that they lend themselves to constant measurement. Examples include guest complaints, maintenance calls, walked guests and the like. Class B standards require a conscious act to measure. Guest room cleanliness and long waits at check-in or check-out are examples. Class C standards are the most difficult to measure because they concern guest-employee interaction which may happen out of public view – a bellhop rooming a guest or an operator making a wake-up call. Class A and B standards are relatively easy to measure; class C standards require more thought and creativity but are certainly not impossible to measure. For example, a guest questionnaire asking for feedback on class C standards might be useful.

The Cost of Quality

A word about the cost of quality (or more precisely the cost of the lack of quality) is in order before we examine how American hospitality quality programmes work. We have stated that the service industries in general, and the hospitality industry in particular, lagged behind the manufacturing sector in terms of implementing QI programmes. One reason was the commonly held belief that it was really impossible to measure the true cost of quality and that it would probably cost more to implement a QI programme than it would save. These notions now appear to be more in the order of an excuse or a justification for inaction, as opposed to being based on fact. It is no exaggeration to say that lost business due to customer dissatisfaction can amount to 10 to 50 per cent of current revenues. And as for measurement of costs, Hall (1990) and others have outlined clear methods for quantifying costs (*ibid.*).[3]

The American hospitality industry has come to realize that, as Deming stated years ago, quality pays. But how does it pay? First, conforming to market driven standards will inevitably increase customer satisfaction. And in an industry where hotel executives believe that they only execute perfectly between 85 to 90 per cent of the time, that leaves a lot of room for increased customer contentment. Second, almost all successful quality management programmes are process-oriented. That means that they concentrate on the root causes of problems and not simply the symptoms. As we shall see, simply 'satisfying the customer' is not enough; finding out why the problem occurred in the first place and what can be done so that it will not happen again is the real goal. In most cases the root causes are simple and the solution will save money too. Thus, good quality programmes increase customer satisfaction and therefore increase sales, *and* they usually reduce costs as well.

A MODEL TQM PROGRAMME FOR HOSPITALITY FIRMS

What are the components of the American hospitality TQM Programme? The answer to that is as varied as there are companies that have installed them. A good way to start an examination of components of many programmes might be to review the model quality management programme designed by Kenneth Heymann, vice president of the Hospitality Group, a management consulting firm in Denver, Colorado (Heymann, 1992). Heymann suggests that the hospitality industry cannot look to manufacturing firms for guidance in designing a quality programme. A different model is needed. While not all hospitality firms' TQM programmes include all the following components, many include several or variations of his model. Most would do well to incorporate them all. His model is as follows:

- Establish a culture of quality;
- Develop a team orientation;
- Develop leadership skills;
- Develop customer-driven policies and procedures;
- Set standards;
- Develop human resources;
- Plan for quality;
- Build systems to measure achievement;
- Evaluate performance to improve performance;
- Build reward and recognition systems.

We will allow this model to serve as a guide as we examine in more detail how a good TQM programme works.

A Quality Culture

One thing common to almost all TQM programmes is the need for top management commitment to quality improvement – a compact with the entire organization to totally eliminate all deviations from established standards. Making a TQM programme work requires an obsession with eliminating errors. Management must provide the vision, communicate that vision, and then provide employees with the tools to achieve that vision. The corporate culture of firms that are committed to continuous improvement is one in which 'everyone is treated with respect, everyone is encouraged to contribute and is recognized for his or her contribution' (Heymann, 1992).

Team Orientation

The key to developing a team orientation is management stability and continuity; without it, teams tend to break down and lose focus. Once management has set the direction, it must deliberately create situations in which people are forced to work together to solve problems, many of which will be guest-related. These situations will inevitably lead to conflict. Management must learn to resolve conflict, usually by re-focusing the team on the ultimate goal – guest satisfaction. Quality circles or groups of people, usually from the same work area, who meet regularly on a voluntary basis to identify, analyse, and solve quality and other problems in their area (Hall, 1990), have proven a most effective technique in this regard. As Deming pointed out, barriers must be broken down. Where teamwork is effective, shared responsibility and synergy between team members is apparent.

Leadership

What makes a good leader? Certainly we could all agree that, at least, it is a person who achieves desired results from a group. But how do you know when one has achieved the 'best' results or 'maximum' results as opposed to merely 'getting the job done'? Remember that it is the goal of QI to eliminate all errors. Bass in *Organizational Dynamics* (Winter, 1990) has made a useful distinction between what he calls 'Transactional Leaders' and 'Transformational Leaders'. Transactional leaders watch and search for deviations from standards and take corrective action. They assume the role of boss or policeman. Transformational leaders tend to communicate high expectations, and promote intelligence, rationality and careful problem solving. They assume the role of coach and counsellor. The former focus on ends; the latter on process or means. While each may be successful at achieving today's 'desired results', it is the transformational leader who can build effective teams, create Deming's (1986) 'synergy', and achieve the 'maximum' results for the long term.

Customer-Driven Policies

Probably nothing distinguishes today's hospitality QI programme more than its customer orientation. Heymann (1992) points out that many policies are in place to serve the needs of the firm and not the guest. For example, many hotel companies have a policy that requires desk clerks to 'upsell' arriving guests. One wonders how receptive the average guest is to it. Or the policy that protects the hotel from the poorly trained employee, sometimes creating more paperwork or more steps to a procedure than may otherwise be needed. For example, the credit clerk in the accounting office who asks the customer for company information already given and on file in the sales or front office. Clearly, the hospitality industry has erred in the past by not always looking at the way they do business from the guest's point of view.

But customer-driven policies and procedures may be a double-edged sword. Hall (1990) warns that there are pitfalls in a completely customer-driven orientation. He suggests four:

- It may mean an over-focus on ends rather than means; QI should be process-oriented;
- Focusing only on ends may mean accepting considerable waste; Hall suggests interim inspections;
- Overly focusing on customer service may reduce the time and emphasis to be placed on cost savings;
- Many hospitality employees earn a large proportion of their wages from gratuities; gratuities may be higher when service is better. That fact may cause better service to go to 'big tippers' whereas all guests deserve the same treatment.

Still, more emphasis on customer wants and needs can only improve customer service and the overall quality of a hospitality operation. Despite the pitfalls, most would agree that customers need to come first.

Standards

Heymann (1992) states that:

> well-developed standards define both completeness and timeliness in terms that are meaningful to customers and consistent with their needs.

While standards for completeness are common, timeliness standards are not.

He suggests that more emphasis be placed on this area. He also proposes that there are two kinds of standards breakdowns: mechanical and interpersonal. Almost anyone can be taught the mechanics of a procedure. Interpersonal skills – the friendly smile, the caring attitude – are largely a matter of personality and are difficult, at best, to teach. The careful selection of guest service personnel seems to be the best way to reduce this type of error and employee selection is an important component of any human resource programme.[4]

Human Resources

Human resource development is a topic so complex as to be a subject in its own right. Suffice it to say that in a service business where up to 50 per cent and more of each dollar earned may be spent on personnel and related costs, human resources development is of vital importance. Training and performance-appraisal systems are at the heart of good human resource management. Still this is an area where studies have shown that more needs to be done in the typical US hospitality operation. In an interesting article in *Cornell Hotel and Restaurant Quarterly,* George Conrade, Robert Woods and Jack Ninemeier point out that while 97 to 98 per cent of all corporate respondents to a survey they conducted see a relationship between training and knowledge, about 92 per cent believe that training affects skill-levels and, 85 per cent perceive that a relationship exists between training and attitudinal factors, only 23 per cent spend more than 1 per cent of sales on training and 15 per cent spend less than 0.5 per cent.

Still, training of guest-contact personnel is important enough to some companies that a separate training budget is established so that managers are encouraged to train newer and typically less productive employees. As more hospitality managers realize the logical inconsistency of not planning and budgeting for training and how well-trained employees can give their operation a competitive edge, it may be that a higher percentage of sales will be spent on this vital area.

Planning

One of the central management functions is to forecast short-term business volume so that the organization can provide for expenses and staffing. But the question at times is whose needs are really being provided for, the owners or the guests. In the past it was not at all unusual for managers to allocate an amount of money to be spent on staffing based on a more or less fixed percentage of forecasted sales. Whether this level of staffing was adequate to meet the guest needs was not always a determining factor. Guest service typically suffered during low demand. Another kind of planning is budgeting for capital expenses. Many firms have learned that by targeting capital improvements towards guest concerns, customer satisfaction can be improved and sales can be increased.

Measurement Systems

Building systems to measure achievement is important because the tools that are readily at hand, the income statement and guest comment cards, provide little or no help in identifying root causes of problems. Income statements may simply show the result of a problem but usually give little insight as to its source. Customer comment cards may tell you what 3 to 5 per cent of your customers think, but studies have shown that they are typically inaccurate predictors as to what the majority of guests may think. It is particularly important that systems be built that measure performance in those areas vital to customer satisfaction. In hotels, that would include; check-in and check-out performance, guest room cleanliness, wake-up call accuracy and the like. In a food service operation, it might include; speed of service, plating specification conformance, bill accuracy, etc.

Evaluation and Reward Systems

Evaluation and reward systems finish Heymann's (1992) model QI programme. Evaluation systems, states Heymann, should flow logically from the achievement measurement systems. Just as it is folly to rely on guest comment cards and income statements to evaluate quality, so too is it foolish and probably even counterproductive to evaluate and reward staff based on these criteria. If an organization is truly committed to quality improvement, then it should reward those who contribute most to the unit's quality-centred goals. The other point that Heymann (1992) makes is that reward systems need to be consistently applied, and not just 'trotted out' when times are especially good or bad.

THE RITZ-CARLTON TQM PROGRAMME

Heymann's (1992) model probably does not exist anywhere, at least exactly in the form as stated above. But one TQM programme that does exist and that has been recognized as exemplary is the Ritz-Carlton Hotel Company's 'TQM' programme. Much of the following material is taken from Partlow (1993). First, a word about the award it achieved, the Malcolm Baldrige National Quality Award. Established in 1987 and administered by the US Department of Commerce, this award recognizes US companies that have achieved excellence through adherence to quality-improvement programmes. There are seven categories that all applicants are evaluated on:

- leadership;
- information analysis;
- strategic quality planning;

- human-resource development and management;
- quality assurance;
- quality operating results; and
- customer satisfaction.

It is interesting to note that in the first four years of its existence, of the 12 award recipients only one service company (Federal Express) was chosen. Ritz-Carlton was the second. It is possible that many of those aspects that make hospitality and other service-oriented QI programmes unique and difficult to manage also made it difficult for the Baldrige judges to evaluate them.

The Ritz-Carlton TQM programme is, in many respects, not unlike Heymann's (1992) model. Its basic component parts include:

- Top management commitment and involvement;
- Hiring the right people;
- Clearly proscribed standards, called 'Gold Standards';
- Building effective employee teams;
- Empowering employees;
- Detailed data reporting systems;
- Forming strong supplier relationships.

Top Management and the 'Right' People

At Ritz-Carlton approximately 25 per cent of each top executive's time is spent on quality-related matters. Horst Schulze, COO of Ritz-Carlton Hotel Company, initiated the TQM programme (with the goal of attaining the Baldrige award) by examining the QI programmes of other Baldrige winners; he visited Milliken & Co. and Xerox Corp. He found much to copy, but also determined that they had much to do themselves (Schulze, 1994). In particular, he realized that he had to improve what he called the 'employee interface'. He established a four step programme:

- Hire the right people, matching new hires to detailed job profiles.
- Orient them to the way we want the job done (two full days of orientation upon hire).
- Teach them the skills they will need to succeed.
- Inculcate appropriate behaviour.

Standards

Next top management established the Ritz-Carlton gold standards, both a general statement of what they believed in:

- genuine care and comfort for our guests;
- a warm, relaxed yet refined ambience;

and specific steps of service and procedures expected to be followed by all employee:

- Use proper telephone etiquette, Answer within three rings . . . ;
- Escort guests rather than pointing out directions . . .

Management met weekly to review these standards and the progress being made in 'inculcating appropriate behaviour.'

Teams

Unit quality teams with designated leaders were established in each hotel. Each was charged with setting objectives and devising action plans that were subject to corporate review. Each QI team had three subgroups for each work area under review:

- a problem solving group;
- a strategic planning group; and
- a quality-certification standard setting group.

This level of detailed review led to maximum employee commitment.

Empowerment

Patrick Mene, Ritz corporate director of quality, says that employee empowerment came easily for Ritz-Carlton. He states:

> To us, empowerment means giving employees the responsibility for solving guests' problems. We found that . . . the employee will have to break away from his or her normal routine to take an immediate positive action, to investigate what went wrong, and straighten it out. We would rather have a guest room attendant, for example, deal with fixing a guest's problem on the spot rather than having the director of marketing fix it later. It's the 1–10–100 rule that we believe in: What costs you a dollar to fix today will cost $10 to fix tomorrow and $100 to fix downstream.

Of course, empowerment does not come without some risk and ultimately requires something of a 'leap of faith' in their employees on the part of management. Finding the 'right' employees and training them well, not only in job skills but also in organizational values (the 'gold standards'), is an important precedent to empowerment. At Ritz-Carlton the management has taken the 'leap'; employees are authorized to spend up to $2000 to satisfy a guest.

Data Reporting

Data tracking is important for Ritz-Carlton. Each hotel is divided into 720 work areas and daily quality production reports are derived from an analysis of each of these areas. These reports serve as an early warning system for management. Among the data tracked are percentage of guest check-ins with no queuing, time spent to achieve industry-best clean-room appearance, and annual guest-room preventive-maintenance cycles.

Suppliers

Ritz-Carlton has also developed a supplier certification programme. Borrowing ideas from manufacturers, the Ritz-Carlton programme measures supplier delivery timeliness, conformance to standards and improvement. Ritz-Carlton has also developed a rigorous 100-question supplier capability audit plus they survey other users of the product and their own guests to get an accurate assessment of the supplier. The goal, says Mene, is for the supplier to become a fully integrated partner with Ritz-Carlton.

What has been the result of all this (besides the winning of the Baldrige award)? Since implementation of the TQM programme, Ritz-Carlton has found that operational costs are down, employee turnover has fallen from 100 per cent to an amazing 30 per cent and that profit retention has been dramatic (Macdonald, 1993).[5] In addition, Ritz-Carlton received 121 quality awards in 1991 alone. Perhaps the most important accolade has come from its guests. According to an independent research firm 92 to 97 per cent of Ritz-Carlton guests describe their experience as 'memorable'.

FUTURE IMPLICATIONS

For most American hospitality firms, quality improvement has become an integral part of their overall strategic planning and thinking. Some are doing it today because they understand that not to do so will put them at a competitive disadvantage. Others, like Ritz-Carlton are taking a more proactive approach and setting seemingly impossible goals for themselves.

Schulze (1994) has stated that the future goal for Ritz-Carlton is 'six sigma,' a statistical notation that acceptable quality is less than three errors per million transactions. He estimates that now, even with all the work that has been done, at Ritz-Carlton they are committing 60,000 to 70,000 errors per million transactions (Schulze, 1994) – and remember that most American hospitality managers estimate that they are making between 100,000 to 150,000 errors per million transactions. Schulze has also stated that hospitality companies will be out of business in 7 to 9 years if they have not instituted a TQM programme (Salomon, 1994).

Hoteliers seem to be getting the message. Many of the major US hotel franchisers, including Holiday Inn World-wide and Hospitality Franchise Systems, are installing tough new quality-focused inspection programmes on their franchisees (although a basic tenet of most TQM programmes is to develop processes so that errors are eliminated and so that 'after-the-fact' inspections become largely unnecessary) (Koss, 1992). Still, if these inspections show nothing else, they indicate management understanding that today's customer is expecting, indeed demanding, more than in the past.

Is six sigma an impossible goal? If you think so, do not tell the management and staff at Ritz-Carlton. It is being done today in the manufacturing industry and who is to say it can not be done in the service industries. If Schulze is right and six sigma is not an impossible goal, then the twentieth century has only laid the foundations for dramatic leaps in quality improvement. And the twenty first century holds the promise of truly exciting times for quality improvement in the American hospitality industry.

REFERENCES

Conrade, G. *et al.* (1994) Training in the US Lodging Industry: Perception and Reality, *Cornell Hotel and Restaurant Quarterly* 35(5) October, pp 16–21.

Deming, W.E. (1986) *Out of the Crisis* p 24 Cambridge, MA: MIT Press.

Dube, L. and Renaghan, L.M. (1994) Measuring Customer Satisfaction for Strategic Management, *Cornell Hotel and Restaurant Quarterly* 35(1) February, pp 39–47.

Halberstam, D. (1986) *The Reckoning* p 316, New York: William Morrow & Co.

Hall, S.J. (1990) *Quality Assurance in the Hospitality Industry* pp vii, 31, 84–105, 254, 275, Milwaukee, WI: Quality Press.

Heymann, K. (1992) Quality Management: a Ten Point Model, *Cornell Hotel and Restaurant Quarterly* 33(5) October, pp 51–60.

Kirwin, P. (1991) Speaking out, *Lodging Hospitality* June, p 66.

Koss, L. (1992) The Future of Franchising: Franchisers Answer Questions of Quality with New Programs, *Hotel & Motel Management* 207(14), August, pp 19, 22.

Macdonald, J. (1993) Survival Ties to Quality Management, *Hotel & Motel Management* 208(14), 16 August, p 3.

Partlow, C.G. (1993) *How the Ritz-Carlton Applies*.

Peters, T.J. and Waterman, R.H. (1982) *In Search of Excellence* New York: Harper & Row.

Salomon, A. (1994) Schulze: Focus on quality or fail, *Hotel & Motel Management* 209(13), 25 July, pp 3,9.

Schulze, H. (1994) What Makes the Ritz the Ritz? *Across the Board* 31(5), May, p 58.

Stephenson, S. (1993) Restaurants & Institutions, *TQM: Making it work for you* 1 October, pp 103–111.

Sweeney, J.C., Johnson, L.W. and Armstrong, R.W. (1992) *Journal of Services Marketing* 6(4), pp 15–22.

NOTES

1: Much of the literature makes a distinction between QI and TQM. They really belong on a continuum, with QI a more modest or limited version of a more 'total' TQM approach. For the purposes of this chapter the technical distinction is relatively unimportant although we will be referring here to the more comprehensive TQM approach. An examination of a model TQM programme will be found in this section entitled: 'A Model TQM Programme for the Hospitality Industries'.

2: This definition, with minor variations (e.g. 'the consistent application of standards'), is put forward by a number of academics including S.J. Hall, formerly of The Hotel School at Cornell University and currently founder and owner of Stephen Hall Associates: and Daryll Wycoff of Harvard University, two of the foremost thinkers in the area of service, and especially hospitality service, quality systems. In 1982, the American Hotel & Motel Association (AH&MA) defined quality as 'the consistent delivery of individual standards'.

3: Hall divided costs of quality into three areas: hard costs, costs directly related to the error; soft costs: costs arising as a result of the error; and opportunity costs: or lost sales due to error. All these areas are easily definable and therefore quantifiable or can be quite accurately estimated.

4: As we shall see when we examine the Ritz-Carlton programme later, employee selection is, for them, the essential first step of their TQM programme.

5: The reason why Ritz-Carlton has not been very specific reporting profits is probably due to the fact that, as primarily a management company, profit information is a matter for owners to divulge or not. Many of the Ritz-Carlton's owners are private citizens and are not required by law, as a public corporation would be, to make public this information.

3

Organizational Culture in Luxury Hotels

Paul A. Goodale and Roy C. Wood

From a critique of the prominent literature on organizational culture, this chapter uses case study analyzes of three luxury hotels as the foundation of an examination into culture techniques. The principal contention is that culture management can be instrumental to organizational success.

The 1980s saw an explosion of interest in the concept of organizational culture most notably fuelled by the book *In Search of Excellence* (ISOE) authored by Tom Peters and Robert Waterman (1982). While the Peters and Waterman genre of texts merely describe the common characteristics of successful businesses, culture management is now perceived as being a prescriptive solution to be applied to any given environment and has consequently been transposed from the sphere of the organizational writer into the realm of the practising manager. As Wilson and Rosenfeld (1990) point out:

> firms in the private, public and voluntary sectors have begun to look seriously at their organizational culture and how changes might be brought about to secure strategic success.

The essence of 'culture' approaches is that the workplace can develop as a hospitable environment in which there exists a feeling of mutual dependency between organizational members. Unfortunately, at this point the romantic notion constructed by much culture literature of the manager as guardian of the workers' best interests must be dispelled. Aside from any sense of moral obligation that may exist towards ensuring that the employee's working life is a happy one, managers have sought to achieve financial benefit for their organization by promoting togetherness and shared goals. In this they have been encouraged by the popular organizational culture literature. Peters and Waterman's book alone sold five million copies in fifteen languages in the three years subsequent to its 1982 release (Peters and Austin, 1985).

In Search Of Excellence (ISOE) looked at financial indicators within a 20 year window, such as 'compound asset growth from 1961 through 1980' and 'return on equity 1961 through 1980' to select firms for closer examination.

Peters and Waterman (1982) focused on 43 firms, comparing them in the hope that similarities accounting for this success would emerge. Firms such as McDonald's, Marriott, Caterpillar and IBM have gained notoriety for their selection and all were found to share eight organizational traits, all of which are so well known as to make only a listing of headings necessary here. These traits were: a bias for action; closeness to the customer; autonomy and entrepreneurship; productivity through people; hands on, value driven; stick to the knitting; simple form, lean staff; and simultaneous loose-tight properties.

Throughout ISOE, the suggestion is that organizational leaders and managers are responsible for the success or failure of an organization through instilling the correct cultural values in their employees. In particular, the authors focus on the role of founder figures and charismatic heroes in creating organizations which mimic their own personal beliefs. To some degree, this appeal to the charisma of organizational leaders undermines the sociological commonalities claimed for the firms studied by Peters and Waterman. ISOE has many other contradictions and inaccuracies. Silver (1987) points to three of these:

- First, he questions the methods used to select the excellent firms, 'some of which were studied less extensively than were twelve of the nineteen that were dropped from the original sixty-two';
- Secondly, Peters and Waterman selectively applied aspects of theories to back up each of their findings, a methodological process lacking consistency;
- Thirdly, these theories are borrowed with little suggestion of the criticisms they have collected over the years.

Two further criticisms can be levelled at ISOE. The first is that none of the firms cited as being 'excellent' by Peters and Waterman had themselves initiated culture change programmes in order to achieve this status. Thus the practicalities of implementing the generalized hypothesis derived from examination of these specific firms goes untested in the text. A more fundamental problem is that time has not been kind to ISOE. Not all of the firms that were excellent in 1980 were still excellent in 1993. Most notable was the fall from grace completed by IBM during this period. Despite claims that 'back in the 1960s, IBM set an objective of being able to mount a major reorganization in just a few weeks', the announcement of year end losses for 1992 of $4.97 billion (*The Independent*, 20.1.93) tended to suggest that this was no longer the case in the 1990s. Further, firms that continued to succeed into the 1990s appear to have departed from Peters and Waterman's advice. Indeed, rather than merely 'sticking to the knitting', Caterpillar have since turned to weaving and sewing with the emergence of their highly successful range of clothing.

Despite this, the fact that culture exists within organizations is hard to dispute. If it is true that 'we can only genuinely learn by jettisoning impoverished notions of culture which mistake style as substance' (Thompson and McHugh, 1990), then it may be wise to abandon the managerially biased theories of the likes of Peters and Waterman, in favour of adopting a micro-perspective which focuses on the logistical and practical issues relating to the implementation of a culture change programme. An organization does not simply acquire a culture overnight when a culture change programme is implemented. All organizations possess an informal culture regardless of any official mission statements that may or may not be in existence. Formal countercultures have their origins in the trade unions and professional associations subscribed to by organizational participants. However, the more widespread and intangible sub-culture is that which develops between workers purely as a consequence of social interaction. Indeed, Turner (1973) points out that 'sub-cultures exert influences over their members which may be stronger than the influences of the organization's culture'. The influence of sub-cultures is invariably understated by firms wishing to impose culture management programmes on the organization. One possible reason for this is the impossibility of an external change agent being able to identify, let alone set about quantifying, what is at best a highly intangible subject and at worst a taboo one. This situation has led Morgan (1986) to conclude that 'culture is not something that is imposed on a social setting. Rather, it develops during the course of social interaction'.

ORGANIZATIONAL CULTURE AND THE HOSPITALITY INDUSTRY

The problem with applying culture management theory to the hospitality industry is made apparent by Peters and Waterman (1982), when they state that:

> controlling quality in a service business is a particularly difficult problem. Unlike manufacturing in which one can sample what comes off the line and reject bad lots, what gets produced in service businesses and what gets consumed happens at the same time and in the same place.

The potential impact of an employee's behaviour and attitude in such instances has caused issues relating to culture management to be addressed by hospitality firms. Some academic literature regarding hospitality culture management has appeared in response to, or as a consequence of, this trend.

Reyes and Kleiner (1990) begin by outlining Roger Harrison's (1972) four distinct organization types showing 'how each of these cultures attempts to instil purpose in their employees'. These four cultures, namely:

- power oriented;
- rule oriented;
- achievement oriented; and
- support oriented,

each bring both positive and negative aspects to an organization. Reyes and Kleiner (1990) enthuse that:

the way to build an organizational purpose is to create a mission statement with a vision that brings all of the positive aspects of the four cultures into the corporation.

As with much popular culture literature, Reyes and Kleiner (1990) are overly concerned with management roles in culture change at the expense of other staff. They state that:

after top management has determined what the customer wants and how all levels of the organization envision meeting the needs, and organizational purpose coloured by a vision and mission statement exists then, guided by the mission statement they helped develop, the employees will adopt the organizational purpose. The employees will work with management when the vision is real to them.

The apparent ease with which organizational culture can be directed, as suggested by these statements, is in contrast to the majority of work on this subject, which emphasizes the complex nature of such tasks and:

suggests that anybody who tries to unearth a corporation's culture, much less change it, is in for a rough time. The values and beliefs people espouse frequently have little to do with the ones that really hold: these tend to be half-hidden and elusive (*Fortune*, 1983).

In the light of this evidence, the value of Reyes and Kleiner's contribution to the hospitality culture debate is questionable. Much more interesting is the contribution of Robert H.Woods (1989). Woods begins by stating that:

there is no such thing as a 'right' culture. Cultures that work for one company may not work for another.

Furthermore, he claims that:

a restaurateur should not try to duplicate the culture of a, say, successful airline company. Most likely such a cultural transplant would not be effective.

Woods still seeks to find comparable traits between the five restaurant chains he studied in the hope that they will make possible the construction of an outline of 'some of the elements of the restaurant industry's culture'.

Woods (1989) openly admits the application of his work to be motivated by improving financial returns for shareholders, stating that 'the result should be a better guest experience and a stronger bottom line'. The link between culture and profit in the context of the hospitality industry would appear to be an obvious one to make, given that in many instances, the organizational member is the product. However, Siehl and Martin (1990) conclude that:

in addition to these limitations in the definition and measurement of culture, these studies have not definitively established an empirical link to financial performance.

Woods (1989) does deserve merit for his recognition that organization culture is difficult to change and, more importantly, for stating that:

> a commonly held misconception about culture is that top management can somehow drive or build a company's culture. While management can greatly influence many elements of company's culture, all members of an organization exert influence over your culture.

In contrast, Lundberg and Woods (1990) leave behind the consideration of staff involvement in culture change processes, in favour of focusing on the role of the manager as cultural leader. Building on Woods' (1989) earlier work concerning investigation of the culture of five US restaurant chains, the authors argue that culture manipulation should be considered to be the new financially attractive option for restaurant managers to pursue, and add that there are 'three broad managerial roles for doing this:

- the roles of cultural spokesperson;
- cultural assessor; and
- facilitator of cultural modification.'

Lundberg and Woods' (1990) ideas place heavy emphasis on the quality of the manager and highlight well the problem facing many organizations attempting culture change. The UK hotel industry is characterized by the dominance of single unit operations. In such instances, culture management techniques are likely to be unnecessary and inapplicable, as the organization will be personally run and will reflect the owner's attitudes. Staff may feel as though they work for the owner, not the business. In such a situation, the culture of the firm may be so directly connected to the personalities involved that a culture change programme (besides being prohibitively expensive) would have to change the core beliefs and schema of the manager before any organizational change could be effected. Alternatively, if the possibility exists that a culture change programme does not need to penetrate 'the level of deep meaning' (Lundberg and Woods, 1990) in an organization and should not seek to change organization members' attitudes, then is it enough to simply change their behaviour? Lundberg and Woods, while leaving some aspects of hospitality culture unresolved, at least attempt to attend to some of its complexities and in doing so raise some interesting questions regarding the realities of initiating a culture change programme.

Quality

CASE STUDIES

Three luxury hotels were selected to form the basis of an examination of the extent to which culture techniques have been or could be adopted. The hotels were selected on the basis of known personal contacts in the respective Personnel/Human Resource Departments willing to co-operate in this research. Also, hotels of a relatively similar size and market segmentation were selected in order that comparisons could more easily be drawn than would be the case if markedly contrasting units were juxtaposed.

Data gathered in the period November 1993 to January 1994. Initial intervention comprised interviews with the personal contact in each unit. These interviews were pursued in accordance with a questionnaire interview schedule, although this framework was intermittently departed from, as and when related areas of interest for discussion became apparent. In the case of each hotel, a sample of thirty questionnaires were left with the personal contacts, whom it was agreed would disperse them randomly to staff attending non-departmental specific training sessions in the ensuing fourteen days. These questionnaires were to be completed by the respondents and returned to the personal contact at the conclusion of the training session. Accordingly, the response rate was 85 per cent, although no data are available for one hotel (The Hardy) as the distribution of questionnaires was not permitted. Completed batches of questionnaires were returned in reply-paid envelopes, within which it was requested that any literature relating to mission statement, organizational chart, induction or general human resource objectives should be included. A brief description of the three hotels now follows. Although one of the hotels was prepared 'to go public', the others requested anonymity and so in each case, pseudonyms have been used. The hotels are as follows.

The Thomas Hardy Hotel

The Hardy is a five-star luxury hotel located in London's West End. The hotel has 252 rooms, 590 employees and is independently owned by an investment agency. Personal contact at this hotel was established with the hotel's Senior Personnel Officer.

The Charles Dickens Hotel

The Dickens is a four-star deluxe hotel located in London's West End. The hotel has 200 rooms, 292 staff and is branded accordingly by its company. Personal contact at the hotel was established with the hotel's Area Training Officer.

The Walter Scott Hotel

Walter Scott is an 830 acre golf and leisure resort in countryside near Scotland's Central Belt. The hotel has 236 rooms and 500 staff. Personal contact at this hotel was established with the Director of Personnel.

MAIN FINDINGS

1. Mission Statement

The most apparent indicator of an organization's priorities and values, a mission statement, immediately demonstrates its cultural orientation and agenda. In each of the units studied, a mission statement was in place. The essence of these statements is concentrated in tabular form below.

	Hardy	**Dickens**	**Scott**
Wordcount of Statement	86	119	17
Operational Excellence	✔	✔	✔
Improved Profitability	✔	✔	
Financial Accountability	✔		
Quality of Service	✔	✔	
Development of Staff		✔	
Innovation and Initiative	✔		
Specific Commitments to Staff		✔	✔

From this it can be seen that both the Hardy and Dickens encompass the majority of sentiments in their statements and only wordcount prevents the Scott from similarly accommodating these concerns. Attention will now, therefore, turn to the expression of these policies in terms of the formal organization charts of the hotels.

2. Organization Charts

The flattening off of organizational structure and devolving of decision-making authority from management to employee level have become synonymous with the cultural technique of 'empowerment'. However, such a policy is not expressed by the Hardy's organization chart, where it was clear that executives, heads of departments and supervisors were intended to ensure that teams functioned smoothly; and that any situation that might arise was promptly and correctly handled by an appropriate member of the hierarchy. The Dickens exhibited a similarly hierarchical organization chart although reference was made more generally to a structure implying an 'inverted pyramid' design to be in place. In 1992 a significant 'headcount rationalization', forced by the consequences of economic recession, manifested itself in the form of an organizational flattening exercise at the Dickens which removed all layers of personnel between line manager (now retitled 'supervisor') and staff (now retitled 'assistants'). In the restaurant, for example, the effect of this action was than an operation previously embracing demarcations such as 'Commis Waiter' and 'Assistant Restaurant Manager' now simply comprised of Food and Beverage Assistants and a single Food and Beverage Supervisor.

The Scott Hotel had a fivefold increase in profits in the ten year period to 1992, but saw business levelling out. Management at the hotel consequently embarked on an introspective analysis to ascertain from staff what could be done as a team to deliver a better service and identify possible distractions to service delivery. The hotel consequently revised the classic pyramid-shaped management structure that had been in place. Essentially, the thirty operations teams of the new structure were distinguished by serving either 'external customers', 'internal customers', or 'tomorrow's customer', and were supported by a second layer of departmental managers. Interestingly, this new order was created without widespread compulsory rationalizations, although certain middle management posts were eliminated, involving some voluntary redundancies mainly among those staff who felt they could not cope with the new structure.

3. Language

The extent to which language is utilized in a luxury hotel to reinforce guest perceptions is made apparent if front-of-house phraseology and staff canteen discussion are contrasted. However, the language employed for departmental specification and job description is also an expression of organizational culture. For example, 'the term human resource management is . . . frequently used to connote a progressive form of personnel management' (French and Bell, 1984).

The language of Thomas Hardy is that of a highly structured organization. Job titles such as 'Senior Assistant Food and Beverage Manager' illustrate the significance attached to seniority and rank within the hotel. This is in contrast to The Scott, where consideration was given to the abolition of job titles entirely, although it was concluded that guests would feel uncomfortable with such an arrangement. However, signatory titles have been removed from internal mail and the use of first names is widespread. While The Scott consciously avoided labelling their culture initiative, language has constituted an element of this change process, with all job titles and descriptions being adjusted. For example, the name of the switchboard room was changed to communications department, which the staff and the department felt described their role more precisely.

Besides employing the culturally aware job titles previously outlined, The Dickens operate 'quality through people', 'job enrichment' and 'multi-skilling' procedures, and sold organizational restructuring to staff by reiterating the benefits of these initiatives over moving notice boards within the hotel. Similarly, The Hardy use language to reinforce company values by encouraging staff to think of residents as being 'guests, not customers'.

4. Sustaining the Design – the Recruitment and Appraisal Process

Considering the previously cited problems associated with any attempted manipulation of an individual's behaviour (let alone core values), a logical method of controlling the complexion of employees within an organization is to focus on the processes selecting individuals for entry into the organization. Indeed, given their exhaustive recruitment procedures, the hotels in this study would seem to concur with the view that: 'in the long term, according to many human-resource specialists, the key to culture is whom you hire and promote', particularly considering that attempted cultural change 'will cost you between five and ten per cent of what you already spend on the people whose behaviour is supposed to change' (*Fortune*, 1983).

The three hotels all pursued similar recruitment strategies. Vacancies are filled either from advertisements placed in relevant journals or else by returning to speculative applications held on file. In each instance, eligible candidates are sought from existing personnel or personal recommendations before any external recruitment is initiated. Results from survey research conducted indicate that 56.5 per cent of respondents at The Scott and 28.6 per cent at The Dickens knew somebody at the hotel prior to entering the organization. Given the contrasting geographical locations of these units, the difference between the two figures is unsurprising. Approximately 15 per cent of positions at The Dickens are filled internally from the wider company. The hotel is currently operating at minimum staffing levels, so that everybody that leaves needs to be replaced.

The hotels all operate interviewing procedures involving an initial 'screening' meeting with Personnel, followed by a further possible four interviews with the relevant departmental managers – depending on the seniority of the vacancy. According to the Senior Personnel Officer at the Hardy, this system operates effectively, with 'a minimal number of people leaving after entering the hotel through Personnel'. Emphasis is placed on potential entrants possessing an attitude for the industry, with The Hardy and Scott hotels both believing that while skills can be inculcated, the attitude must be right from the outset.

In addition to selection by interview, The Dickens and Scott hotels employ personality typing inventories to ascertain the suitability of an applicant to the organization. Having identified the requisite outcomes for the various tasks within the hotels, The Dickens categorize staff as belonging to either an 'action', 'need' or 'team cluster'. These conclusions are reached by inviting respondents to 'think of a time when you were very busy or under pressure' and locate the emotions generated by this incident on Likert scales ranging from one-to-nine and polarized by adjectives such as 'enjoyable or unenjoyable'. Besides assisting the hotels in decision-making, these selection processes also led 42.9 per cent of survey respondents at The Dickens and 69.6 per cent at The Scott to record a positive response to the suggestion that the initial impression gained during selection was an important factor in choosing to assume employment at the establishments.

While it is comparatively easy to control an individual's cultural exposure at the recruitment stage, reinforcement of espoused values becomes more difficult once the organization has been entered. All three hotels operate induction processes, typically operating for twelve weeks and focusing on development of product knowledge and operating procedure. In addition to this, 'new starts' at The Scott are assigned a 'buddy', in order that initial cultural experiences are positive ones.

Once this period of induction has elapsed, The Hardy utilizes an annual appraisal system to monitor employee development, although this process does not contain input from Personnel, it is largely dependent for its accuracy and validity on the professionalism of the supervisor, and 'is not a brilliantly executed system' (interview with the Senior Personnel Officer). The Dickens attempts to maintain the momentum of cultural transmission to staff through an ongoing process of training. Besides operating the company 'gateway' and 'revenue guarantee' sales strategies – which teach staff how to capture and keep business – a 'training guarantee' scheme will soon be implemented. This programme will provide participants with an exhaustive checklist of multi-skilling targets covering points in detail, in making a bed, for example. Completion of the programme will be rewarded with the receipt of a company qualification, which will soon gain NVQ accreditation.

The Dickens has had some success in transmitting the significance of these values to staff. Survey evidence shows that respondents at the hotel unanimously recorded positive responses to the suggestion that customers are important, be they external or internal. However, while 100 per cent of Scott staff believed their skills to have improved since entering the organization, only 78.6 per cent of respondents at The Dickens expressed similar sentiments (of whom 64.3 per cent believed the hotel to have contributed significantly to the acquisition of these skills). Furthermore, the importance of personal development as a work motivation was rated more highly by Scott employees than by Dickens staff. The question of motivation at work will now be examined in greater detail.

5. Staff Motivation

The independent status of The Hardy and Scott hotels reduces the possible sources of motivation available for utilization by the units. The reputation of the properties serves to attract quality staff looking to improve their CV. The Scott offers 'better than average' pay, while The Hardy's remuneration package is worth approximately 30 per cent more than comparable London hotels.

The branding of The Dickens as a high class property serves to attract staff from other company properties, a fact supported by survey evidence demonstrating a 92.9 per cent positive response to the suggestion that the reputation of The Dickens was an important motivating factor in coming to join the hotel. Similarly, the significance of promotion as a motivation was also recognized by 92.9 per cent of respondents. The possibility of advancement through an international chain encourages staff to be motivated by training, as 'pay is average, certainly not the best' (interview with Area Training Officer). This fact is reflected in survey feedback which shows 42.9 per cent of Dickens respondents to regard pay as an important reason to stay at the hotel and 26.6 per cent to value tips. Comparable figures for The Scott show pay to be twice as important as at The Dickens, while only 4.3 per cent of staff considered income from tips to be of consequence.

The independent status of The Scott and The Hardy disqualifies the possibility of maintaining staff motivation through promotion because of limited opportunities in more senior levels of the organization. The Scott concentrates training on developing staff horizontally, encouraging employees to focus on achieving personal growth, not personal advancement. The average length of service of respondents to survey research at The Scott was 67 months, compared with 18 months at The Dickens, and illustrates the success of this policy.

While an individual's actions will be partly determined by commitments external to the organization, culture does play a part (be it positive or negative) in determining these behaviour patterns. An acid test of any organization's culture is, therefore, its labour turnover rate. The Hardy, Dickens and Scott hotels have labour turnover rates of 20 per cent, 66 per cent and 34 per cent respectively. The industry average is variable around 80–100 per cent, although higher figures have been recorded (Wood, 1992). These figures are unsurprising if they are considered in the context of previous evidence which showed The Hardy and The Scott to pay markedly above the going rate for hospitality workers, the unique status of these hotels and the possibility of vertical development offered by working for a chain hotel such as The Dickens. Nevertheless, survey data show The Dickens to perform consistently worse than The Scott in terms of respondent attitude to aspects of organizational life, such as approachability of supervisor and perception of work. Also, the labour turnover rate at The Hardy is perhaps surprising, given the 'traditional', formal structure outlined here.

DISCUSSION

The experiences of the three hotels explored above indicate the apparent pros-
perity of organizations operating within organizational culture frameworks.
The Scott was formerly arranged in a hierarchical structure, but the time delay
involved in processing guest requests provoked a review of this situation. The
Senior Personnel Officer (SPO) at The Hardy viewed the structure of the hotel
as presenting operational problems. 'Senior management are traditional
Hoteliers' she explained, 'and they feel threatened by empowerment. But things
must move on.' A reliance on hierarchy at The Hardy created two main problems, not least the dependency on coercive power as a work motivation. The
SPO's concern was that control through pulling rank was not the answer to
operational human resource management because 'you have to ask yourself how
long whipping will continue to work'. A powerful structure provides, moreover,
relatively little room for personal development – while blocks to promotion
mean that quality staff can be attracted to the hotel by remuneration, ambitious
individuals cannot ultimately be retained.

Leadership and charismatic figureheads tend to accompany instances of positive organizational culture. Accordingly, each of the formal organizations studied had been shaped by key individuals pending cultural impetus. The presence
of inspiring leadership may be required if resistance to cultural change is to be
minimized. While leadership is an important factor in overcoming the 'we've
always done it this way' syndrome among staff, the persistent over-emphasis of
the role of management in shaping organizational culture can lead to a failure
to identify the role of sub-cultures in steering organizations. Sub-cultures do not
apparently originate solely from the lower ranks of the organization.
Management at The Hardy appeared to be split into factions, with 'individual
pockets of excellence' but little common consensus. Given that certain managers
were lost during the transition period at The Scott, it seems fair to assume that
these individuals were resistant to change. Thus there may be evidence to support the earlier suggestion that it is extremely difficult to change attitudes, but
easy to change personnel.

It has been claimed by certain functionalist authors previously cited, that
interest in culture is motivated by a genuine commitment to worker welfare.
However, firms hitherto opposed to rationalization, such as IBM and Nissan
have recently abandoned such sentiments and, in 1992, the owners of The
Dickens did not so much terminate as murder theirs. The combined effect of pay
rises at The Dickens being postponed, the loss of a dedicated Personnel
Department, and staff leaving without authorization being issued to replace
them, has left employees feeling 'neglected'. 'Cultural change' claims *Fortune*
(1983), 'costs a fortune and takes forever', yet the realization by a member of
staff that they will not be getting a pay rise is rather more immediate, the financial consequences of which in the context of hospitality sales could be similarly
instantaneous. The reputation of the UK hotel industry as a whole suggests

that culture programmes should not be viewed as a 'quick-fix' solution to compensate for the absence of a reasonable human resource policy. This is especially so as the propensity for staff to change jobs rapidly in search of marginally better conditions brings into question the logic of directing funds at creating an organizational culture in staff who are unlikely to stay with the organization for any length of time.

Modern organizations have little alternative but to achieve outstanding levels of quality. All of the hotels discussed here had structures and policy to ensure that this quality could be achieved. Whether or not this policy was transposed into practice and quality actually achieved depended on the abundant contingencies outlined in the previous pages. If these considerations are recognized, then the answer to whether or not culture can be managed appears to be yes – but with the greatest difficulty (Pettigrew, 1990). The positive experiences of The Scott would suggest that there exists the possibility of re-engineering culture in the hotel industry, but while the possibility of influencing hotel organizational culture exists, the potential for changing this culture has been less convincingly proven. If culture management has a contribution to make in the hospitality context, it is the way in which it draws the focus away from the structure and nature of work, in favour of the structure and nature of the organization's members. In this context, culture management may appear to be a tremendously complex and intangible phenomenon but it is one that can clearly be manipulated effectively in the pursuit of organizational success.

REFERENCES

Fortune (1983) *The Corporate Culture Vulture* 17(10), pp 66–72.

French, W.L. and Bell, C.H. Jr (1984) *Organisation Development* p 204, Englewood Cliffs, NJ: Prentice-Hall.

Harrison, R. (1972) How to Describe your Organization, *Harvard Business Review* Sept–Oct.

Lundberg, C.C. and Woods, R.H.(1990) Modifying Restaurant Culture: Managers as Cultural Leaders, *International Journal of Contemporary Hospitality Management* 2(4), pp 4–12.

Morgan, G. (1986) *Images of Organization* p 127, Beverly Hills, CA: Sage.

Peters, T. and Austin, N. (1985) *A Passion for Excellence* New York: Fortuna.

Peters, T. and Waterman, R. Jr (1982) *In Search of Excellence: Lessons from Americas Best Run Companies* p xi, New York: Harper & Row.

Pettigrew, A.M. (1990) *Is Corporate Culture Manageable?* In D.C. Wilson and R.H. Rosenfeld (eds) p 268.

Reyes, J.R. and Kleiner, B.H. (1990) How to Establish an Organizational Purpose, *International Journal of Contemporary Hospitality Management* 2(4), pp 26–29.

Siehl, C. and Martin, J. (1990) *Organization Culture: A Key to Financial Performance?* In B. Schneider (ed.), (qv) p 268.

Silver, J. (1987) The Ideology of Excellence: Management and Neo-Conservatism, *Journal of Political Economy* 24, pp 105–129.

Thompson, P. and McHugh, D. (1990) *Work Organisations* p 235, London: Macmillan.

Turner, B. (1973) *The Industrial Subculture.* In G. Salaman and K. Thompson (eds), People and Organizations p 68.

Wilson, D.C. and Rosenfeld, R.H. (eds) (1990) *Managing Organizations* p 235, New York: McGraw-Hill.

Wood, R.C. (1992) *Working in Hotels and Catering* London: Routledge.

Woods, R.H. (1989) More Alike than Different: The Culture of the Restaurant Industry, *The Cornell HRA Quarterly* Aug, pp 82–97.

SECTION TWO
DELIVERING THE ADVANTAGE

4

Empowerment in the UK Hospitality Industry

Gillian A. Maxwell

Empowerment merits discussion due to its general topicality and particular applicability to hospitality organizations. This chapter discusses empowerment in the UK hospitality industry in contextual, cultural and experiential terms.

THE EMERGENCE OF EMPOWERMENT

That the business operating environment in mature economies is complex, dynamic and competitive is widely acknowledged (e.g. Norburn *et al.*, 1988; Nixon, 1995). The source of many of the contemporary pressures facing businesses is the changing nature of the service markets in which organizations operate. Principal among these changes are increasingly refined and sophisticated consumer buyer behaviour, skill and labour shortages, the impact of technology, fierce competition and the drive for quality and value. All of these contextual factors have a bearing on UK service organizations and, in duration and combination, have acted to precipitate a re-examination of organizational decision-making processes.

From scrutiny of traditional methods of decision-making emerged the notion of empowerment in the early 1990s as, so it was levelled, an effective strategic response to facilitate competitive advantage (Goski and Belfry, 1991). Empowerment is asserted to provide the interface between an organization's product/service offerings and the wants of individual customers. Thus it is a vehicle for tailoring customers' experiences and, as such, forms the basis of relationship marketing and competitive distinction.

Empowerment has been variously described:

- 'the process through which one individual helps another to acquire and use power' (Fisher, 1993);
- 'enabling people at all levels to feel they can make a difference, and giving them the confidence and skills to do so' (Clutterbuck, 1993);

- 'ensuring that the employee has the authority to do his or her job' (London, 1993);
- 'managed participation' (Frohman, 1992);
- 'sharing with front-line employees . . . the power to make decisions that influence organizational direction and performance' (Bowen and Lawler, 1992).

The common denominator of the definitions and descriptions – and indeed the key tenet – of empowerment is the devolution of decision-making to staff who previously had no responsibility for it. Whereas decision-making was once the exclusive preserve of managers, empowerment extends decision-making to other employees (e.g. Ripley and Ripley, 1992; Eccles, 1993). The advent of the principle of decentralized decision-making was, however, not a radical and sudden departure from deeply rooted, centralized decision-making practices. Rather, it was the culmination of:

> the steady management trend during the past 30 years [towards] a work culture in which all employees take a personal responsibility for the work and for improving the effectiveness of their jobs (Andrews, 1994).

Recognizing the need to respond to contextual changes and eager to secure competitive advantage, empowerment was readily embraced by many employers. Enticingly, empowerment also promised resource economy by delayering management structures in the 'redistribution of organizational power to achieve corporate objectives' (Tam, 1994) and by raising employee productivity (Scott and Jaffe, 1991). More indirectly, empowerment can also be an enabling vehicle for learning companies, where there is 'a climate in which individual members are encouraged to learn and to develop their full potential' (Pedler *et al*. 1988). Employers can promote empowerment to their employees as an extension of industrial democracy and employee involvement in general terms, and a means of personal development in individual terms. From the employee's perspective, the attraction of empowerment lies in the prospect of increased personal autonomy, development and job satisfaction.

For human resource specialists in the hotel sector, empowerment holds the potential of offering a new-found, much needed source of organizational legitimacy and value. In the UK industry as a whole, managerial perceptions of the contribution of personnel management – or human resource management (HRM) as the function is now more commonly known – is historically and typically low. Reflecting this low status is Tyson and Fell's (1986) commentary on:

> the crisis in personnel management . . . the crisis in confidence among personnel managers themselves and a related crisis over their credibility among their managerial colleagues.

Personnel management has even been dubbed as having a 'Cinderella image' (Davis, 1987). In the UK hospitality industry in particular, perceptions of the organizational contribution of human resource functions are markedly lower than those for industry in its entirety. Beyond the widespread and deservedly poor public reputation of the hospitality industry with regard to employment conditions and practices (Price, 1994), it has been asserted that 'the personnel function remains largely ignored in hotel and catering organizations' (Wood, 1992). Lucas (1995) implicitly concurs with this assertion in her proposition that; 'the personnel function in the [UK] hotel and catering industry is poorly developed, unsophisticated, simplistic and reactive'.

However, with ever-intensifying competitive pressures in the marketplace (Connell, 1994), hospitality organizations may be increasingly inclined to review the organizational contribution and status of the human resource functions (Price, 1994). Ultimately, hospitality employers may even use human resource management itself as the basis of competitive advantage like other, innovative employers (Sparrow *et al.*, 1994). In the meantime, however, it is more realistic that human resource management will provide a vehicle for, rather than a direct means of, competitive advantage through the introduction of new initiatives like empowerment. Lashley's (1995) research supports this contention:

> managerial interest in employee empowerment in the hospitality industry
> has generally been associated with concern to gain competitive advantage
> through improvements in service quality.

Thus the launching pad for empowerment in the UK hospitality sector was established: the changing nature of service markets, employer and employee receptiveness, and the search for organizational legitimacy for the HRM function. Empowerment was, indeed, soon established in management jargon and practice (Hogg, 1993), becoming 'one of the corporate buzz words of the 1990s' (Eisman, 1991). In 1991, Jones and Davies were predicting that: 'the 1990s will continue to see more and more hotel companies "empower" their managers and their employees', and – rather optimistically – went as far as claiming that there is evidence to suggest that "empowerment" will become a significant factor in how hotel and food service firms are managed in the 1990s.' By early 1992, it was levelled that empowerment was 'widely recognized as an important method for improving hospitality employees' performance' (Sternberg, 1992).

Examples of empowerment in practice, like Gleneagles Hotel in Perthshire (Goymour, 1993), have begun to emerge, following on from the lead taken in the United States (Brymer, 1991). For organizations such as Marriott Hotels, empowerment was seen as important in securing competitive advantage through a total quality management (TQM) drive (Clutterbuck and Kernaghan, 1994). Additionally, empowerment was the focus of a Marriott advertising campaign. A major TQM initiative was introduced by Marriott Hotels in the mid-1980s, focusing all business efforts on customer satisfaction. Integral to the TQM initiative was allowing front line staff greater freedom to satisfy guests' individual needs and wants as they became apparent. Hence empowerment became a medium for the wider TQM effort. The relationship between empowerment and TQM may be described as symbiotic in that 'empowerment is essential for successful TQM, just as the TQM culture will provide an environment for empowerment' (Hillman, 1993). Marriott were pioneering in recognizing this mutuality before many other hospitality organizations. By the late 1980s, the TQM initiative was sufficiently mature in the Glasgow Marriott for quality management to be described by the Training Manager as a 'way of doing business . . . part of the business culture permeating all management activities'.

THE ORGANIZATIONAL ENVIRONMENT FOR EMPOWERMENT

Beyond the fanfare that greeted the concept of empowerment, enlightened employers, like Marriott, have recognized that empowerment involves more than simply introducing employees to greater authority and independence in decision-making at the point of contact with customers. Dobbs (1993) for example, contends that 'conditions must be right for empowerment to thrive'. He suggests that organizations should encourage the following conditions for successful empowerment.

Empowerment – 'A Hospitable Climate':

- **participation**: all employees are 'actively and willingly engaged in their jobs';
- **innovation**: innovative ideas are encouraged, 'curiosity is highly regarded';
- **access to information**: employees at all levels determine the information they need to do their jobs;
- **accountability**: 'employees should be held accountable for behaving responsibly towards others, operating with a positive approach, producing desired, agreed-upon results, their own credibility and integrity, and giving their best' (summarized from Dobbs, 1993).

Benson (1992), as a further example, adopts a more strategic approach in his specification of the organizational elements in supporting and promoting empowerment:

- compelling vision;
- clear definition of success;
- timely performance feedback;
- established rules of play;
- valuing diversity;
- delegating decision-making authority;
- allowing individual and team initiative;
- sound organizational structures.

Another way of framing empowerment, developing Benson's model in organizations, is to delineate the conditions of successful empowerment. Most fundamentally, a pre-requisite to empowerment is the competence of every employee in their job. Empowerment practices cannot compensate for incompetence, but only operate and build on the basis of competence. A common means of achieving job competence and consistency is reliance on clearly defined operational practices. A key support to operating standards and procedures is a defined organizational structure, which represents the relationships between different functional teams and levels of job. In turn, organizational structures are a reflection of the organizational culture and vision. Ultimately, the organizational vision will influence the implementation of empowerment, and, conversely, the decisions empowered employees take at the customer interface will ultimately affect organizational performance and development. This model of the organizational context of empowerment, represented below, reflects the aforementioned notions of organizational growth and learning organizations, as articulated by Critten (1993), for example. It also embraces and extends aspects of empowerment identified earlier in the definitions of empowerment proffered by Ripley and Ripley (1992), and Bowen and Lawler (1992).

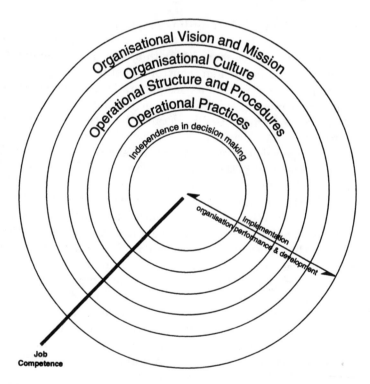

Figure 4.1: Model of contextual empowerment   *(McLean and Maxwell, 1994)*

EMPOWERMENT EXPERIENCES

With employers developing experience of empowerment, the concept and principles of empowerment can be more closely examined and re-defined: the theory can be informed by practice (Terry and Hadland, 1995). Thus the thrust of
commentary has inevitably moved from the promotional to the more critical,
tracking the 'depressingly predictable pattern followed by the reactions to new
organizational and management developments initiatives' (Lowe, 1994). Fault
lines have started to be aired by commentators like Belasco and Stayer (1994).
More damning still are the charges of empowerment being 'one of the most over-
worked buzzwords of the 1990s' (Pickard, 1993); and 'a dirty word' (Anon, 1994).
After a few years of ascendancy, the notion of empowerment could clearly be
seen to be in critical decline. Empowerment, its seems, is proving not to be an
organizational panacea but a more complex, multi-faceted phenomenon than
initially appreciated. Attention has now been drawn to a number of potential
barriers to successful empowerment. In particular, employee reluctance to
accept responsibility and management resistance to relinquishing power have
been highlighted.

According to Maccoby (1992), front-line employees are likely, in fact, to be
more 'fearful of taking responsibility' than senior managers. However, as
Maccoby (*ibid*) suggests, this is more likely to be the case when employees are
used to a high degree of management control and supervision. In contrast, one
of the characteristics of service industries generally and hospitality organizations specifically is a more flexible degree of job autonomy (Mullins, 1992).
Another explanation for employees' reluctance to accept empowerment may,
with some justification, be cynicism about their jobs being enlarged in assuming a degree of managerial responsibility for the same remuneration. This may
be counteracted, as Hogg (1993/4) points out using an example of the Grosvenor
House Hotel in London, by employees' gains in job satisfaction and/or revised,
more flexible performance management, as Goodwen (1993) advocates.

Because delayering is often one of the concomitant factors of empowerment
(e.g. Tam, 1994), it is not altogether surprising that managers may feel personally threatened by the advance of empowerment. Even where it does not lead to
management job losses, it at least calls for the re-engineering of the nature of
management jobs (e.g. Arkin, 1995). Furthermore, empowerment may represent a fundamental challenge to managers' perceptions of their role; an inherent necessity of empowerment is managers accepting that they can no longer
control employees but must instead trust them (Brymer, 1991). In pragmatic
terms, while managers may dislike empowerment, they may have little choice
but to accept it as part of contemporary organizational life. Any 'hidden contempt' (Nicholls, 1995) for empowerment may be overcome, however, to some
extent, by training and role clarification (Chaudron, 1995).

The Glasgow Marriott Hotel

The 298 bedroom Glasgow Marriott exemplar represents a longitudinal case study analysis. Empirical evidence, gathered in the year November 1994 to December 1995, has been garnered from a series of interviews with personnel and training management staff, and two employee surveys. One survey was conducted by Scott's Hotels Ltd (the franchiser) in November 1994, as the unit's annual general survey on employee attitudes/opinions. This survey is standard for all Marriott hotels and is administered by a management research company based in Philadelphia, USA. The other survey, completed on a self-selection basis, was also administered in November 1994, although it explicitly canvassed views and experiences on empowerment and was designed by the author. The completion rate for the general attitude survey was 88 per cent of the hotel staff, and 30 per cent for the empowerment survey.

As outlined earlier, Marriott Hotels introduced its TQM drive in the late 1980s. To support and extend this drive, the Glasgow Marriott, one of the group's 300-plus hotels, introduced empowerment in late 1990. This action was founded on the recognition of the centrality of staff in achieving, ultimately, competitive advantage in a mature market through their direct contact with guests. The unit's experience of empowerment follows a learning cycle from employee awareness, to training, to working with empowerment and, finally, to acceptance of empowerment. In the early stages of introduction of the TQM drive, most employees readily accepted their enlarged decision-making capacity. Where employees were unwilling to adapt to empowerment, they disengaged their services from the hotel. In recruiting replacement staff, an attempt is made to identify the potential to take personal initiative to support empowerment.

Initial investigation by Marriott into the impact of the newly introduced, structured empowerment practices, showed that the employees' decisions were proving expensive. Many freshly empowered employees were making hasty decisions to rebate meals or accommodation costs, for example, no sooner than even a suggestion of a complaint was heard. With greater role definition, as advocated by Arkin (1995), and more training and experience, this problem eased significantly. Empowerment practices have since matured to the point that they are now described by the Personnel and Training Manager as 'an ingrained, integral part of how business is done [in the unit] . . . part of our operating philosophy and, in effect, a cultural change'. This statement can be validated in two ways. First, by the cessation of training sessions on empowerment *per se* and, instead, the inclusion of an empowerment dimension in the training sessions conducted, where relevant. Second, in the empowerment questionnaire 61 per cent of respondents recorded that they consider themselves to be empowered to either a very significant or significant extent, principally in making decisions affecting customers.

That employees are satisfied with empowerment being an integral element of their job is reflected in the job features that they like best. The most popular feature of working for Marriott was recorded in the empowerment question-naire as the physical working environment (by 96 per cent of respondents). The next most popular features were: customer contact (80 per cent), team working (73 per cent), making decisions (71 per cent) and accepting responsibility (67 per cent), all of which reflect the very purpose and nature of empowerment. The general satisfaction with empowerment is underlined by the 75 per cent of respondents who recorded that they actively enjoy being involved in decision making (24 per cent of respondents are neutral about it and only 1 per cent dis-like it).

This overall satisfaction with empowerment is likely to be attributable, at least in part, to the framework within which the empowerment practices operate (cf. the model of contextual empowerment). Most respondents (88 per cent) consider that they receive appropriate guidelines on the decisions they take, for example through coaching and employee handbooks. Further, most (94 per cent) consider that the management trusts and supports their decisions.

The employees' positive approach to empowerment is also manifest in the survey finding that the benefits of empowerment outweigh the disadvantages in number and significance. The recorded advantages are improved personal job satisfaction (69 per cent of respondents), improved customer service (65 per cent), speedier decisions (63 per cent) and personal development (53 per cent). Sixteen per cent of respondents even recorded that fewer staff being needed is a perceived advantage, which may be rather surprising from their perspective. Enthusiasm for empowerment was expressed by additional comments from the employees for example:

- 'empowerment practices make my job more exciting and challenging';
- 'empowerment practices develop my personal job experience'.

Thus empowerment for the majority of the Glasgow Marriott employees appears to coincide with Clutterbuck's (1993) definition of empowerment in par-ticular, as they are given the requisite 'confidence and skills' to be effectively empowered. Further, the employees' perspectives generally mirror the theoret-ical case made earlier for the attraction of empowerment to employees.

Nevertheless, a proportion of employees do have a degree of criticism of empowerment. The main criticism evident from the empowerment survey, cited by 53 per cent of respondents, is that communication problems can arise. Related to this, at times, work practices can be disorganized, as indicated by 37 per cent of respondents, and staff can feel more pressurized, according to 39 per cent of respondents. Also, 35 per cent noted that empowerment can give rise to competition among staff and a 'bottleneck' for a reduced number of promoted posts. As employees' confidence and perception of their ability grows, so too may their desire for promotion; some 58 per cent of the respondents noted that they dislike lack of opportunities for promotion. Similarly, the managers level a degree of criticism at empowerment. Their criticisms centre on their quantity of work due to the delayered management structures, the increasing reliance on systems and the constant pressure to keep staff motivated.

The Marriott group clearly recognizes the centrality of their 'front-line' employees in commercial terms and, hence, in employee management terms. This is in marked contrast to the general hospitality industry marginalization of employee management as outlined earlier. Indeed, one of the five strategic goals towards which the Glasgow Marriott strives is to be above the company average for associate [employee] fulfilment as measured by the employee opinion survey. The regular implementation of the company attitude survey and the response to the survey findings underlines this commitment. Furthermore, these surveys reflect recognition that empowerment may have associated issues/problems and requires an organizational/contextual framework, as discussed above. Questions in the company attitude survey seek to gauge the employees' views on the identified key aspects of empowerment, viz.:

- management listening and acting;
- management fairness and respect in dealing with staff;
- communication and co-operation;
- job opportunities and performance;
- job satisfaction.

The company attitude survey conducted in November 1994 highlighted the [then] pressing issue of high levels of dissatisfaction with pay. As a result, pay was increased across all levels of staff the following March, echoing Goodwen's (1993) position on flexibility in reward management. Other issues raised in the survey are addressed more indirectly but, arguably, no less effectively. For example, the other two key issues highlighted by the November 1994 company survey was the lack of fairness and respect shown by a few departmental heads to staff, and the lack of opportunities for promotion (raised also in the empowerment survey). The approach to solving this issue was, first, to de-personalize it. This was achieved by stressing that the survey responses were perceptual, not factual and involving all departmental heads in the solutions to the negative perceptions. All departmental heads were then invited to identify up to three personal commitments which could improve the negative perceptions. The commitments included more regular, formal involvement and participation with staff – in, for example, meetings chaired by staff themselves on a rotating basis and one-to-one appraisals – and internal advertising of company-wide vacancies. At the time of the last interview with the Personnel and Training Manager, in December 1995, the commitments were still in operation. Their effect will be assessed in the next employee opinion survey.

It can be seen, therefore, that empowerment for the Glasgow Marriott means investment in staff through a constant process of review of their perceptions and subsequent refinement of their management. Business performance results – by hard and soft measures – continue to demonstrate a high return on the investment.

CONCLUSIONS: EMPOWERMENT IN THE FUTURE

The Marriott empowerment experience in particular suggests that empowerment, if managed effectively and sensitively, can help secure, but not guarantee the all-important competitive advantage. Adopting empowerment is, however, a double-edged sword. In addition to the commercial gains, inherent in empowerment are far-reaching financial, HRM and cultural consequences.

The tension between the benefits and consequences of empowerment are illustrated in Newton's (1993) summation of empowerment in Harvester Chain Restaurants: 'empowerment is not an easy route to take but the rewards of real empowerment are inestimable'. These rewards must be offset against Harvester's investment of 'about £1 million per year in the training, development and empowerment of all 3,000 of their team members' (*ibid*). For an industry renowned for its lack of training, the training requirements of empowerment may act to discourage or even deter its potential adopters.

Equally the role of, and emphasis on, HRM in empowerment may require too radical a shift in policy and practice for some hospitality employers. The HRM implications are potentially wide-ranging. They cover the spectrum of employee resourcing (e.g. recruitment and human resource planning), employee development (e.g. training, management development, appraisals, career and succession planning) and employee relations (e.g. communications and reward management). Furthermore, the relationship between line managers' and human resource specialists' responsibility for HRM is called into question. As Holpp (1995) points out, a pivotal element in empowerment is line managers acting as employee coaches and facilitators; they should be attuned and responsive to their staff needs. Thus HRM becomes a significant part of the line management jobs. For HRM specialists, empowerment may mean enhanced or diminished responsibility. Their fate will depend on the organizational expectations of the potential contribution of the personnel function in the 'changing values and culture, work processes, structures, role and responsibilities within and between organizations' (Fonda and Rowland, 1995), that are associated with empowerment. Re-examining the contribution of HRM in strategic, cultural and practical terms is, it appears, an inevitable part of empowerment. The essential focus of change due to empowerment is, however, in organizational culture. As Werner (1992) emphasizes, 'empowerment cannot work without . . . purposeful cultural change'.

As empowerment is currently still 'more talked about than practised' (Fonda and Rowland, 1995), many of the consequences of empowerment may never be realized. Ironically, if empowerment practices were adopted widely in the UK hospitality industry, empowerment may cease to offer a primary means of sustained competitive advantage. The basis of any commercial success due to empowerment is largely – and arguably – the service standard and differentiation that empowerment secures from its competitors. If all competitors rely heavily on empowerment for service differentiation, by definition, there will come a point where there is no differentiation (or novelty), so forcing hospitality organizations to seek alternative means of competitive advantage. Empowerment cannot then be a key determinant of competitive advantage; instead, it may be an element of the service offering. Thus in the long-term, empowerment should not be judged by its organizational prominence but by its integration into the organizational culture and operating procedures. In this way, empowerment may facilitate competitive advantage by allowing customers to receive a 'differential' mix centred around their particular requirements.

REFERENCES

Andrews, G. (1994) Mistrust, The Hidden Obstacle to Empowerment, *H R Magazine* 39(9), pp 66–70.

Anon, (1994) Empowerment: Why Has it Become a Dirty Word? *Involvement* Summer, pp 8–9.

Arkin, A. (1995) Empowerment: The Bumpy Road to Devolution, *People Management* 1(24), 30 November, pp 34–36.

Belasco, J.A. and Stayer, R.C. (1994) Why Empowerment Doesn't Empower: The Bankruptcy of Current Paradigms, *Business Horizons* 37(2), pp 29–41.

Benson, T.E. (1992) Quality Congress Legislates – Focus on People, *Industry Week* 241(14), pp 11–13.

Bowen, D.E. and Lawler, E.E. (1992) The Empowerment of Service Workers: What, Why, How and When, *Sloan Management Review* 33(3), pp 31–39.

Brymer, R.A. (1991) Employee Empowerment: A Guest-Driven Leadership Strategy, *The Cornell HRA Quarterly* 32 (1), pp 58–68.

Carr, C. (1994) Empowered Organizations, Empowering Leaders, *Training and Development* 48(3), pp 39–44.

Chaudron, D. (1995) The Authority Matrix: Empowerment and Role Clarification, *H R Focus* 72(5), pp 22–23.

Clutterbuck, D. (1993) Clarify Your Purpose, *Managing Service Quality*, pp 5–6.

Clutterbuck, D. and Kernaghan, S. (1994) *The Power of Empowerment* London: Kogan Page.

Connell, J. (1994) Branding Strategies for Food and Beverage Operations. In B. Davis and A. Lockwood *Food and Beverage Management* p 48, Oxford: Butterworth-Heinemann.

Critten, P. (1993) *Investing in People – Towards Corporate Capability* pp 203–240, Oxford: Butterworth Heinemann.

Davis, T. (1987) How Personnel Can Lose Its Cinderella Image, *Personnel Management* 19(12), pp 34–36.

Dobbs, J.H. (1993) The Empowerment Environment, *Training and Development* 47(2), pp 55–57.

Eccles, T. (1993) The Deceptive Allure of Empowerment, *Long Range Planning* 26(6), pp 13–21.

Eisman, R. (1991) Power to the People – A Hotel Company Places Guest Satisfaction in the Hands of People on the Front Line, *Incentive* 165(10), pp 116, 140, 218.

Fisher, D. (1993) *Communications in Organizations* (2nd edn) pp 413–415 St. Paul, MN: West Publishing, .

Frohman, M. (1992) The Aimless Empowered, *Industry Week* 241(8), pp 64–66.

Fonda, N. and Rowland, H. (1995) Empowerment – Take Me to Your (Personnel) Leader, *People Management* 1(25), pp 18–23.

Goodwen, M. (1993) Rewarding Empowerment, *Involvement and Participation* (*UK*) 618, pp 8–9,11.

Goski, K.L. and Belfry, M. (1991) Achieving Competitive Advantage through Employee Empowerment, *Employee Relations Today* 18(2), pp 213–220.

Goymour, D. (1993) All Change at Gleneagles, *Caterer and Hotelkeeper* 186(3789), pp 30–33.

Hillman, P. (1993) Unleashing the Right Potential, *Managing Service Quality*, pp 53–56.

Hobbs, J.H. (1993) The Empowerment Environment, *Training and Development*, pp 55–57.

Hogg, C. (1993/94) The Pow in Empowerment, *Human Resources*, pp 70–74.

Holpp, L. (1995) New Roles for Leaders: An HRD Reporter's Enquiry, *Training and Development* 49(3), pp 46–50.

Jones, P. and Davies, A. (1991) Empowerment: A Study of General Managers of Four Star Hotel Properties in the UK, *International Journal of Hospitality Management* 10(3), pp 211–217.

Lashley, C. (1995) Towards an Understanding of Employee Empowerment in Hospitality Service, *International Journal of Contemporary Hospitality Management* 7(1), pp 27–32.

London, M. (1993) Relationships Between Career Motivation, Empowerment and Support for Career Development, *Journal of Occupational and Organizational Psychology* 66(1), pp 55–69.

Lowe, P. (1995) So You Want to Empower Your Organization . . .? *Journal of Strategic Change* 3, pp 277–280.

Lucas, R. (1995) *Managing Employee Relations in the Hotel and Catering Industry* p 45, London: Cassell.

Maccoby, M. (1992) The Human Side – Creating an Empowered Organization, *Research Technology Management* 35(3), pp 50–51.

McLean, M. and Maxwell, G.A. (1994) The Impact of Empowerment on Store Performance in UK Retailing. Paper presented at European Institute of Retailing and Services Studies (EIRASS) Canadian Institute of Retailing and Services Studies (CIRASS) Recent Advances in Retailing and Service Science Conference Lake Louise, Canada.

Mullins, L.J. (1992) *Hospitality Management – A Human Resources Approach* p 185, London: Pitman Publishing.

Newton, S. (1993) Empowering the Front Line, *Training Officer* 29(8), pp 252–254.

Nicholls, J. (1995) Empowerment: Tackling Hidden Contempt, *People Management* 1(24), p 36.

Nixon, B. (1995) Training's Role in Empowerment, *People Management* 1(3), pp 36–38.

Norburn, D., Manning, K. and Birley, S. (1988) Why Large Corporations Must Change, *Management Decision* 2(4), pp 44–47.

Pedler, M., Boydell, J. and Burgoyne, J. (1988) London: Prentice Hall.

Pickard, J. (1993) The Real Meaning of Empowerment, *Personnel Management* 25(11), pp 28–33.

Price, L. (1994) Poor Personnel Practice in the Hotel and Catering Industry, *Human Resource Management Journal* 4(4), pp 44–62.

Ripley, R.E. and Ripley, M.J. (1992) Empowerment, the Cornerstone of Quality: Empowering Management in Innovative Organizations in the 1990s, *Management Decision* 30(4), pp 20–43.

Scott, C.D. and Jaffe, D.T. (1991) *Empowerment: Building a Committed Workforce* London: Kogan Page.

Sparrow, P., Randall, R.S. and Jackson, S.E. (1994) Convergence or Divergence: Human Resource Practices and Policies for Competitive Advantage World-wide, *The International Journal of Human Resource Management* 5(2), pp 267–297.

Sternberg, L.E. (1992) Empowerment: Trust vs. Control, *The Cornell H.R.A. Quarterly* 33(1), pp 68–72.

Tam, H. (1994) Empowerment: Too Big a Task? *Professional Manager*, pp 8–9.

Terry, A. and Hadland, M. (1995) Empowerment: Reaping Benefits from Development, *People Magazine* 15(1,) pp 30–33.

Tyson, S. and Fell, A. (1986) *Evaluating the Personnel Function* p 8, London: Hutchinson.

Werner, M. (1992) The Great Paradox: Responsibility Without Empowerment, *Business Horizons* 35(5), pp 55–57.

Wood, R. (1992) *Working in Hotels and Catering* p 94, London: Routledge.

5

Management Development in the UK Hospitality Industry

Sandra Watson

This chapter is designed to provide an overview of factors which have influenced recent trends in management development in the UK hospitality industry. It examines external and intrinsic factors which have led to the emergence of contemporary approaches to management development. Within this framework, examples of divergent current practice are discussed. Exigent issues which have implications for hospitality educators and managers, and the industry as a whole, are analysed.

MANAGEMENT DEVELOPMENT – DEFINITION AND PHILOSOPHY

Management development can be identified as the process by which an organization ensures that it has the management, in terms of both quality and quantity, it requires to meet present and future needs.

Many definitions exist of management development which include Armstrong (1993) who states that management development:

> is concerned with improving the performance of existing managers, giving them opportunities for growth and development, and ensuring, as far as possible, that management succession within the organization is provided for.

Many writers including Torrington and Hall (1987) address management development in terms of examining processes and procedures which can be seen to fall within the concept of management development. Many of these procedures and processes can be seen to co-exist at other levels within the organization, so that discussion and examination centre around the specific approach which is taken when relating these to management. Examples include 'Recruitment and Selection', 'Training' and 'Appraisal'. This approach enables management development to be analysed in tangible terms, rather than the adoption of a more holistic focus.

Armstrong (1988) proposes seven elements within management development, namely:

- Organization Review;
- Manpower Review;
- Performance Review;
- Management by Objectives;
- Training;
- Succession Planning;
- Career Planning.

In contrast, Torrington and Hall (1987) suggest that management development can be seen to encompass nine separate procedures, namely:

- Selection;
- Appraisal and Self Development;
- Education and Training Courses;
- Action Learning;
- Mentoring;
- Peer Relationships;
- Natural Learning;
- MBO;
- Organization Development.

More recently, attention has been given to the conceptualization of management development. This requires that management development is viewed as a total concept, which should not be dissected into component parts. It should be viewed as a continuous process, which seeks to develop individuals within the context of a business environment. Management development involves managing the total process by which managers learn and develop. Most particularly, learning from work experience and learning from education and training must be integrated activities (Mumford, 1993). Arguably, the recent trend to utilize the terminology of 'Management Education, Training and Development' has arisen as a result of this change in focus. Management education can be viewed as structured, formal learning, which often takes place within an institutional framework. Management training encompasses the manner by which a manager acquires the knowledge and skills related to work requirements by formal, structured or guided means; whereas management development is a broader concept concerned with developing the individual rather than emphasizing the learning of narrowly defined skills. It is a process involving the contribution of formal and informal work experience (Delloite *et al.*, 1989).

As can be seen from the above definitions, management development embraces the following fundamental philosophies:

- It is a wider concept than management training;
- It focuses on future as well as present needs;
- It is an active, rather than a passive process;
- It requires an organization to address individual as well as organizational requirements;
- It encompasses training, education and experiential learning;
- It is an integral component of organizational development.

It can be seen, therefore, that management development is a complex process. In addition to the complexities attached to the process aspects, management development should be viewed in the context of the strategic direction of the organization. Therefore, there needs to be a strong link to organizational development. Litteljohn and Watson (1990) propose that the strategic future of the organization is dependent on appropriate management being available to drive the organization forward. This can only be achieved through management development being inextricably linked to organization strategy. Mumford (1993) contends that there is a continuum on which management development can be placed in relation to its maturity. Figure 5.1 provides an outline of Mumford's model.

1	2	3	4	5	6
No systematic management development	Isolated tactical management development	Integrated and co-ordinated structural and development tactics	A management development strategy to implement corporate policy	Management development strategy input to corporate policy formation	Strategic development of the management of corporate policy
No systematic or deliberate management development in structural or developmental sense, total reliance on natural, *laissez-faire* uncontrived process of management development.	There are isolated and ad hoc tactical management development activities, of either structural or developmental kinds, or both, in response to local problems, crises, or sporadically identified general problems.	The specific management development tactics which impinge directly on the individual manager, of career structure management, and of assisting learning are integrated and co-ordinated.	A management development strategy plays its part in implementing corporate policies through managerial human resource planning, and framework and direction for the tactics of career structure management and of learning education and training.	Management development processes feed information into corporate policy decision-making processes on the organization's managerial assets, strengths, weaknesses and potential and contribute to the forecasting and analysis of the manageability of proposed projects, ventures, changes.	Management development processes enhance the nature and quality of corporate policy-forming processes, which they also inform and help implement.

Figure 5.1: Levels of maturity of organizational management development

(Mumford, A., 1993)

The 1990s have seen much attention focused on management development, both at national and organizational levels. This has resulted in a change of emphasis within management development, with a move away from the process and procedural approach of the 1970s and 1980s to a conceptual approach in the 1990s as discussed above. In addition, there has also been a shift towards addressing management development in relation to successful performance in the workplace. This has led to a competency approach to management development being suggested as the way forward. A competency approach is based on the notion of identifying a range of specific skills and knowledge which encompass all aspects of a manager's work. The ability of a manager to function successfully in the workplace is measured against these competencies.

Schroder (1989) defines competencies in the context of organizational effectiveness. Managerial competencies are personal effectiveness skills, which vary from entry through 'basic' to 'high' competencies. 'Entry' competencies are the abilities and skills which individuals bring to the organization, 'basic' competencies represent personal effectiveness skills and are more task related, and 'high' competencies form a relatively stable set of behaviours which produce significantly superior work groups in organizational environments. Boyatzis (1982) defines competencies as 'skills, types of behaviour, knowledge and traits that are employed successfully by managers in discharging their duties'.

There are numerous reasons for this recent attention to management development. The following section of this chapter focuses on some of the external and internal environmental issues influencing management development.

EXTERNAL FACTORS INFLUENCING MANAGEMENT DEVELOPMENT

Business Performance

The 1980s saw a period of consolidation in the area of management development. Although the majority of UK businesses are aware of the influence of management development on the improvement of their competitive position, management development has been addressed in a sporadic and fragmented manner: 'too little, too late for too few' (Handy, 1987). Evidence from research into this area suggests that:

> when the economy runs into difficulty, tight control of expenditure by employers resulted in the contraction of training budgets, including those for Management, Education, Training and Development' (Deloitte *et al.*, 1989).

This approach to management development, with industry viewing money spent on management development as a cost, can be seen to be fundamentally different to main UK competitors (Handy, 1987).

A number of research reports conducted in this area in the 1980s found that in the USA, West Germany and Japan, industry perceives a clear link between investment in management development and competitive success (Handy, 1987; Constable and McCormick, 1987).

One of the underlying philosophical aspects of management development is that it is concerned with the future as well as the present, as outlined earlier. In industry, the benefits from management development may not be realized immediately, which results in industry being unwilling to invest in management development in its broadest sense. This has resulted in a focus on management training emerging (Litteljohn and Watson, 1990). This emphasis on training is due to the more immediate manifestations of training benefits, which can be more easily measured than those derived from management development.

Management Lessons from Recession

The effects of the 1980–1982 recession included the identification of deficiencies and weakness in management. The reduction in the number of staff during these periods meant that management were required to develop a much broader skills and knowledge base. This move towards 'flatter and leaner' organizations continued over the decade and the recession of 1992 saw organizations reducing the number and levels of middle management in an attempt to maintain competitive advantage. This has further increased the scope of management. Within the hospitality industry this has been realized through line managers and heads of department taking responsibility for roles previously carried out by the now redundant assistant managers.

With the reduction in the number of middle managers, many organizations have taken the opportunity to review the structure and role of support services. Personnel and training, finance and sales have seen the most reorganization with many employees being removed from unit level to provide a wider, more strategic cover, while others have been moved from 'core' activity to a 'peripheral' position. Companies like Forte Hotels, Gardner Merchant and Stakis Hotels exemplify this restructuring.

Another aspect of restructuring which has occurred over the last five years has been the slimming down of head offices in the form of decentralization. Companies, for example Forte Hotels, have not only being focusing attention on the support activities within units but have looked at rationalization strategies at their central head office in the form of reducing the numbers employed in support services.

The restructuring policies adopted in both the 1980s and 1990s have resulted in a wider role for management to realize, in an effort to maintain a competitive edge.

STRUCTURAL AND DEMOGRAPHIC CHANGE IN EMPLOYMENT

Much has been written on the effect of demographic changes in industry, with particular focus on the decline in the number of 16–19 year olds. Although the recent recession did much to diffuse the 'demographic time-bomb', the decline in the number of school leavers has nonetheless affected management development. This can be seen in relation to the changes in the labour force which are occurring and are likely to continue for the next few years. The hospitality industry has traditionally recruited many of its employees from the younger end of the labour age spectrum. In 1992, 29.7 per cent of the industry's employees were less than 25 years of age (Ralston and Lucas, 1995). There are now trends within the industry to recruit older workers, especially married women. Women have always represented the majority of the labour force within the hospitality industry, but there is now a growing trend for older workers to be employed in sectors like fast food, which was historically seen as a young person's sector (Mogendorff *et al.*, 1992). In addition to the nature of the industry's workforce, there is also the issue of the industry being able to attract the managers it requires to meet its current and future needs. Research into hospitality graduates' career paths has already indicated a decline in the number of graduates entering the hotel sector of the industry (Worsford and Jameson, 1991).

One of the features of the hospitality market is the fluctuations in demand for products and services. The industry has traditionally dealt with this unpredictability of demand through the utilization of 'flexible working practices'. Atkinson (1984) advocates three forms of flexibility:

- numerical;
- functional; and
- financial.

Functional flexibility can be seen to be increasing the scope of the skills of workers and is often referred to as multi-skilling. The hospitality industry has utilized multi-skilling in an ad hoc manner for many years, but the recent trend is to implement it in a more coherent and structured way throughout many organizations, e.g. Forte Hotels and Hyatt Hotels (Bartlett, 1993).

Financial flexibility addresses the manner in which employment practices influence the degree of control an organization can have over payments. The utilization of performance related pay schemes and individual contracts can be seen to be approaches which fall under the banner of financial flexibility. TGI Friday's are a prime example of an organization who have successfully implemented financial flexibility in the hospitality industry.

The third dimension of the Atkinson (1984) model is numerical flexibility which encompasses approaches to contractual arrangements which enable organizations to increase and decrease numbers of staff in relation to demand.

The hospitality industry has used numerical flexibility for a number of years so that it can meet fluctuations in demand. Core employees form the nucleus of the labour supply which is supplemented principally by peripheral employees in the form of part-time and casual workers, with further flexibility being derived from secondary peripheral groups of contract workers.

Handy (1994) proposes that the number of people in full-time employment will decline to represent 50 per cent of the total workforce in the UK. The remainder of these workers will be employed on a temporary and/or part-time basis or be self-employed. These changes in the labour market will require not only amendments in skills and knowledge in terms of organizations' ability to attract and recruit the correct management, but also the adoption of a management style which will ensure that the best results are obtained from these employees.

By the year 2000, Handy (1994) predicts that '70 per cent of all jobs will be "cerebral" jobs, with 50 per cent of these requiring a university degree or a professional qualification'. This is having a fundamental effect on the approach to management development. On the one hand there is a greater emphasis being placed on management education, both at undergraduate and post-graduate level. This can be evidenced by the increased number of managers undertaking educational development and, also from increased attention being paid to the content and delivery of educational provision. This can be seen to be receiving attention from both government and industry alike. However, on the other hand there is also the need to develop management approaches which will ensure the development of individuals whose career development is shaped by the 'Contractual Culture' of the 1990s.

GOVERNMENT INTERVENTION

In December 1988 the government released a White Paper entitled 'Employment for the 1990s'. The paper recognized the importance of training for all and the need to foster a 'training for life' philosophy in the UK workforce in order to maintain economic growth. The government identified its role in this process as providing a facilitating framework. The framework which was proposed operates at three levels, namely national, industry and local.

The National Training Task Force (replaced in 1993 by the National Advisory Council for Education and Training Targets) was established at the national level to develop policies to promote training development at industry level, through Industry Training Organizations, known as Lead Bodies. These are employer-led organizations which are responsible for the identification and establishment of national standards of competence. These can be either sector or occupation specific: e.g. The Council for Management Education and Development has developed standards relating to the generic field of management, whereas the Hotel and Catering Training Company has developed sector specific standards for hotel and catering. The final level in the framework was to provide localized training provision and support through the establishment of Training and Enterprise Councils (TECs) (England and Wales) and Local Enterprise Companies (LECs) (Scotland).

The philosophy behind this proposal was to ensure that the quality of training provision meets the needs of the local labour markets. The TECs and LECs are led by private sector employers who are supposed to form two-thirds of the membership of the councils. There has been much criticism on the composition and operation of these bodies, which is beyond the scope of this chapter. Key here is a recognition of the government's strategy to encourage employers and individuals to take responsibility for training and development:

> It is up to employers and individuals by their actions to ensure that the jobs come about; and in reskilling the labour force there are new partnerships to be created between enterprise, vocational education and training, between delivery at local level and policy and priorities at national level, and between employers and Government, customers and providers' (Department for Employment, 1988).

Management development provision falls within this framework, and has led to the emergence of the Council for Management Education, Training and Development which developed the Management Charter Initiative (MCI), with reinforcement being provided by a series of Management Charter networks. The development of the Management Charter Initiative has led to the production of competency standards for two levels of management, junior management (MCI.1) and middle management (MCI.11). Research is currently being undertaken to produce standards for senior/strategic managers.

There are nine Units of Competence, which are grouped into four Key Roles:

- Manage Operations;
- Manage Finance;
- Manage People; and
- Manage Information.

Each of the units consist of a number of Elements of Competence which are intended to reflect the skills, knowledge and abilities which experienced competent managers should possess. Performance Criteria specific to each level or standard of performance are set, along with Range Indicators, which describe a range of instances in which each element of competence applies. The MCI framework also includes four clusters of personal competence, which are not included in any assessment. These are:

- Managing Others to Optimize Results;
- Managing Oneself to Optimize Results;
- Planning to Optimize the Achievement of Results;
- Using Intellect to Optimize Results.

The comprehensive competency approach has received considerable criticism. The principal criticisms are noted below:

- The functionalist approach fails to take into account recent developments in sociological and organizational theory and the complex reality of human work performance (Holmes, 1990).
- Ashworth and Saxton (1990) contend that not all work-related activity (i.e. critical thinking and initiative knowledge) fits the competency model.
- There is no cognizance taken of more recent research on the complex reality of management (Stewart, 1993).
- Burgoyne (1988) and Pye (1990) see the competency approach as promoting reductionism and demonstrate that this prevents an holistic view of the manager's role.
- Talbot (1993) and Baker (1991) critically reveal the unscientific way in which the MCI national standard managerial competencies were derived.
- Burgoyne (1988) and Holmes (1990) highlight the limitations of a list of 'static' managerial competencies in the rapidly changing unstable environment in which most organizations exist.
- Jacobs (1989), Baker (1991) and Reynolds and Snell (1988) emphasize the limitations of a set of competencies which can be verified through objective measurement and highlight the importance of the 'soft personal qualities' such as creativity, sensitivity and mental agility which are difficult to measure objectively.

The now infamous Norman Tebbit phrase 'on your bike' epitomizes the Conservative government's approach to training and development in the free market economy of the 1980s and early 1990s. Individuals were encouraged to take responsibility for their own destiny and 'entrepreneurship' was flavour of the decade. This was evidenced by initiatives to encourage business development and to develop enterprise skills in Higher Education.

INTERNATIONALIZATION

Although this chapter examines management development in the UK, issues pertaining to the international nature of the hospitality industry require to be addressed. The hospitality industry is international in context and character. Many academic researchers have commented on the international dimension of the industry (e.g. Dunning and McQueen, 1982; Dave, 1984; Litteljohn, 1985 and Litteljohn and Beattie, 1992). Such commentary enables an understanding of many hotel operators' international strategies and actions. In relation to management development, there are two aspects which need to be highlighted.

First, there is the issue of the industry being able to develop managers who can survive in an international, complex environment. Watson and Litteljohn (1992) propose a two-tiered approach:

1) At a tactical level, organizations will have to ensure that managers can operate in different locations in a way which is sensitive to the local environment.

2) At a strategic level managers are required who can think 'globally' and view the organization in an international context.

The creation of the Single European Union in 1993, together with the opening up and restructuring of Central and Eastern Europe, have given rise to the need to ensure that managers are equipped to manage across boundaries. The Hotel and Catering International Management Association (HCIMA) has been working on the development of a European Certificate and Diploma of Hospitality Management, which is work-based and designed to provide for a pan-European qualification (Logie, 1995). Many education providers have incorporated languages and cultural awareness programmes into hospitality management qualifications in an attempt to meet the needs of the industry. The requirement of a broader knowledge base and the development of managers who can operate in an international context will warrant the provision of a wider range of management development opportunities and career counselling. With this, managers can reach their full potential.

Second, there is the issue of the industry being able to attract and retain the calibre of management required. Research into hospitality management recruitment has found that many graduates are seeking employment in other industries (NEDC, 1992; Brotherton, 1993). There is concern over the differences in expectations between students/graduates and the industry. Management loyalty will be a key business focus for the 1990s as the skills/abilities of managers who are able to perform effectively in the international market become more complex (Watson, 1991).

INTERNAL FACTORS

Organizational Design

It is argued by some commentators, including Watson and D'Annunzio-Green (1994) and Cannon and Taylor (1994), that the restructuring which is occurring in industry is one of the major factors influencing management development. The move towards the development of 'flatter and leaner' structures will result in organizations having to address the increased knowledge and skills required by managers through appropriate management development. There is also the issue of bridging the gap between tactical and strategic levels of management as there will no longer be the stepping stones for managers to move up the career ladder. This is likely to lead to a 'bi-polarization of the knowledge base' (Watson, 1991).

Focus on Quality and Customer Awareness

The increased competitive environment of the industry coupled with a more discerning customer have resulted in organizations focusing attention on 'quality' as a tool to gain a competitive edge. The labour-intensive nature of the hospitality industry requires that much attention must be directed towards the motivation and development of staff to provide quality service. The Investors in People (IiP) initiative is a vehicle which is designed to help industry improve performance by realizing the full potential of their staff, through the continuous development of their management and staff. Many hospitality companies are in the process of implementing IiP, with De Vere Hotels, for instance, having already achieved this award throughout all their hotels.

Attention can also be seen to be increasing in the area of customer care. This can be evidenced in organizations like Forte Hotels, with customer care being placed at the top of operational managers' job descriptions. At a national level the adoption of the 'Welcome Host' customer awareness programme by the Scottish Tourist Board, the Wales Tourist Board and the English Tourist Board can be cited as examples in this area. Sweeney (1995), in reviewing this initiative, cites it as an example of an industry taking a national focus on the behavioural/'soft' aspects, rather than focusing on technical skills as can be seen in other national initiatives.

In relation to a more comprehensive focus on quality, many hospitality organizations have developed their own quality management programmes. These include: Forte Hotels, Hilton International and Sheraton Hotels; while other organizations including Scandic Crown Hotels have successfully pursued the nationally recognized quality kitemark of BS5750 (now ISO9000).

Information Technology

Some commentators, including Worsford and Jameson (1991), propose that the increased utilization of information technology has had less impact on the hospitality industry than in other industries. The nature of the hotel industry makes it less compatible than other industries with the automation of all its services. However, there are opportunities within the industry to increase the level of technology and augment the personal service. This can be seen in the utilization of complex front-office systems which enable check-out from guest bedrooms, which many hotels now offer (Baker *et al*, 1994). There are numerous examples of the implementation of increased technology in the industry which results in a decrease in the personal service. Another important aspect in relation to technology is the increased availability of multi-media and interactive technologies. This is influencing traditional styles of employment and has the potential to have an impact on management in the industry. This can be seen at two levels. The first is in the employment of managers who are computer literate in terms of managing and utilizing the technology to assist in the development of the organization: e.g. the utilization of interactive computers in organizational communication and information retrieval. Second, there is the related aspect of 'the demand for more skilled personnel, more graduates and new approaches to management' (Worsford and Jameson, 1991). This will have implications for the development of appropriate management skills. Traditionally management styles in the industry can be seen to be either 'autocratic' or 'paternalistic' which may no longer be appropriate in providing leadership for this type of employee (Woods, 1994).

PRODUCTIVITY

Much has been written on the area of productivity in the hospitality industry in the 1990s. Well-known commentators include Jones and Lockwood (1989), Witt and Witt (1989) and Johns (1994). The increased competitive environment of the industry combined with the recent recession has resulted in industry focusing on productivity enhancement as a means of survival and a key to competitive success.

> In general, manpower productivity throughout the UK industry is too low, most notably in hotels. The industry suffers from too many cases of indifferent standards and a vicious circle of low pay leading to high labour turnover, little training and low productivity. Practitioners in the industry should improve training and performance. (NEDC, 1992).

The management of staff and the ability of management to have both the technical expertise and the management skills to identify and implement productivity improvements is imperative to operational success. Attention needs to be paid to both systems and people in the operation. This requires attention to be paid to the 'hard' or technical aspects of management and the 'soft' or behavioural characteristics as proposed by Jacobs (1989).

MANAGEMENT DEVELOPMENT IN THE HOSPITALITY INDUSTRY

Only 10 per cent of hotel and catering managers have a Higher National Diploma, a degree or equivalent qualification, compared with 41 per cent of managers in UK industry as a whole; and 30 per cent of hospitality managers have no qualification, compared with 12 per cent in industry as a whole (HCTC, 1994). Price (1994) comments that:

> the hotel and catering industry remains fragmented with relatively little concentration of ownership and a dearth of the sophisticated human resource management practice which is associated with large, modern organizations.

The industry is renowned for its ease of entry with the result that operators require no qualifications to enter the market and many are poorly qualified. This is resulting in a perpetuation of 'limited, traditional management techniques and an insularity within the industry' (Price, 1994).

There is now a questioning of the appropriateness of the traditional, if somewhat sporadic, provision of hospitality management development. Guerrier and Lockwood (1989) question the validity of the traditional approach to developing hospitality managers, that has led to an operational perspective being developed which is reinforced by the education, training and experiential learning patterns of the industry. At the time of publication of their report, there was little evidence of any focus on 'the development of human relation skills for managers and indeed little acceptance for this sort of development'. In concluding their discussion, Guerrier and Lockwood (1989) propose that what is required is a reappraisal of management development, but, more importantly, 'reappraising the whole basis upon which we currently judge our managers, challenging our beliefs about the kind of managers we want to develop'.

A study conducted by Brotherton (1993) into hospitality management education and graduate training found that there were a number of key issues which required to be addressed by both educationalists and industrialists in order to 'seek greater efficiency and effectiveness in the education and training of hospitality management graduates'. These include:

- **Expectations:** There appears to be a lack of congruence between the expectations of students, education and industry, which is leading to a waste of resources and dissatisfaction for all parties;
- **Transition:** This is in relation to the transition from education to industry, with graduates finding this phase difficult. Obviously there is the problem of expectations which influence this transition, but a contention forwarded is that there are not the type of 'progression linkages' between education and company training programmes which should exist to ease this phase of development;
- **Education-Industry Liaison:** The report found that either specific linkages were non-existent or confined to specific institutional –company collaborative schemes.

Brotherton (1993), argues that what is required is an effective and ongoing dialogue which seeks to define the respective roles and responsibilities of these two stages/parties in the individual's developmental process. The diverse nature

of the industry and the divergent approaches to the academic provision i
hospitality education makes this laudable suggestion difficult to realiz
However, there are examples of industry-wide initiatives in the area of man
agement development and training, which fall under the umbrella c
Brotheron's (1993) framework. These have mainly been developed as a result c
government intervention strategies in the general area of management, educa
tion, training and development, or due to the availability of grant and funds t
support these.

Johnson (1977) defined the need of hospitality managers in the 'Corpus o
Professional Knowledge in Hotel, Catering and Institutional Services'. It out
lined the scope and range of knowledge required by a competent hospitalit
manager. These were divided into primary/core and secondary/important area
and split between technical and general management aspects. The core area
included management aspects of Marketing, Finance, Personnel, General
Industry and Legal; while the technical area encompassed Purchasing
Provision and Service, Sales, Control, Premises and Facilities, and Lega
Aspects. In 1988 the HCIMA reviewed its framework of professional qualifica
tions in order to devise a scheme which would take on board recent develop
ments in the field of education and training and serve the industry into th
1990s. It has developed alongside the management competency and Vocationa
Qualifications framework. There is a certificate course aimed at supervisor
with a high degree of technical orientation and a Diploma course for first line
managers or supervisors. Both courses are designed to provide development
opportunities to more senior levels of management. These programmes involve
input from industry in the form of work-based projects. There is also the provision of a mentoring infrastructure for industry-based students. Provision was
also made for the accreditation of prior learning in order that managers do not
need to re-learn job competencies in a classroom setting. In addition, there is a
focus on widening access and the development of flexible delivery of material in
order that participation rates can be maximized. Although the HCIMA framework is not competency based it has built into the provisions many of the characteristics expounded by the Management Charter Initiative and can be seen to
be developing a UK framework for hospitality managers. It will be interesting
to note the extent to which the NVQ/SVQ level 5 standards currently being
developed by the Hotel and Catering Training Company either impinge upon or
dovetail into this provision.

Criticism has been levelled at hospitality management development provision, in that approaches are not always appropriate to the majority of the industry, due to the predominance of small employers and its fragmented nature. In
a previous article by the author in 1991, it was contended that 'networking' was
an approach that should be developed in order that the small employer sector
of this industry could capitalize on management development opportunities. It
is, therefore, interesting to note the development of one such initiative from
Tourism Training Scotland (TTS). TTS has developed a national management
development programme aimed at small tourism providers. It is available to the
visitor attractions sector of the industry and hospitality companies who employ

less than ten employees. It is a tutor-led programme with a distance learning focus. TTS is composed of representatives from a wide range of organizations who have an interest in the tourism training field. These include Scottish Enterprise, Highlands and Islands Enterprise and the Scottish Tourist Board, the central government agencies with responsibility for training, SCOTVEC, with its role in validating and promoting vocational qualifications, training providers and a wide range of representatives from different sectors of the industry and professional and trade bodies. TTS's role is to develop and promote a national strategy for human resource development and training in the tourism industry (Brogan, 1994). This is an exciting initiative which is a prime example of the industry-wide liaison proposed by Brotherton (1993). It is also an approach where a perceived link between performance and people has resulted in action, rather than words, at a national/strategic level. Brotherton's (1993) proposals can also be seen being implemented in the UK Hospitality Partnership programme, which was launched in October 1993 by the HCIMA. This has the specific purpose to encourage links between education and industry under five broad banners:

- Student Work Experience;
- Staff Development through Industrial Updating;
- Adult Training and Development;
- Hospitality Research;
- Programme Design and Quality Assurance.

This initiative has received universal approval from both employer representative bodies, e.g. Hotel Employers' Group and Hospitality Retail Employers' Group, and the UKs hospitality management educators' representative body of the Council for Hospitality Management Education. The Hospitality Partnership achieved a membership of 73 organizations in the first year of operation, with many collaborative initiatives being developed within the proposed framework.

Although there is an apparent tendency to focus on management training at the expense of management development in the hospitality industry, the emergence of a Continuous Development Programme (CDP), in line with Handy and McCormick's recommendations, will act as an catalyst to change this focus. The HCIMA are currently promoting CDP which may eventually form part of the criteria for Fellowship Membership. This will also encourage a 'virtuous circle' rather than a 'vicious' circle to develop in the area of hospitality management development (Senge, 1990):

> It can, therefore, be seen that within the hospitality industry there are examples of national and strategic initiatives being developed in line with UK-wide generic management propositions.

Organizational change in the form of delayering, empowerment and contracting out, is resulting in a new and complex set of relationships emerging at the workplace (Cannon and Taylor, 1994). Managers will have to provide an environment where employees can develop and flourish. This will require hospitality organizations to examine present management styles. Brownell (1992 suggests that 'today's manager is not characterized by personality or dealing with defined tasks, but rather by the response he or she is able to elicit from others'. Nadler and Tushman (1990) on the other hand contend that: 'vision and charisma are not enough to sustain business growth, what is required is attention to detail'. Fulmer (1992), in commenting on management development into the millennium, proposes nine areas which need to be addressed, encompassing both technical and 'soft' (behavioural) aspects of management. These are:

- the challenge of learning;
- the power of teams;
- time as a competitive weapon;
- dramatic leadership;
- globalization and transnationalization;
- flexibility and resilience;
- customer responsiveness, service and quality;
- technology and information systems;
- systems thinking.

It appears that there is now an emerging consensus on both the key issues affecting management development, and the attributes, skills and knowledge required to move industry into the millennium. The following section provides an overview of the current trends in the hospitality industry in relation to the above management development aspects.

The Challenge of Learning

Botkin *et al.*, (1979) contend that there are three types of learning:

- **maintenance learning:** reinforcing what is already known: i.e. better and more efficiently;
- **shock learning:** which is responsive and often leads to additional problems. Creativity can often be a feature of this learning;
- **anticipatory learning:** which is both future-oriented and participative in nature. It tries to anticipate creative solutions to problems which have not yet happened. It is based on the principle that no individual or 'power-elite' has all the answers, and that capable well-intentioned people working together can produce better alternatives than any single individual.

It is questionable as to the extent that 'anticipatory learning' has penetrated the UK hospitality industry. This is not surprising considering the recent economic recession, resulting in a focus on the first two forms of learning. However, there are isolated examples where anticipatory learning has occurred. For example Forte Hotels' rebranding initiative. Nonetheless, the extent to which this is a continuing strategy is less obvious. The increased utilization of work groups in the industry by companies like Harvester Restaurants and TGI Friday's (Ashness and Lashley, 1995) is likely to result in the increased utilization of anticipatory learning.

The Power of Teams

Kanter (1989) contends that 'in the 1990s' organization, the team is the competitive weapon'. Managers' perceptions of themselves will have to change; they will have to become team leaders in a consensus environment (Cannon and Taylor, 1994). There are some examples of organizations in the hospitality industry realizing the benefits of team work and the power of the team. TGI Friday's and Harvester Restaurants are two. Other organizations, including Forte Hotels, are developing organizational structures and management practices which encourage a focus on teams. However, many more organizations are utilizing traditional management styles (Price, 1994; Worsford and Jameson, 1991).

Time as a Competitive Weapon

Much has been written on the subject of time based management in manufacturing in terms of increased productivity, risk reduction and increased volume of business. In relation to service industries time can be utilized in many ways to gain competitive advantage. This can be seen to be most prevalent with the introduction of management information systems, which increase both the speed and accessibility of information on which to base business decisions. However, these benefits can only be realized if management have the technological skills to enable them to take a holistic view of this information. This will warrant attention in hospitality management development.

Dramatic Leadership

The previous discussion on current hospitality environments indicates that a change in leadership styles is urgently required. It is important, however, that the distinction between leaders and managers is clarified. Kotter (1991) articulates the difference as being that 'managers administer large bureaucracies and ensure stability, while leaders are vital forces in bringing about change'. Both are necessary at various stages in an organization's life cycle. In many hospitality organizations the management role has been predominant, but what is now required is a focus on leadership. A prime example where this can be seen to be occurring is in Stakis Hotels, with the appointment of a Managing

Director to lead the company. This has resulted in a change of focus and a revival of its portfolio, which has transformed the company. This 'leadership' focus is now filtering down through the organization with moves to develop leadership rather than management qualities in management.

Globalization and Transnationalization

Many companies in the hospitality industry can be seen to be multinational in their operation, but few are truly global in their strategy. Intercontinental hotels have taken a global dimension to their management development strategy. They have adopted a two-tiered approach with a Fast Track for its international managers and a Corporate Management Development programme for operations management. Hilton International provide a range of management development opportunities to cope with globalization.

Flexibility and Resilience

The dramatically changing operating environment for hospitality managers requires that management development approaches address both flexibility and resilience. Lombardo (1988) distinguishes between 'arrivers' and the 'derailed'. Arrivers are those who achieve their foreseen potential early in their careers, while the 'derailed' are those with similar potential which is not realized. The difference between the two is not in the quantity of mistakes made, but the individual's ability to learn from them, and to come back with greater energy and enthusiasm. The hospitality industry needs to address this issue in terms of addressing the manner in which we judge managers (Guerrier and Lockwood, 1989).

Customer Responsiveness, Quality and Service

This has been recognized as one of the key business success factors in the hospitality industry, as discussed earlier. Increased attention on these is resulting in a change of emphasis in terms of management development. Organizations like Sheraton Hotels and De Vere Hotels are reappraising the way in which they measure managerial effectiveness. Sheraton Hotels utilize Customer Satisfaction and Staff Satisfaction Indexes as performance indicators, which focuses attention on quality, service and customer responsiveness when evaluating management performance.

Technology and Information Systems

'The area of technology and information systems cannot be ignored by any future-oriented management scholar, educator or practitioner' (Fulmer, 1992). Many advances are being made in terms of technological applications in the hospitality industry (Baker *et al.*, 1994; Johns 1994). Multimedia is becoming popular as both a training tool and as a means of accessing information by both guests and staff. Organizations like Holiday Inn and Marriott are using multimedia technology to increase efficiency, empowerment of employees and effective customer services through the use of immediate, consistent and accurate information (Harris, 1993). In terms of management development, it is imperative that hospitality managers keep abreast with these developments to ensure that productivity can be enhanced and that business decisions can be made effectively. However, the resultant employment patterns will also need to be managed, possibly through management development which focuses on 'soft' aspects of management (Jacobs, 1989).

Systems Thinking

Systems thinking attempts to break down the artificial barriers between the business firm and its customers or suppliers and proposes that artificial distinctions between departments should be either eliminated or integrated. Jones and Lockwood (1989) propose a thinking systems approach to the hospitality industry. This involves a critical reappraisal of the traditional functional aspects of hospitality management. They propose that managers need to focus on:

- improving employee performance;
- protecting assets;
- managing demand and supply;
- managing customer service;
- increasing income;
- improving productivity;
- managing quality.

This would lead to the integration of many artificial barriers within hospitality operations. In addition, it would ensure that management performance can be viewed in relation to critical success factors.

The above commentary has shown that there are moves occurring within the hospitality industry in terms of management development, which fall in line with national concerns and issues, as well as those raised by researchers in hospitality education, training and development. However, there is no room for complacency. Many key issues require further development and attention. The final section of this chapter highlights some of these issues in relation to the key players within the industry: i.e. education, industry and individuals.

EDUCATIONAL ISSUES

The government is keen to encourage the adoption of a competence approach within course provision. Some scepticism exists, though, as to the appropriateness of competencies in relation to education provision. However, if a holistic view of management development is taken, education should realize some of the characteristics of the competence movement in the form of focusing on the effective performance of management. Jones (1992) proposes a conceptual model for curriculum development which demonstrates the inter-relationship between the competencies for an effective hospitality manager and relates those competencies to the realistic work environment. Technical levels of understanding are related to this framework and set in the context of the wider business and economic environment. The intention is to provide the opportunity for students to develop a 'holistic understanding of the business activity' (Jones, 1992).

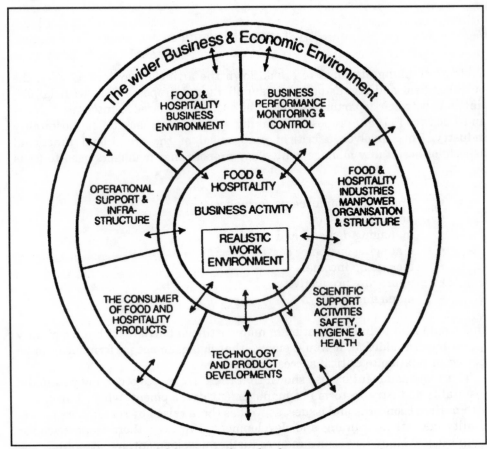

Figure 5.2: Conceptual model for curriculum development

(*P. Jones,* Hospitality, *November 1992*)

Many educational institution courses are looking at moving towards writing courses in 'outcome terms' which may assist in the transient phase of students moving from education into industry. However, the author cautions against moving too far down this route as the competency movement has its base in training, while the focus for education is quite different. Although it can be argued that moves into the competence movement will have short-term complementary benefits, the longer-term benefits from a broad educational base may be lost in the process. One of the key benefits from education is the opportunity to study and research wider issues than those primarily related to a specific discipline. It is imperative that the UK hospitality education system does not lose this characteristic and serve as a 'training' provider in the development of hospitality managers.

Flexibility in Course Provision

Many educational institutions are developing flexible delivery of courses through open-learning packages, part-time course provision and distance learning approaches. This in turn is widening the access to education establishments. Further moves in this area are required in line with the HCIMA initiatives and the Tourism Training Scotland initiative for the provision of educational inputs into management development. It is only with this approach that there will be a significant increase in the number of qualified managers in the industry.

Course Content

Tourism and hospitality courses have developed a cohesive discipline that demonstrates scholarship, research and application to the operational, tactical and strategic issues that surround the industry (Jones, 1992).

It is necessary that course content in hospitality management courses both reflect and influence approaches and trends in the hospitality industry. This requires academics to be involved in research in this area and to undertake their own continuous personal development. This can be realized through a variety of means but needs to be addressed by both educational managers and individuals.

The generic management issues identified by Cannon and Taylor (1994) and the characteristics proposed by Fulmer (1992) should be encompassed into current course provision: e.g. quality, team working, leadership, productivity, technology, systems thinking.

In addition to these, it is imperative that educational providers focus on encouraging students to take responsibility for their learning, which will be a necessary requirement for their own future development. Figure 5.3 provides an analysis of traditional education and an alternative approach to learning. Hospitality educators should move towards the 'new paradigm of learning' (Ferguson, 1989).

The emergent paradigm of learning implies a new kind of learner for a new kind of society. Where the old assumptions generate questions about how to achieve norms, conformity and 'right' answers, the new assumptions lead to questions about how to develop autonomy, how to be open to new concepts, how to motivate for lifelong learning.

Assumptions of the old paradigm of education	Assumptions of the new paradigm of learning
• Learning as a product, a destination.	• Learning as a process, a journey.
• Emphasis on content, acquiring a body of knowledge.	• Emphasis on learning how to learn. What is now 'known' may change. Importance of context.
• Labelling (e.g. remedial, gifted) contributes to self-fulfiling prophecy.	• Labelling used only in minor perspective role and not as a fixed evaluation that overshadows the individual's educational career.
• Concern with norms.	• Concern with the individual's performance in terms of potential. Interest in testing outer limits, transcending perceived limitations.
• Primary reliance on theoretical, abstract 'book knowledge'.	• Theoretical and abstract knowledge heavily complemented by experiment and experience (eg field trips, apprenticeships, demonstrations).
• Emphasis on analytical, linear, left-brain learning. Divergent thinking discouraged.	• Strives for whole-brain thinking. Augments left-brain rationality with holistic, non-linear and intuitive strategies. Divergent thinking encouraged as part of the creative process.
• Teacher imparts knowledge, one-way.	• Teacher is learner too, learning from students. Autonomy encouraged.
• Education seen as a social necessity for a certain period of time, to inculcate minimum skills and train for a specific role.	• Learning seen as a lifelong process, only tangentially related to schools.

Figure 5.3: Comparative assumptions of learning

(Adapted and abridged from Ferguson, 1989)

One of the problems associated with hospitality education is the inability of courses to respond to the needs of industry and of their being too rigid in format. It is therefore important that educational systems provide a means of ensuring currency in course provision. This can be done through appropriate course review systems in educational establishments. However, moves in education to provide modular course provision should enable course amendments to be implemented quickly with a flexible approach to both content and structure.

Integration in Education

One of the recommendations in the NEDC 1991 report *Developing Managers for Tourism*, is the need for more effective integration of course provision at both undergraduate and post-graduate levels. Although there have been moves in this direction in the provision of a national framework, with the NVQ/SVQ and MCI provision, there is still a plethora of educational provision within hospitality. The National Liaison Group, a sub-group of the Tourism Society, are proposing the development of a national curriculum in line with suggestions from the Cannon and Taylor report (1994). Again the author cautions against going too far down this route otherwise a rigidity may develop which could result in 'tunnel vision'. This could also limit initiative in terms of original thinking and new developments.

Collaboration

The HCIMA Hospitality Partnership is a prime example of good practice in the area of collaboration. Other national initiatives can be found through the Enterprise in Higher Education programme in such areas as Live Projects and Records of Achievement. Education and industry should continue to develop links in this way and focus on national frameworks as the basis for collaborative arrangements.

Industry Involvement

The industry representative bodies should continue to develop industry-wide initiatives in the field of management development in line with the HCIMA professional qualifications provision and the Tourism Training Scotland initiative. The industry representative bodies should also continue to promote CPD as a matter of course in line with the Handy, Constable and McCormick (1987) recommendations.

The industry representative bodies should also look at introducing a minimum standard of knowledge/qualification as a pre-requisite to operators entering into the industry. Moves are already being developed in this area with the Scottish Licensed Trade Association (SLTA) offering specialized training to new licensees. This course is designed to provide basic knowledge in legal aspects, environmental issues, staffing, social responsibilities and business knowledge. This has been developed as a result of the SLTA's concern over the number of licensees going out of business after a short period of time. The intention is to encourage Licence Boards to adopt this as a prerequisite for the awarding of new licences.

At an organizational level, organizations should continue to concentrate on the provision of management development programmes which concentrate on both 'hard' and 'soft' management skills. The dynamic change within the business environment has resulted in some organizations recognizing that there is no uniform way to tackle management development. There needs to be more flexible and varied provisions in order to meet the fast changing development needs of hospitality managers. There needs to be a 'cafeteria style rather than an "a la carte" approach' to management development provision (Watson, 1991).

Small organizations will need to focus on forming networks to provide development opportunities for managers in order to survive into the new millennium. Some organizations are utilizing local professional associations as a forum for providing management development opportunities, through joint utilization of facilities or through joint financial arrangements to cover costs. These should be utilized as benchmarks for good practice in the area of management development. Hospitality companies will need to focus on developing a 'nurturing' orientation. A nurturing organization is one where development and training are seen to be key to the success of the organization and where employees are continuously encouraged to undertake self-development. It is also important that management development is no longer seen as a business cost or a separate activity. It needs to be linked into the corporate strategy and viewed as an integral component of business.

Individual Responsibility

The traditional structure for hospitality management is changing dramatically – the flatter/leaner organizations are resulting in fewer management opportunities being available. The graduate management training opportunities are diminishing with many organizations employing graduates in supervisory positions and enabling them to undertake development opportunities to identify their suitability for management. This will require individuals to take more responsibility for their own development to distinguish between 'arrivers' and the 'derailed'.

Individuals will need to be much more flexible in relation to development opportunities in building a career. This may involve greater movement between organizations and movement between work and education on a far greater scale than has previously been witnessed. In addition, individuals need to adopt a 'learning for life' attitude towards their development.

CONCLUSION

There is much attention being paid to management development at all levels of industry in the UK. The hospitality industry is no different in this context, with issues being raised and addressed in relation to management development from all players within the industry. It can be seen from the previous commentary that there is progress being made in this area with examples of good practice emerging. However, there is no room for complacency. As a key contributor to the UK economy, it is imperative that the hospitality industry addresses these issues in order to ensure a supply of good quality managers to compete in the international market. This demands that a holistic view is taken to management development at all levels of the industry, and that all contributors realize their role in this fundamental aspect of business development.

REFERENCES

Armstrong, M. (1988) *A Handbook of Personnel Management Practice* 3rd edn, London: Kogan Page, pp 523–524.

Armstrong, M. (1993) *Human Resource Management Strategy & Action*, p 157.

Ashness, D. and Lashley, C. (1995) Employee Empowerment in Harvester Restaurants, *CHME HRM Conference* Feb 1995.

Ashridge Management Research Group/Foundation for Management Education (1988) *Management for the Future.*

Ashworth, P.D. and Saxton, J. (1990) On Competence, *Journal of Further and Higher Education* 14(2).

Atkinson (1984) Manpower Strategies for Flexible Organizations, *Personnel Management*, August 1994.

Baker, B.R. (1994) MCI Management Competencies and APL: The Way Forward for Management Education, Training and Development, *Journal of European Industrial Training* 15(9), pp 17–26.

Bartlett (1993) Forte Introduces Flexible Rosters, *Caterer & Hotelkeeper* 19 August 1993.

Baum, T. (1989) Competencies for Hotel Managers: Industry's Expectations of Education, *International Journal of Contemporary Hospitality Management* 2(4), pp 13–16.

Botkin, J., Elmandjra, M., Malitza, M. and Club of Rome, (1979) *No Limits to Learning: Bridging the Human Gap: A Report to the Club of Rome* Oxford: Pergamon.

Boyatzis, R.E. (1982) *The Competent Manager: A Model for Effective Performance* Chichester: John Wiley & Sons.

Brogan, E. (1994) Human resource development in tourism: the Scottish perspective, *Tourism State of the Art* Chichester: John Wiley & Sons.

Brotherton, R. (1993) *Hospitality Management Education and Graduates in Britain & Europe* Blackpool College, May 1993.

Brownell (1992) Hospitality Managers' Communication Practices, *International Journal of Hospitality Management* 11(22), pp 111–128.

Burgoyne, J. (1988) Competency Approaches to Management Development, *IPM Conference* October 1988.

Cannon, C. and Taylor (1994) *Management Development to the Millennium* The Cannon and Taylor Working Reports Institute of Management Research Report.

Constable, J. (1988) *Developing the Competent Manager in the UK Context* MSc Report.

Dave, W. (1984) US Multinational Involvement in the International Hotel Sector – An Analysis, *Service Industries Journal*.

Delloitte, Haskins and Sells (1989) *Management Challenge for the 1990s* The Training Agency.

Department for Employment (1988) *Employment for the 1990s* CMD 540, London: HMSO.

Dewer, W. (1984) US Multinational Involvement in the International Hotel Sector – An Analysis, *Service Industries Journal*.

Dunning, J.H. and McQueen, M. (1982) The Eclectic Theory of International Production: A Case Study of the International Hotel Industry, *Managerial and Decision Economics* 2(4).

Ferguson, M. (1989) *The Aquarian Conspiracy: Personal and Social Transformation in the 1980s* London: Grafton Books.

Fulmer, R. (1992) Nine Management Development Challenges for the 1990s, *Journal of Management Development* 11(7).

Guerrier, Y. and Lockwood, A. (1989) Developing Hotel Managers – A Reappraisal, *International Journal of Hospitality Management* 8(2), pp 82–89.

Handy, C. (1987) *The Making of Managers* London: MSL/NEDO, BIM.

Handy, C., Constable, J. and McCormick, R. (1987) *The Making of British Managers* London: BIM/CBI.

Handy, C. (1994) *The Empty Raincoat – Making Sense of the Future* London: Hutchinson.

Harris, K.J. (1993) Multimedia: Fluff, Fashion or Future? *International Journal of Hospitality management* 12(4), pp 367–384.

Holmes, L. (1990) Training Competencies: Turning Back the Clock, Training and Development, *Institute of Training and Development* Manlow, April 1990.

Hornby, D. and Thomas, R. (1989) Towards a Better Standard of Management? *Personnel Management*, January vol. 21(1) pp 52–55.

Hotel and Catering Training Company (1994) *Catering and Hospitality Industry – Key Facts and Figures* London: HCTC.

Jacobs, R. (1989) Getting the Measure of Management Competence, *Personnel Management*, June. vol. 21(6), pp 32–37.

Johns, N. (1994) Food Service Layout and Design. In P. Jones and P. Merricks (eds) *The Management of Food Service Operations* London: Cassell.

Johnson, P. (1977) *Professional Development and the Corpus of Knowledge in Hotel, Catering and Institutional Services* HCIMA.

Jones, P. and Lockwood, A. (1989) *The Management of Hotel Operations* London: Cassell.

Jones, P. (1992) in *Hospitality*, November.

Kanter, M. (1989) *When Giants Learn to Dance. Mastering the Challenge of Strategy Management and Careers in the 1990s* New York: Simon & Schuster.

Kotter, J. (1991) *The Leadership Factor* New York: Free Press.

Litteljohn, D. (1985) Towards an Economic Analysis of Trans-multinational Hotel Companies, *International Journal of Hospitality Management* 4(4), pp 157–164.

Litteljohn, D. and Watson, S. (1990) Development Approaches for the 1990s, *International Journal of Contemporary Hospitality Management* 2(2).

Litteljohn, D., Watson, S. and Beattie, R. (1991) Corporate Ownership in Europe and its Impact on Management Development, *IAHMS Conference*, April.

Litteljohn, D. and Beattie, R. (1990) The European Hotel Industry: Corporate Structures and Expansion Strategies, *Tourism Management* March 1990.

Lombardo, M.M. (1988) *The Lessons of Experience: How Successful Executives Develop on the Job* Lexington: Lexington Books.

Mangham, L.L. and Silver, M.S. (1986) *Management Training Context and Practice* ESRC/DTI.

Mintzberg, H. (1975) The Manager's Job: Folklore and Fact, *Harvard Business Review* 53(4).

Mogendorff, D., Lyon, P. and Cowls, C. (1992) Alternative Labour Markets and Fast Food. Human Resource Management during a period of Demographic Change: Burger King. In R. Teare, D. Adams and S. Messenger (eds) *Managing Projects in Hospitality Organizations* London: Cassell.

Mumford, A. (1987) The Education and Training of British Managers, *Industrial and Commercial Training*, September–October .

Mumford, A. (1993) Management Development Models. In *Management Development, Strategies for Action* 2nd edn London: IPM.

Nadler, D.A. and Tushman, M.L. (1990) Beyond the Charismatic Leader: Leadership and Organizational Change, *California Management Review* Winter, pp 77–79.

NEDO (1991) *Developing Managers for Tourism* NEDO.

NEDO (1992) *UK Tourism: Competing for Growth* NEDO.

Peters, T. (1987) *Thriving on Chaos* New York: Alfred A. Knopf.

Price, L. (1994) Poor Personnel Practice in the Hospitality Industry – Does it matter? *Human Resource Management Journal* 4(4), pp 44–62.

Pye, A. (1990) Management Competence or Common Sense? *Modern Management* 4, Spring.

Ralston, R. and Lucas, R. (1995) Part-time Youth Employment in the Hospitality Industry, *CHME HRM Conference.*

Reynolds, M. and Snell, R. (1988) *Contribution to Development of Management Competence* Report to MSC, Sheffield.

Senge, P. (1990) *The Fifth Discipline: The Art and Practice of the Learning Organization* New York: Doubleday.

Schroder, H.M. (1989) *Managerial Competence: The Key to Excellence: A New Strategy for Management Development in the Information Age* London: Kendall & Kent Publications.

Smith, B. (1993) Building Managers from the Inside Out, Developing Managers through Competency Based Action Learning, *Journal of Management Development* 12, pp 43–48.

Stewart, J. and Page (1993) Competencies: Are they Useful for Trainers? *Industrial and Commercial Training* 24(7).

Stewart, R. (1976) *Contrasts in Management* Maidenhead: McGraw-Hill.

Sweeney, A. (1995) Improving Interpersonal Relationships between Staff and Visitors with the 'Welcome Host', *CHME HRM Conference.*

Talbot, C. (1993) Twin Peaks? MBAs and the Competence: A Fate of Two Courses, *Management* 2nd edn, 24(4).

Torrington, D. and Hall, L. (1987) *Personnel Management: a New Approach* London: Prentice Hall International.

Vora, M. (1995) Lack of IT Skills an Obstacle to Success for UK Business, *People Management*, February, vol 1(3).

Watson, S. (1991) From A la Carte to Cafeteria Style Management Development, *International Journal of Contemporary Hospitality Management* vol 3(4) pp 42–46.

Watson, S. and Litteljohn, D. (1992) Multi and Transnational Firms: The Impact of Expansion on Corporate Structures, in R. Teare and M. Olsen (eds) *International Hospitality Management* Pitman.

Watson, S. and D'Annunzio-Green, N. (1994) The Influence of Organizational Structure on Personnel Management – A Move Towards Human Resource Management, *CHME Research Conference*.

Wills, S. (1993) MCI and the Competency Movement: The Case So Far, *Journal of European Industrial Training* 14, pp 9–11.

Witt, C.A. and Witt, S.F. (1989) Why Productivity in the Hotel Sector is Low, *International Journal of Contemporary Hospitality Management*, vol 1(2) pp 28–33.

Wood, R.C. (1994) *Organizational Behaviour for Hospitality Management* London: Butterworth-Heinemann.

Worsford, P. and Jameson, S. (1991) Human Resource Management: A Response to Change in the 1990s. In R. Teare and A. Boer (eds) *Strategic Hospitality Management* London: Cassell, pp 99–116.

6

Maximizing Labour Flexibility

Rosemary Lucas

This chapter analyses and evaluates supply and demand characteristics and issues relating to the employment of students in flexible jobs in the hospitality, tourism and leisure industries. Empirical evidence is presented from a major research project, 'Youth, Gender and Part-Time Employment'. The rationale for student labour is discussed and key themes from the topic are identified.

INTRODUCTION

'Almost all young women and men who are employed as well as being in full-time education are in flexible employment' (Dex and McCulloch, 1995). Increasing proportions of students are working in flexible employment in industries such as hospitality, tourism and leisure. Flexible employment means many different things but is basically a term used to describe a shift from permanent full-time employee contracts to various types of non-standard employment forms, including part-time, seasonal, temporary work and government training schemes. Many such flexible employment forms are commonly found in the hospitality, tourism and leisure industries (Lucas, 1995).

The issue of student labour in these industries is related to a number of macro-level factors that are supply- and demand-driven within the constraints of a framework that is influenced by legislative and ideological constraints (Ralston and Lucas, 1994). Here the main labour supply issues are closely related to changes in the youth labour market which stand conterminous with demand conditions that require even greater operational flexibility. Employers' use of flexible employment forms is related to a number of considerations including the need to manage fluctuating demand, to reduce labour costs and to increase productivity (Lucas, 1995). Of particular relevance is a traditional industry reliance on young labour (Hotel and Catering Training Company, 1994), dictating that employers must 'milk' the shrinking youth labour market in new ways in order to increase their yield.

THE CHANGING YOUTH LABOUR MARKET

During the 1980s, Government policies seeking to deregulate the labour market have promoted the growth of flexible employment. Concomitant with these developments, the youth labour market has undergone a fundamental transformation in the last 15 years. In order to deal with the high youth unemployment of the early 1980s, the Government responded with a major intervention in youth training, in order to lower the wage aspirations of young people who were expensive to employ relative to adults and to improve the supply of transferable skills in the labour market (Lee, 1992). Related to this, young workers under the age of 21 were removed from the scope of wages councils in 1986, thereby allowing employers to pay young workers wages that were both lower and closer to market clearing levels and removing the obligation on employers to provide additional remuneration, such as overtime and unsocial hours payments, and paid holidays. The end of the 1980s was characterized by a good deal of hyperbole about the relative shortage of young people under the age of 25 and the implications this would have for employers' employment strategies (Lucas and Jeffries, 1991), including the need for greater flexibility among those already in employment (Employment Department, 1988).

Additionally, increasing proportions of this smaller cohort of young people have been continuing in full-time education after age 16 and, as a consequence, more highly qualified young people have been entering the labour market at a later point in time. By the mid-1990s, two-thirds of 16 and 17 year olds were remaining in full-time education (Sly, 1994), and participation in full-time higher education had increased from one-in-five to one-in-three of the youth population (Thomas, 1994). Consequently, full-time youth employment has reduced considerably.

As a result, the number of part-time workers in the 16–19 age group now exceeds those of full-time workers (Employment Department, 1994). This links with the indication that teenage participation in part-time work has increased over time (Micklewright *et al.*, 1994) and that university students are increasingly having to work part-time to fund their studies (Ward and Meikle, 1993; the *Guardian Education*, 1994; Foster, 1994; Porter, 1994). These trends have led Dex and McCulloch (1995) to suggest that Britain:

> may be in the process of moving to the USA model of part-time employment, where the rates of part-time employment are highest amongst the young who are in full-time education.

EMPLOYERS' INCREASING DEMANDS FOR FLEXIBILITY

Studies based on the 1987 Employers Labour Use Strategies (ELUS) survey by McGregor and Sproull (1991) and Hunter and McInnes (1991) point to the fact that most employers do not plan labour use strategically but, rather, respond pragmatically to product market demands, an issue explored more fully below in regard to hospitality, tourism and leisure. In particular, such employers commonly look to greater flexibility in their use of a permanent core of full-time staff (functional flexibility), than through an increased use of non-standard peripheral workers (numerical flexibility) (Industrial Relations Services, 1994).[1]

For a variety of reasons, this functionally flexible option may be less relevant to many hospitality, tourism and leisure firms. Operating in highly volatile and unpredictable product market conditions, many employ above average rates of numerically flexible workers who are more core than peripheral to business needs (Guerrier and Lockwood, 1989b). Furthermore, some have argued that the lack of functional flexibility in hotels stems from implementation difficulties and because of the barrier of cultural norms such as departmentalization (Guerrier and Lockwood, 1989a; Riley, 1992). Others have suggested that the development of 'quite significant levels of flexibility during the 1960s . . . raises the question of whether or not there is any room left for further functional flexibility on a significant scale' (Bagguley, 1990).

We can attribute a large measure of the increased use of numerically flexible work to structural changes in demand caused by increases in the size of sectors traditionally using non-standard work forms, such as hospitality, tourism and leisure. If these industries seek further to maximize flexibility from their workforces which the more traditional flexible workers, part-time women with small children, are unable to fill (Neathey and Hurstfield, 1995), then students provide a readily available alternative. Although most are, in theory, constrained from working between 0900 and 1600 hours between Monday and Friday during term-time, their availability coincides with peak periods of industry demand, including evenings, weekends, and vacations. Additionally, employing young labour that is relatively cheap compared to adults may further reduce labour costs.

OUTLINE CHARACTERISTICS OF STUDENT LABOUR

The growth of students participating in part-time employment (Crompton and Sanderson, 1990) and the implications this may have for labour market policy (e.g. Micklewright *et al.*, 1994) and educational policy (e.g. Ford *et al.*, 1995), have become issues of increasing attention in the early 1990s. Most of the details about the extent and nature of this employment have been established from national statistical sources, such as the Labour Force Survey (Courtenay and McAleese, 1993a, 1993b; Sly, 1993, 1994), the Family Expenditure Survey (Micklewright *et al.*, 1994) and the Labour Force Survey and the British Household Panel Survey (Dex and McCulloch, 1995). Although these sources do not yield a complete set of consistent data, largely because of their differing methodologies and uses of terminology, they do tell us that most students work less than 20 hours a week for relatively poor levels of remuneration in employment located predominantly in distribution, hotels and catering.

Perhaps most interestingly, they all show that higher female participation is a characteristic of teenage student part-time employment. While this is consistent with women being disproportionately located in flexible jobs (Dex and McCulloch, 1995), it is surprising for two main reasons. First, female teenage students are unlikely to differ fundamentally from their male counterparts in terms of domestic or child caring responsibilities. Second, this difference occurs between two tranches of a segment of the labour force that are ostensibly more advantaged and equal that at any other time in their working lives.

Inconsistencies apart, in highlighting points of interest, analyis of these national statistics also beg a number of fundamental questions:

- How many flexible jobs do students have?
- In which industry sectors do they work?
- What is their employment status?
- How did they get their job/s?
- What type and size of establishment do they work in and what job/s do they do?
- How long have they held their job/s?
- How far do they travel to their workplace?
- What is the nature, pattern and distribution of working hours?
- How much do students earn on an hourly and weekly basis?
- Is their pay satisfactory?
- How was their pay fixed?
- What other elements comprise the total remuneration and benefits package?
- Why do they work, or not work, and what do they enjoy or not enjoy about their employment?
- What is the extent of similarity or difference in the treatment of men and women?

The 'Youth, Gender and Part-Time Employment' project aims to answer these questions. In order to focus on the issue of flexibility, the nature of student labour supply in 46 hospitality, tourism and leisure jobs is identified and discussed within four broad themes. These are:

- the nature of employment;
- employment status;
- hours of work; and
- remuneration.

The data, collected in Greater Manchester in Spring 1994 is, where relevant, compared and contrasted with data about flexible employment patterns of students in full-time education identified from the Labour Force Survey Spring 1994 by Dex and McCulloch (1995) and with hours and pay data from the New Earnings Survey 1994. Further discussion of other supply issues identified by the pilot study and details about the research methodology can be found in Ralston and Lucas (1994) and Lucas and Ralston (1995a, 1995b, 1997).

STUDENT JOBS IN HOSPITALITY, TOURISM AND LEISURE

The Nature of Employment

Student jobs, mainly in restaurants and hotels (65 per cent) and in public houses and clubs (22 per cent), were more likely to be held by undergraduates studying hotel and catering management (78 per cent) than lower sixth form pupils (22 per cent). This finding is to be expected since such undergraduates already possess industry-related skills and licensing laws place restrictions on the employment of young persons under the age of 18. Thirty per cent of these jobs were multiple employment – they were held by students with two or more jobs.[2] The majority of jobs (63 per cent) were located in workplaces employing 25 or more employees, which is much larger on average than typical industry workplace size (Lucas, 1995). Most jobs (83 per cent) were reasonably local – within 5 miles travelling distance. These young persons' jobs were also highly likely to be in workplaces where the majority of the workforce was aged 19 and below (74 per cent).

Two-thirds of the jobs were held by females which mirrors industry employment patterns (Lucas, 1995).[3] Over 60 per cent of jobs were located in workplaces where women made up the majority of the workforce, with 30 per cent employing equal proportions of men and women. There was some indication of differential treatment between the sexes along stereotypical lines, although men and women were more likely to do the same jobs in a department (76 per cent) than in the place of work as a whole (65 per cent). Men were more likely to be associated with cooking and more physically demanding jobs and women with housekeeping, reception and cleaning jobs.

Students were most likely to be employed in more than one department (30 per cent) although restaurant (23 per cent) and bar (14 per cent) work were also significant. The most common occupation was waiting (23 per cent) or general assistant (22 per cent), with a small minority (7 per cent) holding the position of duty or shift manager. A small number of job holders (six) had been promoted. These findings suggest that a sizeable element of student labour is 'doubly' flexible. Not only do they hold multiple employment, but as peripheral part-time and casual workers required to do anything anywhere they are also functionally flexible.

Employment Status

One of the problems about flexible employment is defining what it means (Dex and McCulloch, 1995). We followed the broad approach used in the Labour Force Survey, that of self-definition. Students were asked three questions about their employment status – how their employers and they themselves perceive it (full-time, part-time or temporary) and then to refine their actual status. Here there were clear differences between employers' and students' perceptions. While employers were perceived to classify employment as either part-time (74 per cent) or temporary (26 per cent), 95 per cent of students saw their jobs as part-time and 5 per cent as full-time. Refinements within part-time status were fourfold – employee (56 per cent), casual (26 per cent), seasonal (9 per cent) and sub-contracted (4 per cent), and are consistent with findings from the Labour Force Survey, particularly on the point that casual employment is more likely to be found among the young (Dex and McCulloch, 1995).

Many of these students had reasonably stable employment, with 49 per cent having 12 months' service or longer, more than half of whom had two years' service or longer, thus making them eligible for employment protection (e.g. unfair dismissal and redundancy). However, service length is shorter than for flexible workers in the economy as a whole (Dex and McCulloch, 1995), which is a point that further reinforces the even more highly flexible nature of student employment.

Hours of work

Marginally more jobs (52 per cent) had variable hours (which change from week-to-week) than fixed hours (that do not change from week-to-week), as shown in Table 6.1. Mean weekly variable hours (14.8) exceeded mean weekly fixed hours (10), and involved a sizeable minority of students working more than 16 hours or for three days or more a week. Where students had fixed hours, they were most likely to work on a Saturday, although employment was undertaken throughout the week. In both cases, the hours of most jobs (71 per cent) changed depending on the time of year, and of these, change was predominantly at Christmas, during the holidays and to cover busy periods.

This hours profile shares a number of similarities with the national picture identified by Dex and McCulloch (1995), except that the most flexible students in the pilot study, those with variable hours, were more likely to work longer hours and there was a higher incidence of multiple job holding.

Student Survey*

	Variable hours (23 cases: 52%)	Fixed hours (21 cases: 48%)
Weekly hours		
Mean hours	14.8	10.0
Range of hours	5–40	4–24
Distribution of hours		
< 8 hours	13%	52%
8–15 hours	43%	34%
16+ hours	43%	14%
Daily hours		
Range of hours	1–22	1–12
Days worked		
1+	14%	43%
2+	43%	38%
3+	33%	19%

Daily pattern	No cases	Range
Monday	– 3	3.5–7.5
Tuesday	– 2	4.0–5.0
Wednesday	– 4	2.0–7.0
Thursday	– 3	2.0–4.5
Friday	– 6	1.0–6.5
Saturday	– 15	1.0–12.0
Sunday	– 4	3.75–8.0

New Earnings Survey**

Great Britain	19.50
North West	20.70
18–20	18.70
21–24	18.80
H&C***	17.70

*   Numerical base: 44 jobs
**   Mean hours of part-time manual females on adult rates including those without specified normal basic hours
***   SIC Class 66, Hotels and Catering

Column percentages do not sum to 100 due to rounding

Table 6.1: Hours of work
        (Source: Pilot study, 1994 and New Earnings Survey Part F, 1994)

Remuneration

Basic pay is low on a comparative measure, as shown in Table 6.2. Although the New Earnings Survey has a number of limitations as a comparator, because it excludes around one-fifth of all part-timers who are not members of PAYE schemes,[4] these pay figures serve to reinforce the importance of students as a cheap flexible labour source. Further refinements to the data show pay differences relating to gender and age, trends that are also reflected in flexible jobs in the economy as a whole (Dex and McCulloch, 1995).

In spite of being low, in over 60 per cent of jobs pay was deemed to be satisfactory. Pay dissatisfaction was associated with pay being too low for the type of work done and the conditions under which it was performed, in relation to the skills or knowledge of the job holder, or because there was too much reliance on tips.

Student Survey*	Mean	Range of rates
All cases	3.03	1.25 – 4.95
Men	3.16	1.25 – 4.01
Women	2.97	2.00 – 4.95
16–19	3.02	2.10 – 4.95
20–24	2.99	1.25 – 3.95
25+	3.38	3.00 – 4.01
New Earnings Survey**	Mean	
Great Britain	3.99	
North West	3.96	
18–20	3.76	
21–24	3.74	
H&C***	3.45	
* Numerical base: 43 jobs		
** Part-time manual females on adult rates		
*** SIC Class 66, Hotels and Catering		

Table 6.2: Basic hourly pay (£)
(*Source: Pilot study, 1994 and New Earnings Survey Part F, 1994*)

As numerous commentators have suggested, basic pay alone is an inadequate measure in terms of identifying the total reward package. More specifically, in terms of flexible labour theories that assume that such labour is cheaper, it becomes important to establish what other components are available to make up remuneration and, in particular, to identify which of these components are direct costs to the employer. Given that the deregulation of youth pay in the mid-1980s allowed employers to dispense with practices formerly governed by wages councils, including those related to the timing of wage increases, the provision of meals and breaks on duty, allowance for tips received, and premium payments in certain circumstances, it is axiomatic to examine such issues.

Pay was overwhelmingly determined by management and rarely subject to negotiation, even on an individual basis. In terms of pay structures, there was only minority evidence of wage-for-age or wage increases related to length of service. Where a meal was provided while on duty (61 per cent), in the vast majority of cases it was free. In one-third of jobs there was no meal or rest break. Where breaks were given, they were most likely to be between 15 minutes and half-an-hour duration but the practice was largely unregulated in that it was commonly unspecified how long was to be worked before a break was given. More than half the jobs were reliant on tips, although it is difficult to quantify their worth. Of the eighteen cases which specified figures for daily tips, these ranged from 40p to £50, although seven were between £1 and £5 a day and seven were £10. One in four jobs required the job holder to undertake extra hours for no extra pay, in circumstances that broadly relate to 'finishing off' after closing late. Most of the available perquisites, such as discount or free meals and drinks, had a monetary benefit. However, one of the most frequently mentioned, free transport home, is arguably more a necessity than a benefit if it is needed in circumstances where public transport is unavailable, such as late at night.

EMPLOYERS' DEMANDS FOR FLEXIBLE STUDENT LABOUR

The issue of employers" labour use strategies has already been explored by the author in regard to hospitality, tourism and leisure industries (Lucas and Ralston, 1995c, 1996). This is problematic both conceptually and practically for reasons now summarized. Strategy originated as a market-oriented concept concerned with products and their competitive advantage but the term remains problematic both in terms of definition and meaning, and, for this discussion, in terms of the relationship between strategy and the environment. While Porter (1985) sees strategy as a rational process created and developed in response to the market, Mintzberg *et al.* (1988) conceptualize strategy as a discernible organizational pattern that emerges in response to the environment. More recently, he has argued that strategy is an oxymoron (Mintzberg, 1994).

The next difficulty is whether a market-based concept can be applied to employment decisions in hospitality, tourism and leisure since much of the literature suggests that employment decisions are made pragmatically or on an ad hoc basis (Lucas, 1995). In particular, strategy as a concept in regard to labour use oversimplifies the complexities and vagaries of the labour market.

And at a more practical level, we still understand relatively little about the dynamics of employer decision-making, even if we can observe a pattern that is apparently associated with such decisions.

These difficulties apart, it was possible, in seeking to answer whether part-time student labour is a matter of strategic choice or pragmatic response, to move the debate forward. We did not discern any evidence of 'McDonaldization', a more extreme form of labour management strategy particularly associated with fast food (Gabriel, 1988; Ritzer, 1993). Much of the evidence provided by employers tallied with details given by the students. Students and non-student labour were employed in the same jobs, although there was some evidence that students were perceived as bringing with them inherent advantages related to appearance and intelligence. Students were not paid less because they were students but because they were paid as regular part-timers who were paid less than regular full-timers.

Employers were aware of the inherent flexibility of students to work particular shifts, often during unsocial hours. Students provided a ready workforce of part-time and casual labour, regardless of whether they were at school studying for 'A'' levels or at university taking a vocationally relevant course in hotel and catering management and, were actively applying for jobs. Therefore, a combination of strategic choice and pragmatic response, a pragmatic strategy that may be tantamount to 'a coincidence of varying interests', leads hospitality, tourism and leisure employers to employ students.

CONCLUSIONS

Although the findings from one relatively small study in a large urban conurbation in North West England cannot be regarded as authoritative, they do provide firm evidence that students are being used to maximize flexibility. In some ways student employment mirrors female part-time employment nationally in these industries (see Crompton and Sanderson, 1990). But it may be even more flexible because students are more likely to be used to do any job anywhere, to hold multiple employment, and to have a higher rate of turnover. High flexibility may simply be a cover for intensifying effort which is used to raise productivity, a form of 'McDonaldization'. Since our sample contained a high proportion of hotel and catering students, higher in 'human capital' terms because of job-related skills, this may also have the effect of raising productivity.

Additionally a wide variety of daily and weekly hours arrangements are used to manage demand patterns that vary daily, weekly, and at particular times of the year. Students, particularly females, are a cheap labour form because their basic pay is low, they receive relatively few extra benefits and significant numbers rely on tips, demonstrating that employers operate flexible remuneration policies. Lower level work of this kind may be more sex-typed than has been acknowledged (Crompton and Sanderson, 1990). It would seem that flexible student employment is a key issue for the latter 1990s, and once our research is completed, we expect to make a major empirical contribution to understanding its nature and significance.

REFERENCES

Atkinson, J. (1984) Manpower Strategies for Flexible Organizations, *Personnel Management* August, pp 28–31.

Bagguley, P. (1990) Gender and Labour Flexibility in Hotel and Catering, *The Service Industries Journal* 10 (4), pp 737–747.

Courtenay, G. and McAleese, I. (1993a) *England and Wales Youth Cohort Study Cohort 5: aged 16–17 in 1989* Report on Sweep 1. Employment Department Research Series Youth Cohort Report No. 21, July.

Courtenay, G. and McAleese, I. (1993b) *England and Wales Youth Cohort Study Cohort 5: aged 16–17 in 1991* Report on Sweep 1. Employment Department Research Series Youth Cohort Report No. 22, August.

Crompton, R. and Sanderson, K. (1990) *Gendered Jobs and Social Change* pp 135–59, London: Unwin Hyman.

Dex, S. and McCulloch, A. (1995) *Flexible Employment in Britain: A Statistical Analysis*, Research Discussion Series No. 15, Manchester: Equal Opportunities Commission, pp vii, 5–7, 19, 34–5, 55–69, 82–4, 136–7.

Employment Department (1988) *Employment for the 1990s*, pp 5–9 Cmnd 540 London: HMSO.

Employment Department (1994) Labour Force Survey Help-Line, *Employment Gazette* September, LFS1.

Ford, J., Bosworth, D. and Wilson, R. (1995) Part-time Work and Full-time Higher Education, *Studies in Higher Education* 20 (2), pp 187–202.

Foster, J. (1994) Colleges Open up Own Job Centres, *The Independent on Sunday* 6 November, p 10.

Gabriel, Y. (1988) *Working Lives in Catering*, pp 4–6, 93–128 London: Routledge.

Guerrier, Y. and Lockwood, A. (1989a) Managing Flexible Working, *The Service Industries Journal* 7(3), pp 406–419.

Guerrier, Y. and Lockwood, A. (1989b) Core and Peripheral Employees in Hotel Operations, *Personnel Review* 18(1), pp 9–15.

Hotel and Catering Training Company (1994) *Catering and Hospitality Industry – Key Facts and Figures* p 24, London: HCTC.

Hunter, L.C. and McInnes, J. (1991) *Employers' Labour Use Strategies – Case Studies* Employment Department Research Paper No. 87. London: Employment Department.

Industrial Relations Services (1994) Diversity and change – Survey of Non-standard working, *IRS Employment Trends* No. 570, October, pp 7–18.

Lee, D. (1992) The Transformation of Training and the Transformation of Work in Britain. In S. Wood (ed.) *The Transformation of Work* London: Routledge.

Lockwood, A. and Guerrier, Y. (1989) Flexible Working in the Hospitality: Current Issues and Future Potential, *Contemporary Hospitality Management* 1(1), pp 11–16.

Lucas, R.E. (1995) *Managing Employee Relations in the Hotel and Catering Industry*, pp 10, 28–34, 53, 62–9, 71–3, 89–92, London: Cassell.

Lucas, R.E. and Jeffries, L.P. (1991) The 'Demographic Timebomb' and How Some Hospitality Employers are Responding to the Challenge, *International Journal of Hospitality Management* 10(4), pp 323–337.

Lucas, R.E. and Ralston, L.M. (1995a) Part-time Youth Employment in the Hospitality Industry and Elsewhere: Pilot Study Findings in Greater Manchester. Paper presented to the *Human Resource Management in the Hospitality Conference* February, London.

Lucas, R.E. and Ralston, L.M. (1995b) Part-time Employment: Hospitality Undergraduates and Sixth Form Students. Paper presented to the *4th CHME Conference, Hotel School, City College* April, Norwich.

Lucas, R.E. and Ralston, L.M. (1995c) Part-time Student Labour in the Hospitality Industry: Strategic Choice or Pragmatic Response? Paper presented to *Hospitality Industries – Strategies for the Future Conference on the Internet* September/October, MCB Press.

Lucas, R.E. and Ralston, L.M. (1996) Part-time Student Labour in the Hospitality Industry: Strategic Choice or Pragmatic Response? *International Journal of Contemporary Hospitality Management* 8(2), pp 21–24.

Lucas, R.E. and Ralston, L.M. (1997) Youth, Gender and Part-time Employment: A Preliminary Appraisal of Student Employment, *Employee Relations*, 19(1), pp 51–66.

McGregor, A. and Sproull, A. (1991) *Employer Labour Use Strategies: Analysis of a National Survey* Employment Department Research series No. 83, London: Employment Department.

Micklewright, J., Rajah, N. and Smith, S. (1994) Labouring and Learning: Part-time Work and Full-time Education, *National Institute Economic Review* May, pp 73–85.

Mintzberg, H. (1994) *The Rise and Fall of Strategic Planning* New York: Prentice Hall.

Mintzberg, H., Quinn, J.B. and James, R. (1988) *The Strategy Process, Concepts, Contexts and Cases* Englewood Cliffs, NJ: Prentice Hall.

Neathey, F. and Hurstfield, J. (1995) *Flexibility in Practice: Women's Employment and Pay in Retail and Finance* Equal Opportunities Commission Research Discussion series No. 16, London: Industrial Relations Services.

Pollert, A. (1991) *Farewell to Flexibility?: Restructuring Work and Employment* Oxford: Blackwell.

Porter, H. (1994) Best years of their lives? *The Guardian 2* 16 November, pp 2–3.

Porter, M. (1985) *Competitive Advantage: Creating and Sustaining Superior Performance* New York: The Free Press.

Ralston, L.M. and Lucas, R.E. (1994) Youth Employment in Hotels and Catering – Beyond Demographic Phenomenon. Paper presented to the *3rd CHME Research Conference,* Napier University, April.

Riley, M. (1992) Functional Flexibility in Hotels – is it Feasible? *Tourism Management* 13(4), pp 363–367.

Ritzer, G. (1993) *The McDonaldization of Society: An Investigation into the Changing Character of Contemporary Social Life* Thousand Oaks, CA: Pine Forge Press.

Sly, F. (1993) Economic Activity of 16 and 17 year olds *Employment Gazette* July, pp 307–312.

Sly, F. (1994) The Educational and Labour Market Status of 16 and 17 year olds, *Employment Gazette* September, pp 329–334.

The Guardian Education (1994) Results of the Guardian Education Survey into the Attitudes of Final-year Students 15 February, pp 1–6.

Thomas, R. (1994) Students Must Learn Costly Lesson, *The Guardian* 14 November, p 13.

Ward, D. and Meikle, J. (1993) Low Grants Drive Students into Part-time Work, *The Guardian* 15 February, p 13.

NOTES

1: This notion of core and periphery is based on Atkinson's (1984) framework, although this framework has been widely challenged by others including Guerrier and Lockwood (1989a, 1989b), Lockwood and Guerrier (1989) and Pollert (1991).

2: Interestingly, we found a higher extent of multiple employment (15 per cent of students) in the complete pilot (108 students held 125 jobs) than in the economy as a whole, where 7.8 per cent of female and 5.3 per cent of male students have two part-time jobs (Dex and McCulloch, 1995).

3: In the complete pilot, female participation exceeded male participation, but only marginally. It was, however, more marked among teenagers, which is in keeping with the observations of Dex and McCulloch (1995).

4: A pay slip/statement was given for 81 per cent of jobs which may indicate that most students are paid under a PAYE scheme, even though they earned below the income tax threshold − £66.50 a week in 1994.

SECTION THREE
COMPETITIVENESS

7

Privatization and Cultural Change in Hospitality and Leisure Services

Susan M. Ogden

In the context of UK public sector hospitality and leisure services, this chapter examines the adoption of managerialist principles at a strategic level in response to competitive pressure. The impact on the organizational culture at an operational level is then considered. Finally, the extent to which a new, more commercial culture has been created is discussed.

INTRODUCTION

In the public sector, organizational culture has been founded on public service values, traditions and assumptions. In turn these are underpinned by principles of bureaucracy devised primarily to satisfy the need for public accountability. A strong pluralist industrial relations tradition has also been a key feature. Together, these characteristics have been the essence of public sector culture. However, concerns about the failure of the public sector to achieve economy, effectiveness and efficiency have led to the expansion of privatization policies. In hospitality and leisure services provided by both local government and the National Health Services, this has taken the form of contracting out and compulsory competitive tendering (CCT). The latter form of market testing attempts to constrain the strategic choices of decision-makers to the effect that either private sector values, beliefs and practices are imported into the management of public service provision, or that public services are 'exported' to the private sector. The belief is that by amending the constraints under which services operate, organizational culture can be changed to enhance organizational effectiveness. Thus, even if a large proportion of the services subjected to CCT remain in-house, the process of preparing for, and subsequently living in, a competitive environment acts as a major force of change both for the management of the services directly affected and for the organization of which they are a part.

The strategic decision-making process arising from CCT is illustrated in Figure 7.1 (as adapted from Purcell, 1991). It can be argued that the nature of organizational culture is dependent upon a series of upstream strategic decisions. Of particular interest are the nature and implications of 'second-order' strategic decisions relating to modifications to the structural fabric of the organization. 'Third order' strategic decisions which relate to choices in the area of human resource management, are also likely to impact on organizational culture. It can be levelled that policy changes at these two levels will contribute to any transition away from the traditional model of public administration towards a new 'public management' model and, possibly, the future emergence of the 'enabling' authority. At the operational level change is also visible through the introduction of new working practices and conditions of employment and the development of new management styles.

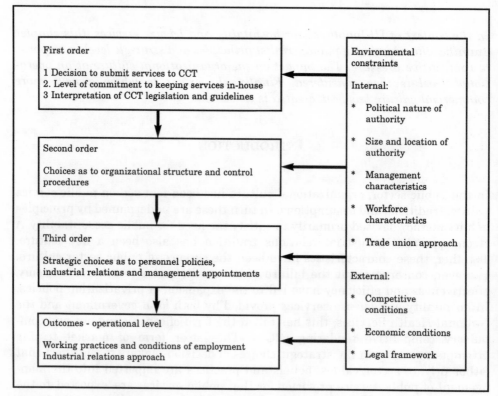

Figure 7.1: A model of strategic choices and constraints in the management of CCT

THE TRANSITION TO PUBLIC MANAGEMENT

The new organizational framework which it is alleged is replacing the breakdown of the traditional bureaucratic model of public administration has been termed 'public management' (Perry and Kraemer, 1983). This incorporates the traditional emphasis within public administration on accountability with modern private sector management principles. The concept is an output from the generic school of management which advocates that the knowledge, techniques and skills necessary for effective administration or management are similar for organizations in a variety of different sectors of society. Although proponents of this school adhere to the view that public administration is not unique, it is generally not argued that business management can be applied directly, without modification, to the public sector. The term 'public management' attempts to make this distinction.

The advent of this new public sector culture has been described as essentially a reaction against bureaucratic formalism and proceduralism (Painter, 1988). Management responsibility is devolved so as to 'let the managers manage', thereby encouraging initiative and, where appropriate, an entrepreneurial spirit. Middle management responsibility centres, which are almost self-contained productive units permitting the devolution of clear duties and the establishment of performance targets, are created. Emphasis is also placed on defining and measuring management performance on the basis of outputs, wherever possible, in quantitative terms. Rather than rewarding public servants for rule conformity, error avoidance and attention to detail, it rewards them for achieving output targets and punishes them for underperformance. The public sector is seen as a productive process and strives for higher productivity through improved efficiency and cost-effectiveness. Matched with this is a conception of the public not as citizens but as consumers and taxpayers, whose stakes and interests in government services are seen as being predominantly economic.

Painter (1988) suggests that the outcome of these innovations is that public servants are now valued for their management skills. The notion that lengthy, faithful service is rewarded by occupancy of a senior position is replaced by the onset of lateral recruitment and 'executive searches'. Thus technical and professional specialists will take second place to the new 'managers'. Furthermore, aspiring public service managers acquire MBAs, learn about marketing and master the jargon of economics. Like their private sector counterparts, they conform to a 'workaholic' office culture and must show an eagerness to accept the risks associated with payment by results and contract appointments (Painter, 1988).

Competition and Public Management

Competition encourages the onset of a managerialist culture in a variety of ways. As Table 7.1 illustrates, the changes CCT is likely to bring about have much in common with the principles contained in the new public management school, as described above. The characteristics listed in the pre-CCT column fit into the traditional, bureaucratic public administration model. Much in the right hand column of the table fits the description of public management. For example, where the decision has been made to attempt to keep the service in-house by submitting a tender in competition with the private sector, the CCT legislation encourages a shift towards greater decentralization. This can be achieved via the setting up of semi-autonomous contracting departments (termed Direct Service Organizations – DSOs) in order to create a degree of separateness between the 'contract' function and the 'client' function. Decisions relating to the degree of autonomy given to these DSOs are likely to have an impact on the role and nature of the centre of the organization. In particular, central service departments may themselves have to become more commercially orientated and more critical of their own costs and services in order to give DSOs value for money. Thus a change in their role from one of control to one of facilitation may ensue. In other words, a shift in control from professionals to managers is encouraged. This has implications for strategic policy-making. In particular, strategic policy relating to employment issues may increasingly become business-led, i.e., be guided by operational needs rather than corporate objectives.

Pre-CCT	Post-CCT
Integrated service departments.	Client/contractor split.
Professionalism – limiting operational autonomy.	Managerialism – enhancing operational autonomy.
No clear performance standards.	Contract specifications; service level agreements.
Budgetary control.	Contract penalties; break even or reach profit target on contact price.
Central support costs allocated: – on a pro rata basis.	Central support costs allocated: – on basis of usage.
Central service control.	Central service facilitation
Tight political control: – frequent reporting back to committees.	Devolution of political control: – more decision-making power to sub-committee & officials.
Payment based on grade and length of service.	Performance related pay – profit sharing.
Promotion by length of service and 'professional' expertise.	Lateral recruitment – executive searches/private sector experience.
Security of tenure	Short-term management contracts
PUBLIC ADMINISTRATION	PUBLIC MANAGEMENT

Table 7.1: Organizational characteristics pre- and post-CCT

A study by Ogden (1994) portrays the organizational characteristics of DSOs in three regional authorities (R1–R3) and eight district authorities (D1–D8). As Table 7.2 illustrates many district authorities have set up a separate DSO for each set of closely related activities; one to deal with environmental health activities (street cleaning, refuse collection and, where carried out, building cleaning) and one to deal with leisure and recreation activities (ground maintenance, and in some cases leisure management). This has meant that the cleansing DSO tends to be the larger and, in some authorities, it also assumes the responsibility for vehicle maintenance since it is the largest user of vehicles. In the study three of the districts had set up what has been termed a 'super DSO', which is one DSO responsible for all of the activities subject to competition under the 1988 Act. Two of these 'super DSOs' also included the operations subject to CCT under the 1980 Act. Pressures were mounting to create a super DSO in one other authority. In the larger authorities studied (the regions and the city council), service areas tended to be kept separate. For example, in two of the regional authorities studied, separate catering and cleaning DSOs had been established. In the small regional authority studied, a combined cleaning and catering DSO was in place.

The creation of the new unitary authorities in Scotland in April 1996, will obviously have implications for the current structure of DSOs (Cost Sector Catering, 1995). In particular, DSOs in large regional authorities face the possibility of being broken up to cover the smaller geographical area of the new authorities. One alternative to such disaggregation would be to supply a cross-boundary service to several new unitary authorities at once. Another possibility would be to transfer the DSO to the private sector by means of a management buyout, although this option is unlikely to be supported in Labour-dominated areas.

Of further interest are the management control structures which are evolving between the DSOs and the centre. The control structures arising from CCT can be categorized using Purcell's (1991) distinction between the administrative control system, the strategic planning control system and the performance control system. The administrative control system arises where corporate office rules and regulations limit unit managers' freedom of action. The performance control system operates where each unit is judged purely on its ability to meet appropriate financial targets. The manner in which the unit manager meets these targets is up to him or her. The incentive to do so is reinforced by monetary rewards for success (i.e., performance pay), or dismissal for failure. Strategic planning organizations, on the other hand, generally place greater emphasis on stamping a corporate character on their constituent businesses. They have long-term aims and are most likely to have an institutional strategy which includes non-economic values and beliefs.

As Ogden (1994) demonstrates, some local authorities have restructured to become performance control organizations very much in line with the public management ethos (see Table 7.2). They have created strategic business units in the form of DSOs and have put incentives in place to encourage a culture which prevents parties from acting against the interests of the organization. Thus, the view of some is that rules and regulations, in the form of corporate policies and procedures, will become unnecessary. However some authorities wishing to maintain public sector values, have either resisted the structural changes which devolve autonomy or, more often, have adopted a balanced view by insisting that key values are adopted via corporate policies and procedures. This demonstrates how the legal framework surrounding CCT is open to interpretation, so that the extent and pace of the introduction of public management depends on the strategic choices taken by the political masters. It is possible that authorities can choose a strategic planning control system to fit in with their political and cultural traditions. Once again the creation of the new unitary authorities will have some impact in this area.

DSO TYPE	AUTHORITY AND SERVICE	CONTROL SYSTEM
Single Service DSO:	R1 – Catering; Cleaning	Strategic Planning
	R2 – Catering; Cleaning	Strategic Planning
	D1 – Grounds Maintenance	Performance Control
	D3 – Grounds Maintenance	Performance Control
Dual DSO:	R3 – Catering/Cleaning	Performance Control
	D1 – Refuse Collection(RC) /Street Cleaning(SC)	Performance Control
	D4 – RC/SC	Strategic Planning
	D7 – RC/SC	Performance Control
	D2 – Grounds Maintenance, Leisure Management.	Administrative
Multi-DSO:	D2 – RC/SC/Vehicle Maintenance (VM)	Administrative
	D3 – RC/SC/VM/ Building Cleaning	Performance Control
Super DSO:	D6 – all services	Performance Control
	D5 – all services*	Performance Control
	D8 – all services*	Performance Control

* Including activities subjected to CCT by 1980 Act.

Table 7.2: Organizational characteristics of DSOs

The Enabling Authority

A step further from the performance control authority is the concept of the 'enabling authority'. Although varying definitions of this concept exist, it usually implies a shift away from direct provision of services to a scenario where the authority is chiefly responsible for the awarding and monitoring of contracts. The phenomenon has been described as:

> a shift from a vertically integrated corporate institutional form of direct service provision by British local government to one of an enabling function within a horizontally co-ordinated network of multi-agency service provision (Bailey, 1993).

These 'agencies' may be private sector, profit-oriented companies, non-profit, voluntary organizations, or internal contracting units. Thus even where work is performed in-house after a CCT exercise, it is anticipated that there will be:

> a shift away from the relatively simple vertically integrated collegial hierarchy within local government to a form of contractual relationships between individual departments operating as competitive internal consultancies charging for professional services (Bailey, 1993).

The concept is seen by some as an opportunity for local politicians to free themselves from the more routine concerns of direct service provision, allowing them to spend more time on matters of strategic concern for their areas – of an environmental, economic, and social nature (Brooke, 1989). Others however see it as a move towards local authorities becoming merely local centres for administering government-determined policies (Platt, 1988).

With the onset of CCT for 'soft' services such as housing management, architectural services and even personnel management, the issues thrown up by this scenario will require further scrutiny.

CHANGING CULTURE AT THE OPERATIONAL LEVEL

The discussion so far has centred around how policy makers have tried to change organizational culture by modifying the structural fabric of the organization, thus changing the environment within which employees operate. At the operational level, however, changes in working practices and conditions of employment are likely to have a more direct impact on the attitudes and behaviour of employees. Whether the effect is of an adverse or a beneficial nature will partly depend on the approach to the introduction of change. As Meek (1994) asserts, culture cannot be easily controlled or manipulated, 'it is not an independent variable, nor can it be created, discovered or destroyed by the whims of management'. It should not be assumed that management creates, changes and imposes 'culture' on a passive and uncritical membership. However, the assumption that people's values, norms and attitudes can be moulded so that they make the 'right' contribution to the healthy collective 'culture', despite any inherent conflict of individual and group interest, appears to be at the heart of much of the new 'public management' ethos. Such a unitarist ideology is unacceptable, especially in the study of the public sector. In this context, the approach to the management of industrial relations is key. As Galbraith (1983) maintains, it is 'conditioned power' which is important for organizational success. It is through persuasions, education or the social commitment to what seems natural, proper or right that the 'corporation' can cause the individual to submit to the will of another. Thus management control over both direct and indirect forms of management employee communication such as mission statements and logos are important in achieving cultural change. The nature of the leadership style at the operational level is also an important variable. The use of these mechanisms for facilitating change in the public sector is now examined.

Leadership Change

It has been argued that the role leaders play in transforming organizational culture is crucial (see Schein, 1985; Fiedler and House, 1988). To aid the adjustment to the competitive environment, local authorities have sought to recruit private sector managers. The aim appears to be to replace those with bureaucratic values with those with performance orientation who are seen to have entrepreneurial rather than administrative skills. The study by Ogden (1994) gives examples of local government DSO managers appointed in catering and cleaning services. Of the five catering and cleaning DSOs studied, three were headed by managers recruited from the private sector and one from the National Health Service (NHS). A change of leader at the strategic level is also important. For example, in one authority radical changes made regarding the introduction of service level agreements and annual hours employment contracts were inspired by the recruitment of a new Personnel Director, who had previously spearheaded the transformation of a newly privatized water authority.

New Working Practices

The traditional culture in public services has been one which has learned to accommodate and placate the multiple internal and external stakeholder groups. In particular, commitment to the 'model employer' tradition (Beaumont, 1981) and to principles of national collective bargaining have conditioned the relations between 'management' and employees (Winchester, 1983). In fact, it is the belief that these principles have encouraged inefficient employment practice which formulated much of the justification for market testing in the public sector (see Forsyth, 1980).

The introduction of CCT has made a big impact on working practices and conditions of employment in both the National Health Service (NHS) and local government. In the area of school catering and cleaning in local government, reductions in the number of part-time hours worked have been widespread.

A study by Ogden (1994) revealed that in one authority this had resulted in reductions in take-home pay of 35 per cent. However another authority had actually increased the number of full-time cleaners and reduced the number of part-time cleaners. The efficiency saving were made mainly from the introduction of new equipment and the intensification of work. The study could find no evidence of performance related pay or profit sharing for this category of worker. Managers were sticking to agreements on pay and conditions of service reached through national bargaining. However, DSO managers recruited from the private sector were finding this part of the public sector culture difficult to accept. Within the bounds of the national agreement more evidence was found of changes being made to rules governing holidays and, although basic entitlement to sick pay was not changing, absenteeism procedures were generally being tightened up. A common change in school catering and cleaning was the ending of summer holiday retention pay. Local conditions such as special rates for travelling time and scrubbing allowances were also being withdrawn.

Kelliher (1995), reporting on the impact of competitive tendering for ancillary services in the NHS, also found that a uniform change across her study was the increased use of numerical flexibility, particularly in relation to the use of part-time staff. On a more disparate level an increasing number of new staff were being employed on short-term contracts. There was also evidence of managers enforcing rules (e.g. over absenteeism) more closely, and some instances of a desire to link rewards more closely to employees' individual performance levels. However, reductions in job security – formerly a major attraction for retaining staff – had also suffered. Evidence was also found of increased absenteeism and labour turnover. Thus, although management had responded to change by becoming more control oriented, there were negative side effects in terms of staff morale and loyalty.

In grounds maintenance and leisure management, an interesting innovation has been the use of annual hours contracts to reduce premium over-time and shift payments. Foley and MacVicar (1995) noted that annual hours contracts for workers covered by recreation contracts had been introduced in at least two Scottish authorities. In one of these authorities the contractual hours per annum for staff is between 1560 and 1595, while for manual employees it is between 1738 and 1777. The study by Ogden (1994) illustrated that this policy had been introduced in six out of the eight grounds maintenance DSOs selected for the study. This had resulted in the employment of a larger number of temporary staff in the summer months to meet peaks in activity, thereby allowing decreases in core staffing levels and reductions in overtime payments.

Communication and Negotiation Process

Top-down culture change begins with the process of communication. One indication of a shift away from the traditional public sector culture has been a shift away from the use of trade unions as the main channel of communication towards direct management communication with the workforce. Both during the introduction of CCT and in the post-contract award phase many managers have put more emphasis on improving management communications. For example, many authorities introduced special CCT information bulletins and/or in-house news-sheets in an attempt to ensure that the management viewpoint was delivered and to help foster a more commercial culture (Ogden, 1994). Joint union-management circulars relating to CCT were only produced in one of the eleven authorities included in the study. However, many managers held joint meetings with the trade union to inform the workforce about the need for change. Other methods of educating the workforce about new managerial values of commercialism such as 'team briefings' and 'quality circles' were not widely evident.

In the area of employment relations, Kelliher (1995) also found diversity of experience in the ancillary services studied in the NHS. In some organizations communication continued to be mainly through trade unions channels, whereas in others managers had moved to using more direct methods of communication with staff, such as staff meetings, individual counselling and the setting up of working groups. Instances were also found of deliberate union avoidance.

Internal Marketing

Symbols have been described as key to the notion of culture both at the national and the organizational level. They are important in that they try to summarize the ethos of the society or organization they represent. In response to CCT, there is evidence that management have introduced new symbols such as logos, mission statements, and staff uniforms. For example, in one catering DSO, an in-house newsletter, annual awards for excellence in a number of categories with prizes sponsored by major suppliers, as well as new logos and uniforms, had been introduced in the post-contract award phase (Ogden, 1994). Even although the contract had been awarded in-house, they felt it important to change the image of the organization portrayed to external customers and to employees.

CONCLUSION

Resistance to change is a natural first response. As Meek (1994) reiterates, norms and values have as much potential for creating conflict within organizations as they do for creating social cohesion. Much of the management literature on the study of organizational culture centres around the need to shape the behaviour of employees to create consensus, loyalty and a general feeling of *esprit de corps*. The process of CCT is an interesting example of 'corporate' culture change. On the one hand the pressure to adapt working practices and conditions of employment is likely to be met with hostility. However, if staff, trade unions and management are not successful in agreeing on new forms of working patterns and conditions of employment to enhance competitiveness, contracts and jobs could be lost to the private sector. Therefore, the manner in which the process of change is managed is vital both to those at the strategic and the operational levels. The evidence suggests that much of the cultural change arising from the competitive pressures brought by privatization policies has been imposed rather than emergent. Some organizations have adopted a top-down, 'evangelical' approach towards change giving employees a clear picture of the direction of culture change which was expected. Others have adopted tactics which encourage a more gradual, emergent change in culture.

The environment within which public sector hospitality and leisure services are provided has been changed quite dramatically. Although choices still exist for policy makers and strategists, constraints have been put in place. Policies which may previously have been rejected due to a commitment to the model employer philosophy can be more easily justified under a competitive environment. However, if the political willpower is strong, the influence of 'corporate' values can be maintained. In short, competitive tendering is likely to lead to greater variation in organizational cultures within the public sector. Despite differences in the extent and pace of change, it can generally be contended that the political contingency and public service values are becoming a less dominant feature of organizational culture in much of what remains of the public sector.

REFERENCES

Bailey, S.J. (1993) Public Choice Theory and the Reform of Local Government in Britain: From Government to Governance, *Public Policy and Administration* 8, pp 7–24.

Beaumont, P.B. (1981) *Government as an Employer – Setting an Example* London: Royal Institute of Public Administration.

Brooke, R. (1989) The Enabling Authority – Practical Consequences, *Local Government Studies* September-October.

Cost Sector Catering (1995) *DSOs Face Breakup Under New Local Authority Structures,* April, p 13.

Galbraith, J.K. (1983) *The Anatomy of Power* London: Corgi Books.

Fiedler, F.E. and House, R.J. (1988) Leadership Theory and Research: A Report of Progress. In C.L. Cooper and I.T. Robertson (eds) *International Review of Industrial and Organizational Psychology* Chichester: John Wiley.

Foley, M. and MacVicar, A. (1995) The Role of Annual Hours Contracts in Local Government Leisure Services. In R. Teare and C. Armistead (eds) *Services Management – New Directions and New Perspectives* London: Cassell.

Forsyth, M. (1980) *Reservicing Britain* Adam Smith Institute.

Kelliher, C. (1995) Competitive Pressures in the Provision of Ancillary Services in the NHS: An Assessment of the Impact on Employment. In R. Teare and R. Armistead (1995) *Services Management: New Directions and Perspectives* London: Cassell.

Meek, V.L. (1994) Organizational Culture: Origins and Weaknesses. In D. McKevitt and A. Lawton *Public Sector Management: Theory, Critique and Practice* pp 265–280, London: Sage Publications.

Ogden, S.M. (1994) *The Impact of Compulsory Competitive Tendering on the Management of Local Government Industrial Relations,* unpublished PhD thesis.

Painter, M. (1988) Public Management: Fad or Fallacy, *Australian Journal of Public Administration* 47(1), pp 1–3.

Perry, J.L. and Kraemer, K.L. (1983) *Public Management: Public and Private Perspectives* CA: Mayfield Publishing, California.

Platt, S. (1988) Skeleton Services, *New Statesman and Society* 17 June.

Purcell, J. (1991) The Impact of Corporate Strategy on Human Resource Management. In J. Storey (ed.) *New Perspectives on Human Resource Management* pp 67–91, London: Routledge.

Schein, E. (1985) *Organizational Culture and Leadership*, San Francisco: Jossey-Bass.

Sinclair, A. (1989) Public Sector Culture: Managerialism or Multiculturalism, *Australian Journal of Public Administration* 48(4), pp 382–397.

Winchester, D. (1983) Industrial Relations in the Public Sector. In G.S. Bain (ed.) *Industrial Relations in Britain*, Oxford: Blackwell.

8

The Changing Role of Marketing in Local Authority Museums

Gayle McPherson

This chapter discusses the social purposes of museums in the UK and how these have emerged since the nineteenth century. In particular, the impact of these values upon approaches to marketing museums in the late twentieth century is evaluated and relationship marketing techniques offered as a prospect for reconciling welfare and commercial objectives.

HISTORICAL ORIGINS AND DEVELOPMENT OF MUSEUMS

Museums in Britain were first developed for the collection of artefacts and only later for visitation by the educated classes and interpretation by curators. The masses were not permitted access to museums and, often, entry was restricted to those who had shoes. Thus, in the early 1800s, museums excluded most of the working class population. The purpose of a museum was to collect and preserve objects, entrusted in the care of the curators. The interest was not in the lay public or the management of visitors but, rather, in the artefacts themselves.

By the 1840s Britain was in the early stages of capitalism and was witnessing its first economic depression (Clarke and Critcher, 1985). With a reduction in bank holidays to just four days a year and increased work time, Britain had become urbanized and industrialized, leaving little time for leisure opportunities. Workers previously employed in agriculture often found it difficult to adopt the work discipline which came with industrialization. Objectives of industrialists and government alike were social containment (Clarke and Critcher, 1985). Now that control was established in the workplace, measures were sought to control the limited time people had free for leisure (Bailey, 1978). The Museums Act of 1845 and the Great Exhibition of 1851 were part of this process. A new middle class was emerging, the desire for more leisure was created, and the opportunity arose for government to control peoples' leisure lives (Hooper-Greenhill, 1990; McLean, 1995). The investment of monies from local authorities for the provision of leisure through museums and libraries was a major change in local government's role and political aims.

Leisure was being used for political means and local authorities were moving from a stance of being prohibitive, through legislative, to acting as enablers. Museums then, were part of an attempt to control people's leisure lives by offering 'respectable' forms of recreation for the masses. Some governmental interventions were rationalized on the basis that consumers were not the best judges of their own, or societal, welfare and that some recreational forms are merit goods (e.g. Storch, 1977; Horne, 1984) due to their educative possibilities. The Victorian ideology that education was delivered in a rigid and disciplined manner was tied up with the ethos of the Protestant work ethic and today some museums still find it difficult to rid themselves of this image.

The Role and Social Purpose of Local Authority Museums

Since the Museums Act of 1845, development has gone largely unquestioned in terms of role, performance and position in society. Why, then, is it that in the 1990s, with the introduction of unitary authorities, local governments feel justified in asking museums to change with the times and account for their *raison d'être*? If this means that museums should change in line with technological advances and adopt multi media approaches to enhance visitor experiences then this may be reasonable and manageable. However, as evidenced in one major authority in Scotland, the emphasis has turned to increasing visitor numbers, introducing performance indicators, increasing efficiency (by reducing the number of museum assistants and opening hours) and effectiveness, and generating further income through ancillary services such as catering and retail trade. These moves are in conflict with the traditional 'professional' approach of museums and emphasizes a change in their role and culture in the nineties. These changes need to be met with appropriate responses which can reconcile 'professional' and 'managerial' ideologies.

Given that in 1991 there were 800 local authority museums in the UK, it is evident and generally accepted that they have a significant role to play in society. Specifically what that role is has been the subject of debate for some time and remains debatable in this chapter. There is no mandatory requirement in the UK for local authorities to provide a museum or a museum service. However in Scotland, under Section 14 of the Local Government and Planning (Scotland) Act (1982), a statutory duty was imposed to ensure that 'there is adequate provision for the inhabitants of their recreational, sporting, cultural and social activities' (HMSO, 1982). Although there was no specific mention of museums and galleries, local authorities had the freedom to interpret this act to suit their service delivery requirements and the needs of their communities. Furthermore, in 1991 the report by the working party on local authorities and museums (Museums and Galleries Commission, 1991) stressed that local authorities should adopt the role of a trustee, and any decisions taken about museums in their care are done so under this auspice.

If museums are to adopt managerialist policies then museum staff should understand what is being managed. The Museums and Galleries Commission (MGC) have advised that museums draw up a mission statement for their museum as a starting point (Museums and Galleries Commission, 1991), leading to a discussion of the role and social purpose of museums. It is widely accepted that museums have an educational role to play. However, the argument lies with their social, political and economic role in the societies they serve. Many museums have adopted political and social policies that bring additional funding and benefits. These include policies to encourage target groups within their community to visit museums and obtaining temporary exhibitions to suit the needs of these communities. This can offer positive achievements to politicians in accordance with their electoral manifestos but does it give museums a social purpose? One view of the purpose of local museums is that they should present a past that is of current importance to its surrounding communities. This being the case, the issues surrounding social purpose develop from whether museums should be object-led or people-led to whether museums should respond to social and political issues. Davies (1994) argues that 'museums must have a social purpose and that to be simply the guardians of, and researchers into, material culture will not command respect in the 21st century'.

He suggests that whether museums are object-orientated or people-orientated will become much less of an issue as political and economic pressure become greater. A possible response to this is that museum professionals should perhaps attempt to take the benefits of both object and people orientation to establish a social purpose for their museum, and exploit the benefits of interest from politicians and members of governing bodies. Others have fuelled this debate, for instance Kavanagh (1989), Lewis (1989) and O'Neil (1991).

O'Neil argues that:

> Museums have the potential to be the brokers or mediators of cultural change for other groups in society . . . but authenticity has to include the social relations as well as the artefact, the viewer's culture as well as the culture of the object, and neither should be obscured by museum culture, which must be as invisible but as omnipresent and effective as a simultaneous translator (O'Neil, 1991).

Lewis (1989) also argues that the fundamentals of museums do not change and asks if there is a conflict of purpose between provider and customer. This, alone, is a significant change in the thinking about museums in the use of the terms provider and customer. The underlying values inherent in terms such as 'customer' place a new emphasis on the status of the visitor or user, and imply a change in approaches to managing museums. Kavanagh (1989), on the other hand, argues that 'the objects (or their absence) can be physical indicators of ideological forces and social positions'. This shifts the debate from one about objects and who sees them to what the objects represent in terms of a social purpose aimed at particular groups.

Clearly it seems that there is general agreement on the benefits of museums to society and that they have a social purpose, albeit one that may differ from museum to museum. It may then be useful if in their mission statements museums highlighted what they believed their social purpose to encompass, and expressed their objectives in terms of objects and representation. In the late twentieth century objects can be viewed from a plurality of viewpoints and are open to different interpretations. Traditionally, interpretation of exhibits was offered through one medium and from the curator's point of view. Museums have changed, taking into account different visitor expectations and catering for interpretation and participation by different methods.

RELATING TO CHANGE ELSEWHERE

The belief that public sector leisure organizations can operate according to commercial sector values has increased recently with the introduction of compulsory competitive tendering (CCT) in sport and recreation management (HMSO, 1988). Under this approach, operations run within agreed performance criteria, involving measurement and penalties for defaults. In 1994, the Minister for Heritage, Stephen Dorrell, ruled out CCT for museums and galleries but emphasized the need for museums to become more financially viable and accountable. Thus it appears museums may have avoided CCT but have not escaped unscathed, and the pressure from central government to move towards self sufficiency is growing. Although opportunities have become available through lottery funding and sponsorship deals, it is unlikely in the short to medium term that these represent either adequate or appropriate replacements for the public purse. There is growing fear, however, that lottery funding will replace some of the capital funding previously given by the central and local authorities, and that sponsorship deals are only viable for attractive ventures, not for general care and maintenance of the building (Middleton, 1990).

If it is accepted that museums are operating on the basis of the merit good argument, then recent government initiatives within public sector services can be seen in two ways, both of which involve a greater emphasis on the application of market forces. The first simply removed businesses from the public to the private sector through privatization initiatives, such as in communication, transport, etc. This approach has not been applied frequently in areas of merit provision where, instead, market forces and values have been replicated within existing approaches. This is witnessed in areas such as the health services, with the introduction of hospital trusts and fund-holding general practitioners. Similarly, in local authorities some services have become subject to CCT, thereby separating policy thrust and ownership of facilities from the actual delivery of services. These initiatives are associated with a search for efficiency and effectiveness, although it is questionable whether both are achievable simultaneously by this route (Litteljohn, *et al.*, 1995). For example, the Museum

Registration Scheme (MRS) introduced in 1992 has a dual purpose: first, it has sought to set minimum requirements for museums; and second, to allow museums to demonstrate that they are worthy of support (Museums and Galleries Commission, 1991). The Museums and Galleries Commission, in its working party report of 1991, indicated that the registration scheme should aim to set optimum standard levels, with the hope that 'these will become a basic standard reference point for museums, for example when developing performance measures' (Museums and Galleries Commission, 1991). The MRS has the backing of central and local government and those who become members of the scheme are then eligible for grants and subsidized services from the appropriate QUANGO – MGC, Area Museums Councils (AMCs) and, in Scotland, the Scottish Museums Council (SMC). This places emphasis on measuring standards by quantitative methods, and upon the preparation of documents such as marketing plans and forward plans. Vanessa Trevelyan, Head of Public Services and Registration at the MGC, argues that 'although forward plans are not mandatory for registration, museums are strongly advised to have one to establish a clear view of where they are heading and how they will get there' (Trevelyan, quoted in Shipley, 1995). Although the registration scheme is voluntary, it places pressure on museums to comply with the requirements set if they are to be awarded the financial benefits traditionally assessed by other means. It would appear then that the QUANGOs, which are government funded, have a potential role conflict; on the one hand to act as a pressure group for museums representing their interests to central government, and, on the other, to reinforce government directives by stipulating criteria for funding and enforcing the new managerialist approach in museum thinking.

CCT has not been introduced in the delivery of the museum service but some services have been put out for bidding and award, mainly in the areas of catering services. It is not inconceivable that cleaning and servitoral services could follow. Traditionally, these have been part of a museum assistant's job in many local authority museums. This could leave the accepted professional province of the curator isolated among contracted out services and introduce pressure to adopt a more recognizably managerial model of action.

Julian Spalding, Director of Glasgow Museums, asserted that 'he would like to achieve one scale, going right through to the curatorial, technical and conservation staff to give more movement' (quoted in MGC, 1991). In an interview with a key member of staff at Glasgow Museums in 1996, it was suggested that Glasgow are about to enter a restructuring stage under the new unitary authorities. With their budget being cut by 14 per cent, new approaches to marketing and income generation were being sought. In Glasgow at present discussions are underway to change the museum assistant's job away from cleaning, catering for visitors and acting as a shop attendant in the retail outlet, towards dealing with visitors only. The aim is to allow museum assistants to focus more on visitors with specialist staff being employed in the retail outlet and cleaning being done by contractors. This may involve redundancies and a cut in hours for museum assistants. On the other hand it may help to move the focus towards visitor management and improve the experience of the visitor. The employment of specialist staff in the retail outlet may lead to better sourcing and merchandising as well as improved and informed assistance, thus enhancing the overall experience of the visitor and the average spend-per-head.

In Scotland all local authority museums have free admission and this appears unlikely to change in the short term. Both Councils in Glasgow and Edinburgh have considered the possibility of a 'tourist charge' but this has been ruled out. Thus, it is essential that ancillary services on offer are exploited fully in order to gain maximum spend from visitors and, at the same time, allow those visitors who want it a fuller experience, by supplying a memento of their visit (*see* Lennon and McPherson, 1995). Similarly, good catering facilities can demonstrate sensitivity to user needs and earn useful revenue for continued development. The contemporary museum experience is not just that of viewing objects but is now a combination of three leisure experiences; objects, catering and shopping. The overall experience will influence how the visitor judges the visit irrespective of the quality of any exhibition (Middleton, 1990). What is needed in response to this challenge is a more integrative approach to management, involving both the curator and professional marketing expertise in the planning of the museum's future. Ancillary services such as retailing and catering should be treated as core to the museum's activities alongside objects and their representation (see Newbury, 1988). Some have gone so far as to suggest that high street retailing now resembles museums due to some aspects of store design and, conversely, that museums are becoming more like shops (Urry, 1993). New approaches to the management of museums are emerging and it is evident that those in charge of museums have a powerful rationale to adopt a more managerialist model and recognize that marketing can be used as a tool to the overall benefit of both the museum and its visitors without posing a threat to curatorial integrity.

Museums with free admission are now being expected to adopt marketing strategies to promote themselves, but it is believed that these strategies need to be specific for museums, not those of the generalist commercial sector (McLean, 1995). Bradford argues that: 'there is a need for inductively derived empirically based studies from which to develop a more appropriate museum marketing theory' (Bradford, 1991).

MARKETING STRATEGIES FOR MUSEUMS

Marketing museums has not emerged as a product of the 1990s. Newbury (1988) highlighted that:

> in 1988 the Minister for the Arts announced that he was providing £270,000 within the MGC's grant-in-aid over three years to be used to encourage better management and marketing in non-national museums and art galleries.

This was the result of pressure over some time from the MGC to improve marketing in museums and, although it is still an important issue, many managers are unsure of what is expected of them in terms of marketing.

The belief by some (e.g. Hoyt, 1986, quoted in Bradford, 1991) that marketing strategies can be transferred from the commercial sector to the public and, further, to organizations that have free admission, appears to be ill-founded in the case of museums. For the reasons given in earlier sections, local authority museums cannot have the freedom to manipulate every variable in the marketing mix in the same way as a commercial organization. Museums are fundamentally different from organizations which exist wholly in the market place and cannot be tested or researched in the same way. They operate under different political and economic climates and any marketing approaches adopted need to take this into account (Bradford, 1991). Certainly, the range of stakeholders is much greater than in the private sector. Local authority museums stakeholders must also include citizens (whose taxes support the endeavour) as well as all other possible dependents (Coalter, 1990). Thus the museum has to be marketed to all of these interested parties: i.e., trustees, governing bodies, sponsors, funding agencies, employees, users and citizens. Rodger argues that even where a museum does not charge for access, there is a surrogate for price in that 'the visitor at museums with free admission is paying through their taxes in the form of public subsidy' (Rodger, 1987, quoted in Bradford, 1991). Whichever of these variants is adopted, it is clear that museums compete with each other for people's time and money and that this element of competition enables marketing concepts to play a part in securing advantage. However it is important to consider what museums are offering and with whom they are competing. Given that most museums are offering an experience of a particular social culture, heritage or elements of historical culture, this alone makes them unique. Some marketing gurus of the nineties would have us believe that it is sufficient to compete on price and value for money, exclusivity and quality of service. However, some museums have free admission and exclusive products but decreasing visitor numbers. How can this be?

Museums are competing for time and money not only with other museums and heritage centres, but also against other possible leisure activities, some of which may be completely unrelated. Museums compete with leisure centres, home-based leisure entertainment, cinema, eating out, etc. (see Austwick, 1993). Essentially, local authority museums are competing for people's leisure time and must convince potential users to come to them rather than, for example, watch a video at home. This dramatically changes the role of museums' professionals and some museums now have their own dedicated marketing officer: most recent figures available suggest that, in 1991, there were only 40 full time marketing officers in museums in Britain, (Museums and Galleries Commission, 1992) and, therefore, that marketing (where recognized) has become part of the job requirement for individuals with other preoccupations. Marketing services, especially those that are free of charge, requires strategic thought as Hooper-Greenhill indicates:

> Museums occupy a particular niche in the leisure industry that is open on the one side to leisure, fun and entertainment, but which is firmly joined to the educational world on the other. This link is strong and it is precisely this link to education that constitutes the appeal to leisure audiences . . . Fun is only possible in an atmosphere where we feel welcome, comfortable, at home and appropriate. A range of frameworks should support and sustain us in order to allow us the freedom to explore, to experiment, to talk and to make sense of our own reactions to the museum (Hooper-Greenhill, 1994).

Museums' professionals are being expected to create this environment. Curators and managers have to attempt this by offering various approaches to the interpretation of objects. It is then up to marketers, in conjunction with curators and managers (in some cases this may be one and the same person), to establish what services should be offered and marketed to whom. It is now the responsibility of museums to allow people the opportunity to participate in this process of interpretation and purpose (Museums and Galleries Commission, 1991), thereby shifting focus towards users. Visitors and their management are becoming more important, as despite visitors to government-funded museums rising by seven per cent, visitor numbers in local authority funded museums in Britain fell by five per cent in 1994 (Mason, 1994).

With the introduction of unitary authorities, museums must not only continue to attract visitors but also to convince stakeholders that it is worthwhile to continue funding against other leisure services and (more importantly) against strategic services such as transport, education and roads etc. For example, parents in Glasgow protested during April 1996 that primary schools were being closed while a new gallery of modern art was being opened. If museums are to continue to develop and maintain an active role in society, then it appears that managerialist policies and marketing approaches have to be adopted into the next century.

The remainder of this chapter will review critically one strategy (relationship marketing) that may be appropriate for local authority museums, especially those with free admission. The initial stage is to analyse the current market of the museum (i.e., who are the visitors at present?), then identify the relationship that exists at present between the museum and the visitor, then secure improvements. This is the essence of the strategy that will be discussed.

Relationship Marketing

Relationship Marketing has been described as a way of understanding marketing itself and Ambler suggests: 'the perception of marketing as managing a network of relationships between the brand and its various customers is fundamental and should be ranked alongside the traditional and strategic paradigms' (Ambler, 1996). This moves thinking from attempting to model a series of individual and isolated transactions towards an understanding of an ongoing relationship over time between suppliers and buyers. Evidence of relaionship marketing may be seen in the development of brands, use of databases to contact and keep customers, and in an increasing concern with the lifetime value of a customer. There are some elements of this approach which have limitations and are difficult to transfer to museums, but its essence, understanding customers and developing relationships with them over a long period, is transferable.

In services marketing there are often reminders that it is cheaper to maintain a customer than to gain a new one (Ambler, 1996). Within this context, museums professionals can continue to use the terminology 'users', but users with spending power in some cases (i.e. market segments). On this basis it would be beneficial to maintain visitor loyalty to the museum by securing repeat visits among the most lucrative segments. This is presently in place with schemes such as 'friends' and 'patrons' of museum. However, once again it brings into question the purpose of the museum. Some museum and local authority agendas may be to allow access to the widest possible representation of the community and these may have to seek a wide audience. How can this be done and visitor loyalty of specific groups maintained at the same time? This has to be answered by individual museums in relation to their social purpose, but there is no operational reason why these approaches of marketing and social welfare need be mutually exclusive. Essentially, appropriate relationships are being developed differently with different groups and users are no longer treated as a homogeneous mass.

Developing relationships with visitors will differ from museum to museum. Determining what the segments are will have to be in terms of type of users: i.e. home-based visitors, school groups, foreign visitors (and which areas of foreign visitors). Identifying non-users should also carried out to allow for future marketing possibilities. Segmentation of current users into similar groups will allow better communication and planning possibilities. By using existing knowledge as a base (e.g. the listing of all 'friends' of the museum), it will be possible to develop relationships with users (and users with spending power) to maintain that relationship, not only at the museum itself but also after the visitor has left the premises. Information technology is transforming thinking, both in terms of multi-media approaches to the interpretation of objects and the ability to improve communication channels. A database of names, ages and addresses of the 'friends' and regular users is the start of the relationship. This is clearly a committed group of enthusiasts for the museum and their generosity in terms of time or money offered should not be taken for granted. Encouraging and rewarding their commitment by providing loyalty cards is one option. In order for this to be implemented the museum would have to have Electronic Point of Sale (EPOS) systems in place. This will store the buying habits of the visitor and give staff a profile of their users. It is possible to send marketing information through the mail that is individually relevant: e.g. if someone regularly visits the museum to view a particular type of art, marketers could mail shot the individual highlighting future events of exhibitions of this nature. Similar relationships can be built with intermediaries, such as tour companies or schools, who themselves market services to museum end users.

Events such as themed dining experiences can be developed within museums. These could be used to develop diversified experiences within the museum's own brand. This approach is highly successfully in American museums. The Museum of Fine Art in Montgomery, Alabama for example, offers a themed dining experience once a month. Management use it as a way of marketing the benefits of the museum and its continued role in the community it serves. The charge for being 'invited' to the evening is anything from $50–100 and is only offered to selected groups. This is viewed as a way of maintaining a positive relationship with users and showing appreciation to important clients of the museum. In British museums, which rarely open in the evening, this could be adapted to suit the purpose of the museum.

Loyalty cards and themed evening invitations are just two examples of how to develop better relationships with existing and committed visitors. The loyalty card could be developed further to encourage all home-based visitors to use the ancillary services more fully and more often. It is also possible to develop a lasting relationship with visitors after they have left the building by considering a wider range of services and products via mail order and Internet marketing opportunities.

REFERENCES

Ambler, T. (1996) Building Brand Relationships. In *The Financial Times Mastering Management.*

Austwick, D (1993) A Wider View. In T. Ambrose and S. Runyard (eds) *Forward Planning* London: Routledge.

Bailey, P. (1978) *Leisure and Class in Victorian England* London: Methuen.

Bradford H. (1991) A New Framework for Museum Marketing. In S. Pearce (ed.) *The Museums Profession Internal and External Relations* London: Leicester University Press.

Clarke, J. and Critcher, C. (1985) *The Devil Makes Work. Leisure in Capitalist Britain* London: Macmillan.

Coalter, F. (1990) The Politics of Professionalism: Consumer or Citizens? *Leisure Studies* 9.

Davies, S. (1994) Back to Basics II *Museums Journal* September.

Davies, S. (1995) *Museums Journal* November.

HMSO, (1982) *Local Government in Scotland (Planning) Act* HMSO.

HMSO, (1988) *Local Government Scotland Act* HMSO.

Hooper-Greenhill, E. (1990) Counting Visitors or Visitors who Count?. In R. Lumley (ed.) *The Museum Time Machine* London: Routledge.

Hooper-Greenhill, E. (1994) *Museums and their Visitors* London: Routledge.

Horne, J. (1984) 'Enforced Leisure' and Compulsory Games in the 1930s: An Exploration of the Social Control of Spare Time. In F. Coalter (ed.) *Leisure: Politics, Planning and People. Volume Three The Politics of Leisure* Brighton: The Leisure Studies Association.

Kavanagh, G. (1989) Objects as Evidence or Not?. In S. Pearce (ed.) *Museums Studies in Material Culture* London: Leicester University Press.

Lennon, J.J. and McPherson, G. (1995) Retailing in UK Museums and Galleries: Developing Revenue Generation Strategies, *Services Management: New Directions, New Perspectives* London: Cassell

Lewis, G. (1989) Preface. In S. Pearce (ed.) *Museum Studies in Material Culture* London: Leicester University Press.

Lewis, P. (1993) The Role of Marketing. In T. Ambrose and S. Runyard (eds) *Forward Planning* London: Routledge.

Litteljohn, D., Foley, M. and McPherson, G. (1995) Trends in the Public Service Sector – the Case of Museums and Art Galleries. Unpublished conference proceedings Bournemouth.

Mason, R. (1995) *Museums Journal* November.

Museums and Galleries Commission (1991) *Local Authorities and Museums Report by a Working Party 1991*.

Museums and Galleries Commission (1992) *Museums Matter* HMSO.

Middleton, V. (1990) Irresistible Demand Forces, *Museums Journal* February.

McLean, F. (1995) A Marketing Revolution in Museums? *Journal of Marketing Management*.

Newbury, C. (1988) Government Funding and Advice, *Museums Journal* 88(3).

O'Neil, M. (1991) After the Artefact: Internal and External Relations in Museums. In G. Kavanagh (ed.) *The Museums Profession* London: Leicester University Press.

Rodger, L. (1987) *Marketing the Visual Arts* Edinburgh: The Scottish Arts Council.

Storch, R.D. (1977) The Problem of Working Class Leisure. Some Roots of Middle Class Reform in the Industrial North: 1825–1850. In A.P. Donadjgrodzki (ed.) *Social Control in the Nineteenth Century* Redwood Burn.

Trevelyan, V. (1995). In P. Shipley (ed.) MGC News *Museums Journal* November.

Urry, J. (1993) *The Tourist Gaze* Sage.

9

Motivational Strategies in Eastern Europe: The Special Case of Service Workers

Michael Riley

Discussed in this chapter are the psychological adjustments of Eastern European service workers in providing service in general, and in providing service to Westerners in particular. The purpose is to address the problems of these service workers in order to illustrate the general case of motivation and the consequences of personal contacts with the West.

Every service worker has to be able to cope with the conundrum of being between 'service and servility' and as such, develops psychological strategies accordingly. In this sense service workers in Eastern Europe are no different to their counterparts anywhere in the world. What is different however is that, at this point in history, they, like all other workers and citizens of the former Eastern bloc, are having to adjust their response to 'obedience and freedom' as the context changes from communist authority to capitalist market determinism. For service workers the adjustment is compounded by their personal contact with Western behaviour and values.

Eastern European service workers are a special case of two orthodoxies. First, they are special to the conventional wisdom of the psychology of service roles because they have had no time to develop intervening strategies that, at the very least, enable them to grant politeness and willingness to strangers who inadvertently cause feelings of inequity simply by being foreign and wealthier. Exposure has simply happened too quickly. Second, they are special to the general problem of adjustment to capitalism for the very same reason that they are exposed at first hand to Western materialism and capitalist values. There is a sense of immediacy in their relationship to the 'new ways'. To put it simply, they can see how free people behave. It is one thing to desire consumer goods glimpsed on satellite television, but quite another to have to deal with embodiments of that consumer culture. Western advisors in sharp suits unintentionally send a message to their hosts. When conspicuous wealth meets deprivation it can hardly avoid paternalism.

The thrust of this argument goes one stage further and presents a strange irony. Solving the problem of service helps to solve the problem of adjusting to capitalism. Exactly because the psychological pressure on service workers is so great and exactly because they have not had the time to develop sophisticated intervening mechanisms, they resort to pure defensive measures such as indifference to work. The way out of these defensive positions is instrumentalism and its concomitant demand for incentives. In other words, the argument is that the only motivation that will work for a worker who has retreated into a legalistic definition of effort is incentive. Once incentive becomes part of a worker's life it reinforces the capitalist values and in this way helps to make the central change from communism to capitalism. The fact that service workers actually encounter Westerners would suggest that they would be in the forefront of demands for incentives.

CULTURE AND BEHAVIOUR

The theoretical argument is based on the principle that culture is reinforced by behaviour. Continuity of behaviour over time maintains the culture. A schism in a behavioural pattern causes the cultural meaning of that behaviour to be questioned (Glenn, 1991). While accepting that capitalism and communism have separated the worker from the output of his or her labour, the communist system has gone further in separating the worker from the consequences of effort. Capitalism has maintained this coupling through incentives. The prediction of Rakos (1991) that the adjustment to capitalism values would be fairly rapid has not been borne out. However, his argument is based on the assumed power of incentives to re-couple work behaviour with its consequences. The fact that such incentives have not been introduced may account for the slow acceptance of capitalist values. It cannot be as simple as this. Indeed, Mokrzychi (1993) points out that the 'learned helplessness' created by communist authority cannot be waived away simply by incentives. The nurturing of democratic responsibility in the citizen is seen as a long-term solution that will eventually have an impact on work behaviour (Tomes, 1992). Whatever the theoretical debate says, one fact above all militates against the acceptance of incentives by workers and that is unemployment (Kovari, H. *et al.*, 1992). The dilemma is clear; on the one hand incentives are the key to unlocking productivity, but they are unacceptable with so much unemployment around (Tausky, 1991). That the two are related is one lesson that the population has learnt quickly.

INVIDIOUS COMPARISONS

Looked at simply, comparisons between Eastern Europe and Western Europe produce a picture of relative deprivation based on wealth differentials

(Runciman, 1966). Although comparisons of nations always carry extra emotion and baggage, the effect of such relative comparisons will be ameliorated by the strength of national culture, but inequity will be there nonetheless. The consumption behaviour of the West is now conspicuous to Eastern Europe and has awoken desires for material improvement. Wealth differentials become personalized where rich and poor meet. The venue for such close proximity is usually tourism where the effects of invidious comparisons have to be coped with psychologically by service workers.

Coping with Invidious Comparisons

For service workers, coping means finding psychological ways of doing their job in a way that satisfies their employers and customers, while simultaneously protecting their ego from the assaults of servility; the universal dilemma of the server. The conventional wisdom of service work is fairly convincing in its two principal tenets. First, that constant exposure to interpersonal communication with new people can lead to anxiety which is avoided by a range of coping strategies. In the capitalist context these strategies produce behaviour that 'looks' positive and fulfils its psychological defence function. Such strategies take time to evolve within the individual as they gain strength through practice. Second, that the coping strategies operate within a set of values. For example, caring for those in pain requires a coping strategy which maintains the ethos of care while protecting the individual carer from continuous anxiety. For such personal strategies to be legitimate they have to be reinforced by the culture of the organization. Such culture has to be described as either supportive or defensive. That is it either encourages the appropriate responses to situations or engenders a defensive closed posture (Larsen and Folgeno, 1993).

Such reinforcement is operationalized by confining expectations of the server solely to the role of server. When service takes place within a commercial framework, the role of the server takes on expectations. The modern trend towards the demand for motivation to go beyond willingness to commitment only exaggerates the expectations of the role (Lincoln and Kallenberg, 1990).

One coping strategy is emotional labour (Hochschild, 1983). Emotional labour is a display of expected emotions by service workers in service encounters. It is performed through surface acting, deep acting or genuine feeling. While this acts as an operational device for getting through the customers, it can lead to self-alienation because of its separation of work emotions from real personal ones. It gets the server through the day but may not protect them from the fragmented feelings of alienation.

The appropriate behaviour is learnt over time through gaining an understanding of the social norms of the role. The power of this acting to cause alienation is moderated through its connection to social identity (Ashforth and Humphrey, 1993). The greater the commitment to work, the greater is the threat of adverse consequences of acting. Full identification with the job is a risk. However, when other forms of identity are stronger, the commitment to a job is decreased. It is possible to speculate that the resurgence of national identity might act as a brake on organizational commitment.

The response to relative deprivation which produces cognitive dissonance is not always negative. The theory of cognitive dissonance does not predict how the dissonance will be removed; only that it will (Festinger, 1957). There is evidence in the literature of clerical work and domestic service to testify that one form of coping strategy is social emulation (Lockwood, 1958; Riley, 1984). This strategy involves the server in internalizing the values and lifestyle of those he or she serves. It is the very opposite of envy. Here dissonance is coped with in a positive way. However, the adoption of such a strategy has to carry with it either an exclusive culture shared by the server and by the served or there must be some realistic chance that the server could one day actually emulate the role model by becoming wealthy. This strategy appears to be out of court as far as Eastern European servers are concerned unless they have ambitions to work in the West.

A VIEW FROM INTERPERSONAL COMMUNICATION

A clearer picture of the limited psychological options open to the server is illustrated by a view from interpersonal communication. There are two important models here. First, the *equilibrium model* which suggests that in interpersonal communication there is an 'ought' in the air. For example a pupil ought to be respectful to a tutor, a waiter ought to be polite to a customer. In other words, both parties agree on the character of the exchange and try to make it work in the prescribed way. By so doing they are either striving for symmetry or avoiding dissonance (Pearce and Stamm, 1973). When it goes wrong the recipe for avoidance of dissonance becomes a retreat into the 'rights' implicit in the 'ought'. For service employees this means retreating into a minimalist interpretation of their job (Riley, 1986). What is important here is that what 'ought' to happen is a culturally derived social norm based on values in society. Why should the customer always be right if everyone is equal?

Second, the *co-orientation model* suggests that the way communication ensues in an interpersonal exchange depends on both parties having a perspective on and expectations of the subject which forms the purpose of their communication. Here the concern is with the mutuality of their orientation towards the subject. How congruent and accurate are both their expectations? It is at this point that culture intervenes. Like the equilibrium model, orientations are built up by experience and are consensually agreed within a culture. Cross-cultural exchange provides the possibility that the server and the served will not have the same orientation towards, for example, 'hospitality' and 'good service'. In a similar vein, the advisor and the client may not share the same orientation to 'market segment' or 'cash flow'. The outcome of this model in such ircumstances is a breakdown in information flow. Not knowing what the Western tourist means or feeling ignorant in the relationship leads to the withholding of information. The study by Markoczy (1993) of a joint management between Western and Hungarian managers is a good illustration of the withdrawal of information and the refusal to take decisions which would be predicted by a co-orientational model.

FOLLOWING A HISTORICAL TREND

f the arguments here are correct, then it follows that the Eastern European server has few psychological options, and in these circumstances it would not be at all surprising to find them retreating into indifference or instrumentalism. There is, however, a rope bridge from instrumentalism to entrepreneurship.

If incentive is the key to transferring values towards market determinism, hen history suggests that service workers may be at the forefront of the conversion. The one mechanism used to cope with 'servility' has been to convert an nstrumental attitude into an entrepreneurial one. The mobility from service to small business ownership is a universal phenomenon. The psychology starts from the negative position of minimal involvement in work and instrumental values. This then turns into a positive instrumental attitude which endeavours to get something out of tourist encounters e.g. big tips. The final stage is to become an entrepreneur. It must be said that along the way the process can be diverted into illegal activity (Mars, 1982).

The expansion of tourism may provide the impetus for change (Stetic, 1991, Lockwood, 1993). If the arguments here are valid, it could be said that the way to learn capitalism is to fleece the tourists! The brakes on that possibility are competition, the responsibility of ownership, and the generally high level of education.

THE GENERAL PROBLEM OF MOTIVATION

The central problem of devising strategies for the management of people is that any strategy will have, in addition to its specific aims, the burden of helping the transition towards the new social values. The idealized solution of incentives produces inequality through the creation of differentials. The problem here is not just that people have recognized that incentives lead to unemployment but that organization policies are translated into consequences for society. It is the intrusion of concern for the broader picture into daily contingencies that is the legacy of communism. Furthermore, if incentives are the only policy, the organizational relationships become merely calculative which then reinforces the instrumentalism of the workers (Etzioni, 1975).

However, the best hopes lies in refocusing the constituency of feeling away from society on to the enterprise. In other words, what has to be de-coupled is the notion of incentives from social values. This suggests that shared ownership and the discounting of consumer goods would be effective motivators because they are not connected to unemployment. More than mere hope lies in the reformation of industrial relations structures. Examples of 'green field industrial relations, literally starting from scratch, are rare but have a good track record of changing attitudes without conflict (Brookshire and Rodgers, 1977). As new structures emerge from the new economic order they will contain opportunities and constraints that may make managers and workers re-focus their attention on life inside the unit of production (Brewster, 1992).

REFERENCES

Brewster, C. (1992) Starting Again: Industrial Relations in Czechoslovakia, *International Journal of Human Resource Management* 13(3), pp 555–574.

Brookshire, M. and Rodgers, M. (1977) *Collective Bargaining in Public Employment* Toronto: Lexington Books.

Etzioni, A. (1975) *A Comparative Analysis of Complex Organizations* New York: Free Press.

Festinger, L. (1957) *A Theory of Cognitive Dissonance* Stanford, CA: Stanford University Press.

Glenn, S. (1991) Contingencies and Metacontingencies: Relations Among Behavioural, Cultural and Biological Evolution. In P. Lamal (ed.) *Behavioural Analysis of Societies and Cultural Practices* London: Hemisphere.

Kovari, H.A. and Nagy, G. (1992) Hungary Faces Unemployment, *International Labour Review* 130(2), pp 165–176.

Hochschild, A.R. (1983) *The Managed Heart Commercialization of Human Feeling* Berkeley: University of California.

Larsen, S. and Folgeno, I. (1993) Supportive and Defensive Communication, *International Journal of Contemporary Hospitality Management* 15(3), pp 22–25.

Lincoln, J.R. and Kallenberg, A. (1990) *Culture, Control and Commitment* Cambridge: Cambridge University Press.

Lockwood, A. (1993) Eastern Europe and the Former Soviet States. In P. Jones and A. Pizam *The International Hospitality Industry; Organizational and Operational Issues* London: Pitman.

Lockwood, D. (1958) *The Blackcoated Worker* London: Allen and Unwin.

Markoczy, L. (1993) Managerial and Organizational Learning in Hungary – Western Mixed Management Organizations, *International Journal of Human Resource Management* 14(2), pp 277–304.

Mars, G. (1982) *Cheats at Work, The Anthropology of Workplace Crime* London: Counterpoint Unwin.

Mokrzycki, E. (1993) The Social Limits of East European Economic Reforms, *Journal of Socio-economics* 22(1), pp 23–30.

Rakos, R.E. (1991) Behavioural Analysis of Socialism in Eastern Europe. A Framework for Understanding the Revolutions. In 1989 in E. Lamal (ed.) *Behavioural Analysis of Societies and Cultural Practices* New York and London: Hemisphere.

Runciman, W.G. (1966) *Relative Deprivation and Social Justice* London: Routledge & Kegan Paul.

Riley, M. (1984) Hotels and Group Identity, *International Journal of Tourism Management* 15(2), pp 102–109.

Riley, M. (1986) Customer Service Training – A Social-psychological Framework, *Tourism Management* 7(2), pp 103–112.

Stetic, S. (1991) Tourism in Eastern Europe: A New Challenge. In C. Cooper (ed.) *Progress in Tourism Recreation and Hospitality Management* 3(10), pp 154–164.

Tausky, C. (1991) Perestroika in the USSR and China; Motivational Lessons, *Work and Occupations* 18(1), pp 94–108.

Tomes, I. (1992) Social Reform: A Cornerstone in Czechoslovakia's New Economic Structure, *International Labour Review* 130(2), pp 191–198.

SECTION FOUR
ETHICS

10

Dark Tourism – An Ethical Dilemma

Malcolm Foley and J. John Lennon

In this chapter the authors explore tourism associated with tragedy, death and disaster, which they have termed 'dark tourism'. Through case studies of sites associated with President John F. Kennedy and the Jewish Holocaust they explore the centrality of simulation, reproduction, repetition and duplication in the presentation of dark tourism. The dilemmas facing those responsible for such sites and artefacts is explored within the contexts of authenticity, commodification and post-modernism.

INTRODUCTION

In writings on tourism there has been an unwillingness to focus on macabre or 'negative' aspects of human interest which often motivate site visitation and which the authors have titled 'dark' tourism. Such 'dark' elements of popular culture are frequently the focus for attractions whether real or created. Writers such as Berman (1983) recognize the potentially lucrative opportunities such developments and their associated connections could offer, and both Urry (1990) and Rojek (1993) identify this as a post-modern phenomenon.

Rojek (1993) describes some sites as 'fatal attractions' and, more particularly, 'death spots', which he identifies as:

> commercial developments of grave sites and sites in which celebrities or large numbers of people have met with sudden and violent deaths.

Such 'dark' attractions are of great significance in our culture and offer sensation and spectacle for the visitor or tourist. Locations cited by Rojek include national and metropolitan cemeteries, Cholame (the site of James Dean's fatal car crash) and Graceland. The method by which some of these locations are developed as tourist attractions (to offer the visitor an experience that is different to that of everyday life) is systematized and socially organized. In this way the tourist gaze is both constructed and developed (Urry, 1990).

This type of cultural tourism which the authors have entitled 'dark' or 'tragic' tourism is an intrinsic part of the post-modern world. The concept embodies the simulation of experiences, the critical importance of reproduction/duplication and the presence of various forms of media at such locations. Media, particularly visual media such as television and film, are central to contemporary attraction treatments. In many cases, media have shaped our views of reality and informed understanding of the dark nature of such sites. Yet within the attractions, through interpretation, media occupies a central position in re-interpretation, display and the oft-quoted educational 'mission' of many such developments.

Thus the contemporary context for dark tourism is that of post-modernism. Examples of simulation and use of repetitive forms were registered by Rojek (1993). The procession of James Dean fans in authentic late 1940s and early 1950s vehicles and dressed in period costume which takes place on the exact time, date and precise location of his death is symptomatic of this phenomenon. This process of projecting oneself into a simulation of reality is furthered elsewhere through audio-visual media blurring distinction of the imagined and the real in a number of other locations. However, gravity and reverence are not always characteristic of such attractions and activities. Jim Morrison's grave in Pere Lachaise questions the Victorian bourgeois cultural view of the cemetery as a place of dignity and respect (cf. Rojek, 1993). Now tourists rather than mourners visit and undertake cemetery tours. In Arlington National Cemetery, Washington DC there is a good example of the changing designation of a 'death' site to convey tourism or leisure significance, where cemetery tours by minibus have been organized to convoy tourists from one celebrated grave to another. In Los Angeles, this is taken a stage further in the 'Graveline' tour, by Cadillac hearse, of sites associated with the deaths and tragedies of the rich and famous.

Dark Tourism – Nature, Definition and Scope

The starting point for the authors in conducting research into aspects of heritage and atrocity was that some common threads could be drawn between sites and events of the last century which had either been the locations of death and disaster, or where such events are interpreted 'off-site' for visitors (e.g. the US Holocaust Memorial Museum in Washington DC). In constructing a vocabulary for these sites and locations, it became clear that the use of the term 'tourist attraction' represented both a judgement about the motives and rationales for making the site available to the public and a commentary upon the experiences of visitors. It was seen as unacceptable that we should proceed from either of those prejudices without any substantive foundation and concluded that a label was needed for this phenomenon which could both describe it and allow fieldwork to be conducted without fear of misunderstanding. That is not to say that some of the sites are not 'attractions' in the tourism sense, simply that we found it easier to open wider debates without the semantics of that label. We chose to establish an overall term, 'dark tourism', encompassing the visitation to any site associated with death, disaster and tragedy in the twentieth century for remembrance, education or entertainment.

The interpretation and representation of deaths, disasters and atrocities associated broadly with the history of the last hundred years appears to be growing throughout the world. The US Holocaust Memorial Museum, Washington DC, is a popular place to visit in a city which contains some of the world's most visited museums. In Dallas, Texas, the Sixth Floor Museum, alleged location of Lee Harvey Oswald's vantage point on 22 November 1963, when John F. Kennedy was assassinated, attracts more visitors annually than any other site in the city (Dallas County Historical Foundation, 1989).

In Memphis, Tennessee, the reconstructed Lorraine Motel interprets years of segregation and oppression in the American south and offers the opportunity to stand on the spot where Martin Luther King was assassinated. The sites of First World War battles in Belgium and northern France interpret the horrors of trench warfare and a number of tour operators offer packages to visit these sites and to the many Commonwealth War Graves Commission cemeteries in the area (*see*, for example, Holts Tours, 1995).

Recent reflections upon the fiftieth anniversary of the end of the Second World War have highlighted the interpretation of heritage at, among others, the beaches of Normandy, former concentration camps located throughout Europe, the islands of Jersey and Guernsey, museums at Hiroshima and Nagasaki and the USS Arizona at Pearl Harbour, Hawaii. London's various Imperial War Museum sites chart the effects and impacts of war upon the UK and its citizens during the twentieth century. The recent successful opening to visitors of Hellfire Corner under the cliffs of Dover demonstrates that there is a continued demand to see 'interesting' and unusual sites. Elsewhere in the UK, near St Andrews in Scotland, the Secret Bunker from which the government of northern Britain would have been conducted during a nuclear war is now open to visitors who can explore the corridors and experience the simulation of a direct nuclear strike upon a local strategic target. Krakow, Poland is a major centre for tourism on a global scale not least because of its proximity to Oswicziem, location of the Auschwitz and Birkenau concentration camps.

In Moscow, it is possible to be given a tour of the Lubyanka, headquarters and prison of the former KGB. North of Ho Che Minh City, the Cu Chi tunnels of the former Vietcong have been widened and heightened to accommodate the growing number of visitors who want to see for themselves these subterranean bases. Chicago boasts a popular Gangster Tour which covers sites of the St Valentine's Day Massacre, Al Capone's headquarters and the cinema where John Dillinger was shot. In Berlin, the site of the former Checkpoint Charlie is being redeveloped into a business complex, but nearby a museum run by a charitable trust interprets the history of the Berlin Wall, its victims and those of other infractions of human rights throughout the world in the twentieth century. Meanwhile, in South Africa, debates rage over the proposed development of Robben Island, site of Nelson Mandela's first prison, as a centre for the interpretation of the apartheid system and its years of dominance over national politics (Schadeberg, 1994).

Understanding Tourist Motivation

The authors have been concerned to establish why some, and not other, events led to certain locations being interpreted, and what is involved in the process of moving from death and disaster to 'attraction'. It was of interest to ask why some 'notorious' sites of the twentieth century are offered as heritage attractions, such as those mentioned above, and others are not. For example, the Watergate building in Washington DC, Hitler's Bunker in Berlin, the Altamont Racetrack in California and the tunnels of the Securitate in Bucharest remain undeveloped as attractions.

It was also of interest to understand how central the primacy of 'the real' was in terms of sites. A site of genocide such as Auschwitz is clearly of international importance but ageing and visitation has created problems of wear and tear. Such issues of decay present curators with problems of authenticity. Furthermore, an alternative to authenticity conceived in this way is the recreation of some events and their implications elsewhere, such as at the US Holocaust Memorial Museum in Washington DC or the Museum of Tolerance in Los Angeles. It is interesting to examine why these seemed to be at least as successful in terms of visitation as the original sites which represent their very reason for existence.

Issues of 'taste' and 'decency' emerge in any attempt to understand behaviours, operation and management of such sites, and the relative age of the properties, fixtures etc., seems to figure as a factor in development. Sites commemorating events within living memory generally require a more sympathetic and measured approach to interpretation and commercial development. Those sites with a greater 'chronological distance' from the tourist generally are interpreted in a less sensitive manner (see, for example, Culloden Moor in Scotland and the sites of the English Civil War in England). These issues were explored within the presentation of artefacts raised from the RMS Titanic at the National Maritime Museum at Greenwich (Deuchar, 1996).

Furthermore, it would appear more than a coincidence that many of the deaths and disasters which gave rise to heritage interpretation had received considerable coverage via global media, especially, but not only, in television, film and popular novels and songs. It appeared likely that where an event received attention via international news and film media, then some form of 'dark tourism' development would be conceivable, even if it was neither desired nor promoted (see, for example, *The Herald*, 1996). Even more powerful, it seemed, was the presentation for cinema audiences of events in the recent past which had been contemporary sensations and news 'events'. A particular example of this which exemplifies the phenomena was the assassination of John F. Kennedy (JFK) and the Oliver Stone film *JFK*. Media is a central focus in interpretation of JFK and this theme is further explored below.

The Centrality of Media – The Case of JFK

The Kennedy phenomena can be seen as both a media product and a result of the, then recent, availability of global news communication at the time of the assassination. Central to the interpretation of JFK are pictorial images. This is clearly evident at two important sites in the US, namely:

- The New Museum at the John F. Kennedy Library, Boston, Massachusetts
- The Sixth Floor Museum, John F. Kennedy and the Memory of a Nation, Dallas, Texas

The focus of interpretation at both of these sites is pictorial with repetitions of such key images as: the assassinations of JFK and Lee Harvey Oswald, Jacqueline Kennedy in mourning at the funeral, John (Jnr) Kennedy's salute at the funeral, the riderless horse, the Walter Cronkite (CBS) news flash intimating the shooting and the eternal flame at Arlington. Such images have become international markers of collective memory. As Knapp (1989) notes, they trigger shared social dispositions relating personal life to the date and time of the assassination (or rather the point at which the media reported the assassination). The multiplicity of roles for media in the Kennedy story in contextualizing, telling, promoting and recollecting are central mechanisms. Known as the 'television president' he was believed to have had one of the earliest grasps of the political importance of that medium. From the initial 'great debate' with Nixon, through the regular live televised news conferences to his ultimatum on US television demanding that Russian missiles were removed from Cuba, he showed an early mastery of TV (Zelizer, 1992). Consequently many exhibits utilize footage from the critical events of Kennedy's lifetime. Television and film are also clearly linked with the assassination and are central to its retelling and interpretation. As White(1982) noted:

> Television was at the centre of the shock. With its indelible images, information, immediacy, repetition and close-ups, it served to define the tragedy for the public.

In the US, TV had rapidly grown as a critically important media for news and by the early 1960s some 88 per cent of all homes owned TV sets. Key events where media (and most particularly, television) had an important role included: the fateful weekend of the assassination, from the point of the shooting to the scenes outside of the hospital; Johnson's 'swearing-in'; the murder of Lee Harvey Oswald, and the Kennedy funeral. Central and notable in the media coverage was the death itself, which offered a spectacle of televisual images defining the 'reality' of that weekend for many viewers. These images which constituted 'touches of pure television' (*Broadcasting Magazine*, 1963, p 50) and have been utilized heavily in both of the sites examined in Dallas and Boston.

The interpretation and re-telling of events surrounding Kennedy's death have shaped perceptions of reality. In projecting visitors into the past, reality has been replaced with omnipresent simulation and commodification. Thus the real is confined in pure repetition (Baudrillard, 1983).

The 'dark' fascination with the assassination and the short period of this presidency has been an enduring one. Within 36 months of JFK's assassination more than two hundred books were published pertaining to the tragedy. This has been joined by a further one thousand books, periodical articles, television retrospectives, more than twelve newsletters, and a number of booksellers now specializing in assassination literature (Zelizer, 1992). Indeed novels and film treatment such as the *Parallax View, Executive Action* and *JFK* have all contrived to feed the growing interest in the events of the Kennedy death as have a number of sites on the World Wide Web devoted to the assassination.

Any interpretation of JFK and consideration of his presidency will inevitably be affected by these repeated images. Television and film have shaped the memory of those events rather than historical data alone. As Connally (1988) noted:

> I don't think the time has come when history will really look at the Kennedy administration with a realistic eye. And how could we? When you see a beautiful little girl kneeling with her hand on her father's coffin, when you see a handsome little boy standing with a military salute by his slain father, how can you feel anything but the utmost sympathy? It's a scene of pathos, of remorse, of tragedy, and that's the way we now view President Kennedy.

Cultural authority is herein defined through the narrative pictorial images clouding historical reality. This process of what Weber called 'rhetorical legitimation' illustrates how the purveyors of this 'history/story' legitimate themselves by the stories they tell in discourse with the public. The authentic newsreels, assembled by curators and museum professionals, along with text, provide and confer meaning. The television/film image is replayed as the historical 'reality' (cf Urry, 1990) yet the professionalism of the curator/museum professional is located in the context of a paid attraction in both the cases of the JFK Museum, Boston, Massachusetts and the Sixth Floor, Dallas, Texas. Financial imperatives for museums and the need for economic efficiency drive the provision of elements such as retailing and catering (Walsh, 1992). The justification for both museums is frequently cited as popularity and educational mission. Yet popularity does not ensure acceptability and cannot be equated with quality. Similarly, the educative mission of both attractions veers very closely towards spectacle. Furthermore, the heavy dependence upon newsreel for interpretive purposes in both attractions reveals a fundamental difficulty of delineating education and entertainment/spectacle and an uncritical approach to history. The criteria of educational quality, critical insight and academic credibility were mainly cited by project directors, managers and curators as central to their 'missions' when interviewed by the authors for this research. Yet what is happening is that the past is being manipulated and relabelled to convey a tourism/leisure orientation.

The holocaust sites across Europe represent a contrasting approach to interpretation and the use of media. They are considered in the following section.

Interpretation of the Unimaginable:
The Case of Holocaust Sites

Sites of mass killing, particularly those associated with the Jewish holocaust, present major challenges for interpretation and invariably questions arise concerning the nature of motivation for visitors. The enormity of the systematic destruction of the Jewish people is beyond comprehension and constitutes an enormous task in the sense of 'interpretation' and 'explanation' (sic). The inadequacy of language, images or art to deal with the holocaust has already been the subject of critical debate (see, for example, Wiesel, 1968; Langer, 1975; Wyschogrod, 1975). The scope of the subject area is difficult to comprehend, yet visitation to concentration camps endures and they continue to receive visits from a huge range of ages and nationalities. Herein the nature of interpretation and documentation presents a potential danger for dealing with the holocaust in artistic/moralistic terms; even documentary/historical approaches have inherent problems in dealing with this subject. As Steiner notes:

> Not only is the relevant material vast and intractable; it exercises a subtle, corrupting fascination. Bending too fixedly over hideousness, one feels queerly drawn. In some strange way the horror flatters attention . . . I am not sure whether anyone, however scrupulous, who spends time and imaginable resources on these dark places can, or, indeed, ought to leave them personally intact (Steiner, 1971, pp 30–31).

There are major problems for the language utilized in interpretation to adequately convey the horrors of the camps. Consequently, and because of the presence of historical records, visual representation is extensively used. Documentary evidence in the form of photographs is employed in sites of mass killing such as the Auschwitz/Birkenau complex at Oswicziem in Poland. Historical photographs and documentation of this nature have been central in transmitting the events of World War II. The visual heritage of the Nazi era is rich: the symbols of the SS, the swastika, the watch towers, barbed wire, the skeletal victims and the gates of Auschwitz. In taking this striking image of the gates and the rail head within Auschwitz II, a useful illustrative example of the use of photographs helps to demonstrate this centrality and the sensitivity necessary in their use. The visitor looks at the documentary photograph showing guards and prisoners at the rail head (the past) to the present empty rails and in this way the camera has had the impact of what Barthes titles 'resurrection' (Barthes, 1981). The photographic image has the ability to transmit the reality of the death camps with an immediacy and shock effect that words can rarely achieve. In this way the visitor can associate 'photographic time' with real time. However, as others have noted, the recurrent use of pictures of the victims and deportation trains can have the effect of an obsessive concentration/fascination with the real that can blur into unreality (see, for example, Lanzmann, 1995). Indeed, there is an inherent danger in constant re-creation of the past, particularly if there is any attempt at stylization which can cheapen or trivialize the enormity of the issues being confronted.

A problem of interpretation and preservation of holocaust sites is dealing with what Steiner titled 'the time relation'. Here he is referring to the contemporary nature of Auschwitz in human culture/history and how incomprehensible that is. It appears as 'the other planet' to the one in which we live our everyday lives:

> Precisely at the same hour in which Mehring or Langer (victims of the camps) were being done to death, the overwhelming plurality of human beings, two miles away on Polish farms, five thousand miles away in New York were sleeping or eating or going to a film or making love or worrying about the dentist. This is where my imagination balks. The two orders of simultaneous experience are so different, so irreconcilable to any common norm of human values, their co-existence is so hideous a paradox – Treblinka is both because some men have built it and almost all other men let it be . . . (Steiner, 1967 pp 156–7).

This unreality, and the problem of temporal and spatial affinity, has been dealt with in a range of ways in the cinema. The controversy surrounding the development of Steven Spielberg's production of *Schindler's List* is illustrative of the problems faced with such use of visual images. In this case, the film-maker had to recreate Auschwitz in the form of a film set on the outskirts of Krakow since he was not allowed to film within the camp. The film set itself became an attraction (quite literally 'The Schindler Tour') for some two years until it was dismantled. It offered the visitor a conveniently located replica of the real camp. A truly post-modern replication for the enormity of the real Auschwitz/Birkenau's sprawling complex. However, the debate surrounding the film itself goes to the heart of this grim fascination with horror and atrocity and the dilemmas of sensitive interpretation. Spielberg not only recreated a film set, but his approach to *Schindler's List* was to recreate actual events e.g. the deportation from the Krakow ghetto.

This approach is not uncommon in works of film of the period (1950–85), this genre of reproducing 'actions' is dominant (for critical examinations see Avisar, 1988 and Insdorf, 1989). The Schindler story of a German who saved 1,300 Jews can never communicate the enormity of the attempted wholesale extermination of the Jewish race. Rather, it operates within the confines of classic Hollywood narrative technique that is central in popular cinema. 'Story' is necessary for effect and market appeal, as indeed is chronological development and a clear 'plot'. The difficulty is that recounting the Holocaust in narrative form will limit and distort representation and visions of that reality (Lanzmann, 1995). Reconstruction and replication are flawed in this context. The approach of Claude Lanzmann in the film *Shoah* is markedly different. It explores the legacy of the final solution by drawing the viewer into the debates of the original experience (Avisar, 1988). The work focuses on the death camps of Chelmno, Belzec, Maidanek, Sobibor, Treblinka and Auschwitz to reveal and document the genocide programme. It is not, however, a historical documentary. Rather, Lanzmann conveys the full amazement of holding in sight an item (a tower, gate, rails) that came from 'the other planet' with the use of extensive interviews with victims, bystanders, perpetrators and survivors. In using contemporary 'real time' and interviews while linking this with long screen takes of camp sites, trains, rails etc., the connection between 'screen time' and 'real time' is established. In this way, rather than providing didactic, historical narrative or Hollywood stylized stories, the viewer is taken into the reality of the 'other planet' through this process of traumatic cultural shock. It ensures that the 'visitor' is able to appreciate the dreadful aspects of the past ('the other planet') by dealing with its symptoms in the present. Lanzmann denies the viewer the dubious privilege of being a witness; the viewer has rather to deal with more uncomfortable questions such as 'what does it mean to have witnessed it?' (Romney, 1995).

The problem of interpretation in concentration camps for visitors is not dissimilar. Orthodox museum displays condone the feeling that one can stand back from the past and be 'educated' about it. Presentations such as the US Holocaust Memorial Museum, Washington DC, promote the idea of the past as 'another country' (cf Walsh, 1992). In this view, the past is a place which is separate from the present, and which one travels to and visits via re-creation of authentic elements. In contrast, the concentration camps themselves represent reality, and here the task of the interpreter is vitally important in terms of allowing the public to differentiate between truth and falsity, replication and reality.

Yet all interpretation is ideological and this is clearly evident in much of the interpretation of concentration camps in the former Communist states in Central/Eastern Europe. In many of these countries, the Second World War was used as an ideological vehicle to expose the evil consequences of fascism and Western capitalist exploitation and to commemorate and celebrate Russia as the force of liberation. This type of political interpretation is still evidenced in concentration camps in the Czech Republic, the former East Germany and in Poland. Thus the authority of interpretation becomes diluted and the displays as representations of the past lose the authority of their command over time and space. The problems of interpretation are akin to the problems faced by the film-maker in this area. They are related to the difficulties of representation (creating a truthful account of the reality of Nazi rule), and presentation (paying tribute to and understanding the predicament of the victims and the context of genocide). The dilemma becomes avoidance of the potential for ideological distortions or deceptions.

The extreme alternative is non-interpretation and non-development of such sites. Literally to adopt the call for silence made by Wiesel (1960) who claimed that 'Auschwitz negates any form of literature, as it defines all systems, all doctrines' (op. cit. p 7). Indeed, Steiner went further in arguing that it is best 'not to add the trivia of literary, sociological debate to the unspeakable' (Steiner, 1967, p 163). However, silence, of course, brings with it the problem of displacement and may encourage future generations to ignore or forget the incidence of the terrible period of human history.

CONCLUSION

The analysis of such dark tourism sites in terms of their selection, interpretation, use of media and the understanding of motivation for visitation is important to developing an understanding of human behaviour and understanding events in the 'other past'. Sociological and literary analysis are necessary for the appreciation of these areas and personal and cultural self-examination are valuable (cf, Avisar, 1988). Yet invariably, one is dealing with a subject so enormous that it threatens to overwhelm the resources of media and language (Rosenfeld, 1980). Dealing with inhumanity, whether it is an act of assassination or genocide, can induce a sense of fatuity and even indecency. However, only through utilization of critical analysis and review of questions and interpretation and concomitant issues of taste and decency, can one contribute to understanding. Only in this way can one move towards avoidance of compromising distortions or inadequate representations.

REFERENCES

Avisar, I. (1988) *Screening the Holocaust* Bloomington and Indianapolis: Indiana University Press.

Barthes, R. (1981) *Camera Lucide: Reflections on Photography.* Trans. R. Howard, New York: Hill and Wang.

Baudrillard, J. (1983) *Simulations* New York: Semiotext.

Berman, M. (1983) *All That is Solid Melts into Air* London: Verso.

Broadcasting Magazine (1963) Comments on Coverage: Well Done 2 December p 50.

Connally, J. (1988) quoted in '25th Anniversary of JFK's Assassination' *Night Line* ABC News quoted in B. Zelizer (1992).

Dallas County Historical Foundation (1989) *The Sixth Floor. John F Kennedy and the Memory of a Nation* Dallas, Texas.

Deuchar, S. (1996) Sense and Sensitivity: Appraising the Titanic, *International Journal of Heritage Studies*, 2(4), Intellect, pp 212–221,

Herald, The (1996) Tourists in Dunblane Asked for Tact 07/08/96.

Holts Tours (1995) *Battlefields and History, January 1996 to March 1997* Sandwich: Green Field Leisure.

Insdorf, A. (1989) *Indelible Shadows Film and the Holocaust* 2nd ed., Cambridge: Cambridge University Press.

Knapp, S. (1989) Collective Memory and the Actual Past, *Representations*, Spring.

Langer, L. (1975) *The Holocaust and the Literary Imagination* Newhaven: Yale University Press.

Lanzmann, C. (1995) quoted in I Avisar (1988) *Screening the Holocaust* Bloomington and Indianapolis: Indiana University Press.

Lanzmann, C. (1995) Why Spielberg has Distorted the Truth. In *The Guardian Weekly* 3 March p 18.

Rojek, C. (1993) *Ways of Seeing Modern Transformations in Leisure and Travel* London: Macmillan.

Romney, J. (1995) Screen Seen: Vital Video – The Holocaust. In *The Guardian Weekly* 13 January, p T016.

Rosenfeld, A. (1980) *A Double Dying: Reflections on Holocaust Literature* Bloomington: Indiana University Press.

Schadeberg, J. (1994) *Voices from Robben Island* Randberg: Raven Press.

Steiner, G. (1967) *Language and Silence: Essays in Language, Literature and the Inhuman* New York: Athenaeum.

Steiner, G. (1971) *In Bluebeard's Castle: Some Notes Towards the Redefinition of Culture* New Haven: Yale University Press.

Urry, J. (1990) *The Tourist Gaze* London: Sage.

Walsh, S. (1992) *The Representation of the Past* London: Routledge.

White, T (1982) *America in Search of Itself* London: Warner.

Wiesel, E. (1960) *Night*. Trans S. Rodway, New York: Avon.

Wiesel, E. (1968) *Legends of our Fire*. Trans S. Donadio, New York: Holt, Reinhart and Winston.

Wyschogrod, M. (1975) Some Theological Reflections on the Holocaust, *Response* 25, Spring.

Zelizer, B. (1992) *Covering the Body – the Kennedy Assassination, the Media and the Shaping of Collective Memory* Chicago: University of Chicago Press.

11

Ethical Dilemmas in Strategic Management

Gillian Broome

This chapter considers the reasons underlying the growing interest in, and importance attached to, ethics in business generally and the hospitality, tourism, leisure industry in particular. Ideas are developed with reference to a survey of hotels in the La Rochelle region, south-west France.

THE GROWING DEMAND FOR THE STUDY OF ETHICS

Why do we need a chapter on ethics in a book on management issues in the area of hospitality, tourism and leisure? If this question had been asked in the 1970s or 1980s, responses would almost certainly have referred ethics to the areas of religion, morality and more recently to politics. The question of 'fair-dealing' in business would have been seen to have had its own set of rules which would have been different from those of a service industry, whether medical, educational, or indeed leisure. So, what is it about ethics that makes it so relevant in the 1990s?

Hardly a week goes by without there being a reference in the British news to the subject. France and Italy are in the process of an ethical investigation politically and in the United States the papers are full of unethical business ventures which have created a specialist legal field in terms of litigation. Yet until recently ethics *per se* was not taught on management courses and indeed it is still frequently seen as a less than essential subject. The change is largely due to the media which has found a never ending source of newsworthy stories in this area.

This is not to say that unethical practices did not occur previously, but with the buzz words of 'accountability' and 'open management' as well as stress on sound basic, moral values, the public are looking more critically at practices previously accepted, albeit grudgingly. A catering manager of a large restaurant complex was told when appointed, 'We don't expect you to buy any food for yourself – we just don't want to see truckloads being driven away'. Hotel managers turned a blind eye to the barman who introduced his own bottle of whisky to sell by the measure for his own profit, so long as the margin of profit reached the level desired.

Are examples such as these examples of ethical/unethical practices? Partly, however, ethics is a much bigger issue.

Ethics could be defined as any area in which questions of safety, fair-dealing and responsibilities, both towards people and the environment, need to be considered. 'Trust, dignity, fairness and honour are ethical virtues. Openness and ethics go together' (Nash, 1990).

The question is often asked that if one is behaving according to the law, isn't one behaving ethically? The answer has to be 'No, not entirely'.

The law is defined as dealing with right and wrong, socially acceptable and unacceptable behaviour. But as our way of living becomes more and more complex, so the rules need to change. In fact ethics *leads* the law. Situations drawing forth ethical questioning are areas which may well become codified later into law. Take for example, the question of computerized information of personal data. The law needed to change to deal with the ethical questions concerning people's right to privacy – hence the Data Protection Act. In the same way laws concerning racial equality and equal opportunities generally, have developed differently in countries such as Britain and the United States where the number of races living in one society is very high compared with, for example, France. The importance of ethics is considerable when seen in this way because it is ethical questioning which will generate tomorrow's laws.

The unethical behaviour of individuals is quick to gain media attention – politicians and church leaders are the first to be toppled from their pedestal. People in public positions cannot afford to have questionable values or even to have behaved in a manner that might be considered unethical before they took up public office. In such situations in Britain, resignation would be expected. However, ethics is more than individual opinions, or sets of values.

For centuries organizational morality (that of business and services) has been based on the idea that people rely on their conscience to direct their actions. But this relies on two factors: first that everybody is willing to listen to their conscience and act accordingly, and, second, that everybody's conscience will respond according to the same principles, which cannot always be guaranteed. There was also an inherent code of: if in doubt, consult your superior. However, a superior in business experience and acumen is not necessarily superior in the reading of a conscience! The whole situation was somewhat haphazard and ambiguous.

As organizations became bigger and developed internationally, the questions loomed larger. 'Mission Statements', 'Guidelines' and 'Codes of Ethics' became increasingly needed. Nonetheless, every aspect of every situation cannot possibly be laid down. Education in ethical principles, therefore, is vital in initial training courses as well as in each organization itself.

So what should be considered ethical issues? The following list applies in general:

- **Safety**: including from supplier to client, management to employee, as well as application of standards from the West to Third World plants or members of the hotel chain;
- **Responsibility to Employees**: including accountability from employee to shareholder, dismissals, redundancies and discriminations, the right to privacy;
- **Responsibility to Clients**: the whole question of quality service;
- **Environmental Responsibility**: pollution, conservation and resource depletion, as well as our responsibility to the future;
- **Global Responsibility**: in terms of varying standards as well as respect for cultural values.

In addition, there is the whole question of personal versus corporate morality.

All these are applicable to the hospitality, tourism and leisure industry, but in particular the areas of safety, standards and responsibility to employees and clients are apposite. Public image can frequently become an area of ethical concern.

It was the Bhopal disaster of 1984, and later Chernobyl, where thousands of people died and where health was, and still is, seriously affected, that brought ethics into the spotlight. The question at the forefront of people's minds was one of responsibility and apportioning blame. Bhopal became a landmark legal case to establish liability for hazardous industries located in developing countries. Union Carbide's public image of a caring company helping to solve India's food shortage plummeted.

It is easy to see why the question of ethics is equated with apportioning blame. Blame implies responsibility, which in turn implies a clear definition of hierarchical roles. However, in terms of management structures, the pyramidal, traditional system typical of the previous century is changing to systems more in line with 'the web' or 'the net' structure, focusing more on corporate decision-making or semi-autonomous smaller units within the whole (Handy, 1985). Thus the line of responsibility is less clearly defined. However, 'blame' and 'responsibility' are only two aspects of ethics:

> Ethics is the study of a particular group of normative judgements that are concerned with what is morally right or wrong, morally good or bad...when internalized, they help establish mutually beneficial systems of conduct and can provide publicly acceptable justification for actions and policies (Velasquez, 1988).

Ethics is concerned primarily with being prescriptive, with influencing behaviour, rather than analysing and justifying after the event. Much of the ethics discussed in the media is of the latter kind. This distorts the true value of ethics.

Survey of Ethical Issues in Six Hotels in La Rochelle

In a small survey of six hotels in La Rochelle, interviews were conducted, in each case with either the manager of deputy manager, in order to identify the current ethical issues. Examples and case studies in the text arise primarily from this study. All names have been changed.

In all hotels training was given, but was informal, not specific. Only one hotel had nothing to contribute, which the manager attributed to two factors one, that it was a small, family concern and two, that he exercised discrimination, accepting only couples and families.

The question of discrimination generally in this area of France has a considerably less high profile than in Britain and therefore did not appear as an issue. In all cases, where a question of personal safety arose – such as one client throwing plates at the room service he had requested, or the alcoholic night manager scaring clients and staff – steps were taken to remove the offender whether the client or staff.

A rapid turnover of staff is usually a sign of dissatisfaction with the working conditions. In none of the hotels was this a problem. In an interview with one assistant manager the professionalism and fair-dealing of the manageress was seen as the direct cause of stability: staff appointed as the opening of the hotel in 1988 were still there and seasonal staff returned regularly. This was a hotel where the personal influence and example of the manageress had permeated all levels and affected the attitudes and behaviour of staff. This and the encouragement of open discussion were sufficient to ensure a corporate response to issues, despite there being no written policy.

It was interesting that almost all interviews started with a statement to the effect that, in terms of ethics, there wasn't really very much to say, and yet in answer to questions they were able to talk of specific instances for an average of an hour and ten minutes. Only one hotel was reluctant to participate.

Analysing Problems – Theory and Practice

In terms of the hospitality, tourism and leisure industry, what makes it particularly susceptible is that it is 'on show' permanently. The very nature of its business means that it is tested by the public continuously. Being a service industry, it needs to court and satisfy its public in order to ensure continuing profits. One of the problems of ethics is that there is no formula that can divide the morally responsible from the morally questionable. We can take the traditional methods of analysing a situation, simplistically those of the deontological or duty based approach and the teleological or right goal approach. With the former, considerations are focused on one's duty towards a certain group of people. However, in a complex service industry there are many groups of people, perhaps with differing duties. Consider the following cases:

A German couple from Hamburg booked a package holiday through their local travel agent. When they had settled into their hotel, they strolled down to the restaurant for dinner. They were ushered to their table which they found they were sharing with another couple. However, they were distressed to find out that both were disabled and suffered manipulation difficulties when eating. They asked to change their table for future meals, but were dismayed to be told that there were no other tables and that they would be sharing with this couple for the rest of their holiday. On return to their home town they took the company to court on the grounds of having caused distress and having ruined their holiday. (In process at the time of writing.)

Compare this case with a similar case in La Rochelle:

A couple with a disabled daughter of ten booked into a hotel. The girl had manipulation difficulties, had unclear speech and was noisy. With the agreement of the parents, the hotel staff created a table away from the rest, in a corner where the girl would be less disturbing to the other guests. However, as Pierre put it, 'We did all we could to compensate, whenever possible helping to cut up her food or shell the langoustines, in order that the parents should be able to enjoy their meal in peace.'

Let us consider the first case in more detail. In this, the hotel management, with a credo of offering a welcome to all, regardless of creed, race or disability, had a duty to the disabled couple to welcome, integrate and treat them equally with the other guests (duty number one). They also had a duty to the other couple to ensure that their stay was a pleasant one and that they were getting value for their money in terms of the holiday they wanted (duty number two). They also had a duty to their shareholders to uphold the ideals of their hotel, maintain good relationships and avoid getting into a situation that could lead to unwelcome publicity or worse (duty number three). You could also say that the management had an implicit duty to their staff to set an example in terms of ethical behaviour (duty number four). As managers they also had a duty to follow the guidelines, whether written or 'understood', laid down by the company (duty number five). A deontological approach therefore throws up conflicting considerations rather than providing a single clear cut solution.

The teleological, right goal approach, equated with the utilitarian 'for the good of the majority' approach, is equally ambiguous. If considering people's rights, it becomes the inverse of the duty approach. When considering the 'majority good', it is clearer that in this case it would be the majority of clients as opposed to the disabled couple. However, it offers no solution of how to deal with their needs and their situation. Thus this approach is equally ambiguous.

This leaves us with a 'basic test' approach, analogous to listening to one's conscience. This is frequently advised as the question 'Would I want my family to see or hear about this on TV or radio?' If the answer is a negative, a hesitation or a qualification, then the proposed action is ethically questionable.

Nash (1990) proposes a list of six questions 'to heighten moral sensitivity':

- Is it right?
- Is it fair?
- Am I hurting anyone?
- Could I disclose this to the public or a respected monitor?
- Would I tell my child to do this?
- Does it pass 'the stink test'?

To these could be added:

- Is there an element of risk taking?
- Am I prepared to take responsibility?

Unfortunately people's thinking frequently boils down to:

- For once it won't do any harm;
- It will be adequate for now . . .
- I was told it was OK/accepted practice/safe, etc . . .

In January 1995, thirteen hotels on the Algarve were cited as having unsafe swimming pools, pools which formed a prominent feature in their advertising brochures. Where did the ethical responsibility lie? With the manager for accepting a sub-standard piece of work or for not checking regularly for safety? With the manager of the pool company for passing shoddy workmanship, or not being sufficiently knowledgeable about safety regulations? With the installation foreman . . . the list could continue. Or was it simply a question of differing safety standards?

In an ideal situation the responsibility is shared, the pride in the quality of work provided is a realistic and perceived aim. But that requires an education, a relationship which is genuine first class team-work, where the ideals of the company are internalized and 'owned' by all the employees – the sort of situation promoted by Peters (Peters and Waterman, 1982; Peters, 1987) in his books *In Search of Excellence* and *Thriving on Chaos*. It is worth noting that, in law, ignorance is not necessarily a mitigating circumstance.

The problem of differing safety standards in different countries was highlighted in an article in the Weekend Telegraph (11/3/95), 'How Safe is your Hotel?' Quoting deaths of holiday makers from faulty gas water heaters and incidents of blocked or inadequate fire escapes, it called for a European Union directive on hotel safety. The ethical questions are 'Is the law sufficient?' and 'Should tour companies use hotels or accommodation where the safety levels are lower than is acceptable in the home country?' (The lower safety regulations in India was one of the causes of the Bhopal disaster.)

Returning to the ideal work situation, ethical behaviour is clearly led from the top and is a question of good leadership. So what are the characteristics of a recognizably ethical manager?

- Someone who acts out, in everyday situations, the principles which he has stated are his, in particular terms of respect for other people.
- Someone who is able to inspire others to emulate this behaviour.
- Someone who is able to articulate and explain ethical issues.
- Someone who is able to stand by ideals in times of stress.

In turn, employees need to feel encouraged to be sensitive to ethical issues and be given a responsibility for these. Velasquez (1988) cites the following as providing job satisfaction (paraphrased):

- Being set a clear example.
- Being given clear guidance.
- Feeling that the job is meaningful.
- Being encouraged to take responsibility.

When these situations are combined, an ethical situation is encouraged.

When examining the hospitality, tourism and leisure industry in the field of ethics, we need to consider its vulnerability. It suffers from two pressures: first, as stated above, being continuously in the public eye, and secondly, being subject frequently to an extreme pace which in turn creates stress.

One hotel manager interviewed about this aspect said:

> This is very much a holiday hotel. At one time, when I was younger, during the season I got an average of four hours sleep a night, making up on my day off. Clients come here to relax and have a good holiday, and it's our job to ensure they do. If this meant staying up with them till the early hours of the morning, I did. Unfortunately we also had clients who were the early risers and who appreciated the warm welcome at breakfast. There was no way I could survive the season without the extra stimulus of alcohol to keep me going. Of course, this was when our hotel was small and the personal touch was all-important.

Truly client satisfaction! However, it raises the issues of seasonal pressures. Under such stress, can a manager be relied upon to give a 100 per cent sound judgement in problematical situations that might arise? If one couples these pressures felt by hotel staff with the short term, ego-centric needs of each client desiring a good holiday, you have a situation which is potentially volatile!

It is pressures such as these that put the ideal relationship between client and staff truly to the test, the relationship of seeing the interaction as being founded on respect and consideration of the clients' needs. It can be a delicate balance too of staff answering these needs, but at the same time not allowing clients, in pursuit of their own happiness, to violate the rights of others.

Invasion of privacy is one such right. It is usually considered in a work context – of employer with employee, colleague with colleague – but in the hotel situation there is the in-house closed community situation as well as the peculiarity that individuals may be deliberately choosing a public place to give them anonymity.

In any organization there are two problematical situations regarding ethics. The first is the situation where, whatever rules or guidelines you apply, you cannot decide what is the right or wrong course of action. The second is the situation where you know what is the right thing to do, but, for various reasons, usually short-term and practical, you consider not doing it. The key here is the difference between the short and long term. Providing a customer service relies on client satisfaction. In turn, they provide word of mouth advertising – good or bad. A wrong course of action, taken for the best reasons, can, in the long term, have disastrous effects. The public enjoys pointing the moral finger at those who have erred!

In the first situation the difference between the right and wrong course of action is unclear and it is therefore a problematical one. In general it is necessary to view each proposed course from the point of view of *all* people involved, directly or indirectly, currently or in the long term. In this way all eventualities are considered and evaluated. In the final analysis, the decision has to be taken for the course of action that causes the least amount of harm to the least number of people (the converse of the utilitarian principle of working for the greatest good for the greatest number of people).

In the second situation, practical expediency over-rules the innate knowledge of what is the right course of action. Often it is influenced by pressures of time or personnel available, and it is usually a situation where the alternative course is not seen as causing any injury.

The problem with the hotel circumstance is that rarely is there the time or opportunity to analyse and reflect as many of the problems are up front, on-the-spot and often of a confrontational nature. It is, therefore, exceedingly important that all employees are given the security of a training of sufficient depth to give them the confidence to act knowing that their actions are commensurate with the values and policy of the organization. Such a response needs to become instinctive.

Frequently a company sets out its ethical policy with a view more to protecting itself and its actions than to following an ideal. Unless firmly anchored to reality and practice, the philosophy stated can be too unrelated to the daily life and routine of employees. 'Credos', 'Mission Statements', or 'Charters of Quality' – whatever the term – are only as good as the employees make them. Ownership, agreement and practice are what makes them a reality. This comes through discussion and working together.

The training, therefore, needs to be more of an experience than an intellectual exercise, and as such needs to be repeated at regular intervals. In this way, values are shared, teamwork is built and a whole way of responding and behaving is inculcated. A well run hotel aims for quality. Quality implies continuous improvement. Both rely on the personnel involved.

Summary

Why should managers bother? There are a variety of reasons based on negative motivation:

1) to avoid unpleasant/distasteful media coverage;
2) to avoid legal investigations (cost, time and energy consuming).

Both of these are detrimental to the reputation of the hotel:

3) to avoid upsetting people – clients, employees, shareholders.

Equally, there are a variety of reasons based on positive motivation:

1) to help promote quality service and therefore client satisfaction, which in turn promotes a good reputation;
2) to provide security and a framework for employees, which leads to job satisfaction, good performance and ultimately client satisfaction;
3) the implications in terms of society and organizations generally.

There are practical reasons against developing an ethical policy – or values:

1) it requires, consistently, a good example set from the top;
2) it is time-consuming to train staff;
3) it is not clear that it is necessary – hotels have been operating successfully without it;
4) it does not provide straightforward solutions.

However, in response:

- public relations are improved;
- the good example set from the top, coupled with the education/training experience, creates:

  a) consistency of behaviour, attitude and conduct, which eliminates some of the problems caused by lack of uniformity;
  b) teamwork, which offsets the time-consuming factor;
  c) for managers, a lack of conflict between what they believe to be right or moral and their work.

If, therefore, one is aiming for more than simple profit making, for excellence, quality and a caring service, the ideas set out in this chapter are essential reading and well worth considering. Ethics is frequently seen as synonymous with good management where respect is a vital element.

REFERENCES

Handy, C. (1985) *Understanding Organizations* Harmondsworth: Penguin.

Nash, L.L. (1990) *Good Intentions Aside. A Manager's Guide to Resolving Ethical Problems* Harvard Business School Press.

Peters, T. and Waterman, R. Jnr (1982) *In Search of Excellence: Lessons from America's Best Run Companies* New York: HarperCollins.

Peters, T. (1987) *Thriving on Chaos. Handbook for Managers' Revolution* London: Pan Books.

Velasquez, M.G. (1988) *Business Ethics* Englewood Cliffs: Prentice Hall.

FURTHER READING

Harley, R.F. (1993) *Business Ethics. Violations of the Public Trust* John Wiley and Sons Inc.

Green, R.M. (1993) *The Ethical Manager. A New Method for Business Ethics* London: Macmillan Publishing Company.

SECTION FIVE
SUSTAINABILITY

12

The Tourism and the Environment Debate: From Idealism to Cynicism

L. Rory MacLellan

The complex relationship between tourism and the environment is examined in this chapter. By focusing on the philosophy of sustainable tourism and associated guidelines and policies, the chapter illustrates some of the complexities and contradictions surrounding the tourism–environment debate. In conclusion, means to advance the debate are proffered.

INTRODUCTION

Tourism was once promoted as a clean, non-resource consumptive economic activity, free of the environmental impacts attributed to manufacturing, mining and intensive agriculture. Since the 1970s this benign view of tourism has been increasingly questioned. Between 1970 and 1990 world tourism grew by nearly 300 per cent (WTO, 1991). It is expected to grow by half again before the end of the century. This growth has reinforced the need to re-examine the relationship between tourism and the environment.

EVOLUTION OF THE RELATIONSHIP BETWEEN TOURISM AND THE ENVIRONMENT

Attitudes towards the relationship between tourism and the environment have gradually shifted from being viewed as coexistent, with minimal interference, through recognition of adverse impacts, to more recent acceptance of their mutual dependence. Where once tourism was seen as essentially a non-consumptive use of resources, it is now regarded as being highly dependent on sometimes fragile, finite natural and cultural resources.

The examination of this relationship goes back over forty years and ha
undergone several shifts in emphasis. Dowling (1992) identifies four phase
since the 1950s when tourism was viewed as a clean industry, with few impact
on the natural environment. This complacent phase, termed 'co-existence', wa
rudely awoken by the advent of 'mass' tourism in the 1960s which led to
period of soul searching research, evaluating a range of tourism impacts. Th
debate widened to include associated relationships between tourism and hos
communities. Thus the term 'environment' expanded to include social and cul
tural environments in addition to the physical (natural and built) environmen

In 1976 official recognition of the diverging views on the tourism-
environment debate came from the Director General of the IUCN (Internationa
Union for the Conservation of Nature), where, in the case of tourism asset
whose value was derived from nature and its resources (the majority of prima
ry attractions), the relationship was seen to be one of either conflict, coexistenc
or symbiosis (Budowski, 1976). The challenge, Budowski suggests, was for con
servation and tourism interests to change their attitudes and work toward
integration of policies, which would in turn lead to a symbiotic relationship
Almost twenty years on, academics and practitioners are still attempting to fin
means by which this basic goal can be achieved.

It is debatable whether much progress has been made towards this goal. A
great deal of literature and theory has been developed involving a wide range o
academic disciplines from social sciences and business studies to pure sciences
However, the debate has increased in complexity and – some would argue –
become confused by the lack of consensus over definitions of the basic terms
'tourism' and 'environment' which remain open to a variety of interpretations
This is reflected in much of the literature, where the analysis has widened and
deepened, but where there remains a high incidence of contradictory evidence
Where previously studies concentrated on direct tourism impacts on destinatior
environments, the analysis has expanded to include all aspects of the tourisn
system, in particular the contribution of increased use of transport services to
global environmental change. Rather than concentrating on the extremes such
as fragile, natural wilderness areas, or mass concentrations at coastal resorts
as tended to be the case in early studies, the less obvious but often equally
important impacts are now examined, for example inner city locations
industrial heritage and rural environments.

The tourism-environment debate has progressed to the extent that the field
of study now appears to have formed discrete subsections, concentrating or
specific disciplines, sectors, locations or issues. These still emerging specialisms
reflect the increased interest and awareness of issues relating to tourisn
development but do not in every case serve to enlighten the debate or offer
meaningful solutions. A comprehensive review of the breadth of these
environment–tourism specialisms is beyond the scope of this chapter, but some
of the more high profile and cohesive are outlined below:

1) Management of Built Heritage – promotion, conservation and interpretation.
2) Management of Natural Heritage – landscape designations (National Parks), access, commercialization, conflicting activities, capacity measures.
3) Rural, Agri, Farm Tourism – balancing economic, social, cultural objectives.
4) Socio-cultural, Anthropological Considerations – community-based decisions, acculturation, staged authenticity, morals, ethics.
5) Tourist Types – consumer behaviour, markets, codes of conduct, tourists (mass) vs travellers (independent), social class.
6) Holiday Products – traditional vs 'alternative' products and associated fashionable terminology (green, ecotourism, adventure, soft, progressive quality).
7) Environmental Regulations, Controls and Legislation – Global, EU, National-measurement, attributing liability, enforcement.
8) Industry Responses – trade associations, voluntary codes, corporate environmental policies, audits, environmental impact assessments, green public relations.
9) Government (Public Sector) Policy Statements – voluntary guidelines, codes of best practice, principles, green charters.
10) Academic Theories and Paradigms – eco-development, integrated, community based, symbiotic, synergistic, green/appropriate/alternative, sustainable.

Most of the above specializations have their own experts, fields of knowledge, academic foundations, specialist journals and research focus. The widening of the subject is, to a large extent, justifiable and necessary in the attempt to identify and encourage participation from all stakeholders in the debate.

The number of recognized stakeholders has increased dramatically in recent years. In addition to tourists, tourist entrepreneurs, local residents and policy makers, the list should include a range of public, private and voluntary organizations. Sommerville (1994) provides an airline industry (British Airways) perspective by identifying three groups of 'players and organizations'.

Many Players and Organizations		
Tourism	**Aviation**	**Environment**
WTO, ETB, ITT, TOSG, PATA, AITO, BTA, ABTA, WTTC, GFI, T. Soc, ASTA	FAA, IATA, ATUC, CAA, IPCC, ACC, ECAC, ICAO, AEA	OECD, CC, D. Env, BTCV, WWF, RSNC, IUCN, UNESCO, NCC, CPRE, RSPB, FNNPE, FOE, UN, WCU

Table 12.1:Tourism and the environment organizational interaction (see acronym list at end of chapter). Source: Adapted from Sommerville (1994).

Somerville maintains that to approach an understanding of interactions of tourism with the environment, it is first necessary to appreciate the complexity of the interactions of the groups involved.

The issue of stakeholders also raises the question of responsibility, classically addressed in Hardin's original essay on 'The Tragedy of the Commons' (1968). Here the tragedy which befell the commons was the inevitability of destruction because of the lack of assigned responsibility, brought on by the fact that each individual user stood to benefit in the short term, by deliberately exceeding the limits of the resource. Some would argue that most tourist resources are 'common' goods, in particular the natural environment or local culture, for which no agency or individual has specific responsibility. In this way all recognize that the environment is being degraded but none are willing to take the first step to save it. To some extent this has been addressed in many developed countries through the creation of heritage and conservation agencies. However, many gaps remain if total tourism resources on a global scale are considered.

It seems that, to date, the tourism–environment relationship is a long way from (and may never reach) the symbiosis of synergistic panacea and we must recognize that the relationship remains fundamentally one of conflict. A number of 'solutions' to alleviate, or at least reduce, the impact of this conflict have been suggested and the list of ten focus issues above reflects some of the diversity of approach. It is important to critically examine these proposals or 'solutions', which admittedly add width to the debate but sometimes confuse issues or tend to baffle stakeholders with a barrage of nebulous terminology. It is also important to identify idealistic but impractical solutions. Butler (1991) summarized these 'solutions' under four headings:–

- *Curb Tourist Numbers:* which may be appropriate at a local level but which is impractical or unacceptable (for economic reasons) at national level and unrealistic in the face of global tourism growth trends;
- *Change Tourist Type:* which reflects the universal condemnation of 'mass tourism' and the desire to offer quality/eco/alternative tourism. This seems to offer dubious micro solutions to macro problems;
- *Changing the Resource for Resistance*: where the resource is made more robust to withstand tourism pressures but which may not be acceptable to tourist tastes or, in the case of sensitive features, be environmentally appropriate. The last 'solution' category is;
- *Educating All Concerned*: (including all stakeholders), which may be the only realistic long term solution but which may take generations to implement and therefore does not meet current, or immediate future pressures on the environment.

THE PARADIGM OF SUSTAINABLE TOURISM DEVELOPMENT

The concept of sustainability and sustainable tourism development emerged from the environmental conservation discussion in the 1980s and has provided a theoretical focus for the debate. It has gained international recognition through the WCED (World Commission on Environment and Development) (1987) and at the United Nations Conference on Environment and Development held in June 1992 in Rio de Janeiro. The WCED 'Bruntland Report: Our Common Future' (1987) defined the term sustainable development as 'development that meets the needs of the present without compromising the ability of future generations to meet their own needs' (WCED, 1987).

This seemingly clear, straightforward definition has spawned a plethora of statements, policies and guidelines refining and adapting the definition for tourism. The above founding principle of sustainable development has been almost universally accepted in all quarters. For example the Scottish Tourism Co-ordinating Group (STCG) defines sustainable tourism as noted below:

> Sustainable tourism emphasizes the need to use and develop our tourism resources in a way which allows enjoyment while, at the same time, ensuring that these resources will be preserved for use by future generations (STCG, 1992).

However, the initially euphoric reception and adoption (at least in principle) by public agencies and industry alike has now been tempered by more sceptical critiques resulting from closer examination of the practicalities of implementation.

It is worth considering briefly the philosophy behind sustainable development rather than concentrating on the term itself. One of the most important principles is the concept of holistic planning and strategy making. Issues previously seen as separate – such as ozone depletion, waste production, water pollution, soil erosion, social and cultural impacts, landscape degradation – are now considered together in the tourism development debate. This integration of issues has been represented in a variety of models by agencies and authors. For example Lane (1994) views sustainable tourism as a triangular relationship between local people and their environment, the visitors, and the tourism industry, where in the past the balance lay firmly in the industry corner which dominated the relationship. Sustainable tourism aims to minimize environmental and cultural damage, optimize visitor satisfaction and maximize long term economic growth. Although recognizing the need for balance is a step forward, in reality two corners (industry and tourists) still tend to dominate, in particular where local inhabitants' desire for economic wealth is greater than their regard for the environment.

Muller (1994) takes the geometry a stage further by representing tourism development objectives as a 'magic pentagon' linked to the magic square in national economies (full employment, stable prices, stable balance of payments and growth). The five factors are seen as of equal importance, the overriding aim being to establish harmony in the 'magic pentagon', maximizing the positive relationships between all factors while minimizing the negative. The five points of the pentagon are:

- economic health;
- subjective well-being of locals;
- unspoilt nature, protection of resources;
- healthy culture;
- optimum satisfaction of guest requirements.

The geometric permutations for representing sustainable tourism principles seem endless, however, as Muller (1994) points out:

> There is nothing as practical as a good theory, but too many over-abstract theories do not get us any further either. In fact, they quickly provoke counter-reactions and rejection.

Some of the counter-reactions have struck a chord and there is a danger of the term 'sustainable tourism' being devalued and discredited completely. Sustainable tourism runs the risk of becoming just an empty cliché. Two key problems have been identified. First, the definitions and implications of sustainable tourism are often confused, misunderstood or even exploited for promotional purposes, as with green holidays for example.

> The inherent vagueness of sustainability is its greatest weakness. At present, it is being used by both industry and the conservation movement to legitimize and justify their existing activities and policies although, in many instances, they are mutually exclusive (McKercher, 1993a).

The second key problem is related to scale, where long term, practical, macro-solutions have yet to be identified.

> The current in vogue 'solutions' to tourism (sustainable policies and principles) are, I suggest, actually further fuelling the rapid spread of tourism without offering any real, lasting answers (Wheeller, 1991).

There is clearly a need to recognize the limitations of sustainable tourism and conduct a more objective appraisal of its applications. However, it is equally important to recognize some of the positive attributes of sustainable tourism and not reject it in its entirety or belittle the progress made so far. In order to make this objective appraisal, it is important first to recognize what McKercher terms 'the fundamental truths about tourism' (McKercher, 1993b), and second identify the contradictions – paradoxes, conflicts, irreconcilable goals – which surround the concept of sustainability.

TOURISM TRUTHS

McKercher (1993b) points out that few authors have attempted to seek out the underlying reasons why tourism development brings with it the inevitable potential for adverse impacts. Further, he argues that the very process of tourism development provides the catalyst for a wide range of potential impacts. Eight factors are examined which, if acknowledged by policy makers, planners and industry leaders, should at least offer valuable insights into understanding the nature of tourism impacts.

---

1) As an industrial activity, tourism consumes resources, creates waste and has specific infrastructure needs.

2) As a consumer of resources, it has the ability to over-consume resources.

3) Tourism, as a resource-dependent industry must compete for scarce resources to ensure its survival.

4) Tourism is a private sector dominated industry, with investment decisions being based predominantly on profit maximization.

5) Tourism is a multi-faceted industry, and as such, it is almost impossible to control.

6) Tourists are consumers, not anthropologists.

7) Tourism is entertainment.

8) Unlike other industrial activities, tourism generates income by importing clients rather than exporting its product.

Table 12.2: Some fundamental truths about tourism   (McKercher, 1993b)

Unfortunately these 'truths' are often ignored in the rush to embrace 'sustainable tourism solutions'. For example, the nature of the tourism industry, based on the profit motive, makes voluntary compliance with environmental conservation policies virtually impossible. Investment, in particular in the initial stages of development, tends to be focused on profit centres (tourist facilities) rather than cost centres (sewage systems). Whereas governments tend to provide support for national tourism promotion, they often shy away from actively policing tourism developments to ensure they operate in an ecologically appropriate manner. This factor is compounded by the fragmented

nature of tourism supply and the unpredictable actions of tourists which mak
effective government control extremely difficult to achieve. The free mark
system, in which most tourism takes place, tends to place growth as a ke
objective. Even where government agencies have attempted to limit or contr
this growth (regionally or nationally), and there is little evidence of this, th
diverse and highly unregulated nature of the tourism industry has continued t
delay efforts to limit its expansion. Effective control can only occur throug
integrated policies that include national and international agreements, backe
by legislation and a will to enforce.

SUSTAINABLE CONTRADICTIONS

The difficulties in understanding the nature of tourism development are com
pounded by the confusion over sustainability:

> At every level of society we seem to be indulging in the rhetoric of sustain-
> able development but our numbers, per capita consumption, and total load
> on the biosphere continue to increas' (ccs in Dovers and Handmer, 1993).

Nowhere is this more applicable than in the case of tourism where we ar
constantly reminded of the meteoric growth projected for the future. It high
lights a paradox in tourism development as economic growth is often viewed a
thoroughly unsustainable in that it is the actual cause of the ecological predica
ment we now face. The objective in reality is not absolute sustainable develop
ment but economic growth that can be achieved in a more environmentall
sound manner. Rather than attempting to achieve tourism development with n
environmental cost (or idealistically environmental enhancement), it is mor
practical to aim to minimize environmental costs.

A second paradox lies in the concept of intergenerational equity where sus
tainable development seeks to meet the needs of the present without compro
mizing the ability of future generations to meet their own needs (WCED, 1987
Justice between generations is the moral principle behind sustainability bu
this tends to ignore the inequalities which exist in the world today or intragen
erational equity. Surely assuring tourism resources for the future must be see
as inadequate if the inequalities that are painfully evident in the world toda
are perpetrated. This elitist philosophy is most obvious when comparin
tourism generated in the industrialized world with that of the industrializin
world, but it also exists within highly developed societies. On the other hand i
the less developed world is brought up to the tourism consumption levels o
industrialized countries, a fivefold escalation in the rate of environmenta
degradation would result.

The only alternative to accepting this paradox as inevitable is to institute a
massive redistribution of global wealth (and tourism generation) which in the
West would be politically impossible in the face of current consumerism. Thi

leads us to the paradox of individual versus collective interests. Individual choice is central to western cultures, as witnessed in the trends towards more private car based holidays, independent travellers and dispersed rather than concentrated tourism. In contrast, environmental conservation groups call for mass public transport, restricted access to fragile environments and greater controls on new developments. But environmental issues are collective problems at individual consumer and government level. Those who consume little bear the costs of total global consumption just as much as those who consume a lot. In this way a responsible approach to sustainable tourism issues at local level may be swamped by global environmental pollution.

On the other hand, in a democratic system with full self-determination and free choice (often to damage the environment), the alternative may be equally unpalatable: in extreme form, world environmental governance or eco-fascism?

These extremes in reality would be tempered by the ability of most modern industrial societies to resist change. In many cases sustainable tourism policies give the appearance of significant change in attitude while in reality they make little impact on underlying trends and institutional structures. Governments have become adept at devising tactics which produce changes at the 'margins' or 'fine tuning', rather than making fundamental policy shifts.

The above discussion seems pessimistic. However, these fundamental truths and contradictions must be confronted if sustainable tourism is to maintain any long-term credibility. Many would argue that sustainable tourism as a concept is fundamentally misguided. However, as Bramwell and Lane (1993) point out, 'one must ask what the alternatives are to developing more sustainable tourism – presumably either to stand back and do nothing or else to criticize without offering any realistic, practical way forward.'

For want of any alternative paradigm, sustainable tourism, if realistically and vigorously analysed, should continue to provide, at the very least, a focus for continued debate.

CODES, PRINCIPLES, GUIDELINES AND ECO-SLOGANS

During the 1990s one of the most high profile manifestations of the sustainable tourism debate has been the explosion of public policy statements, codes of conduct for tourists, and guidelines for industry. These have been produced at all levels, from international organizations, such as the WTO 'Sustainable Tourism Development: Guide for Local Planners' (WTO, 1993), to national and regional agency level where it has become almost obligatory for tourist boards to use sustainable terminology in their development plans (ETB, 1991; NITB, 1993). Industry and voluntary organizations have not been slow to respond with reports, brochures and 'glossies' promoting their green, eco-sensitive, sustainable credentials (Tourism Society, 1991; Tourism Concern 1992). Whether this explosion of literature represents true conversions to the environmental cause or an industry desperately defending itself from a barrage of media criticism (Nicholson-Lord, 1990; Barley, 1990) is highly debatable. On balance, evidence seems to suggest the latter. As Waldstein (1991), reported by Bramwell and Lane (1993), pointed out, all politicians and all large corporations now claim to be pursuing pro-environment policies. He terms this 'limousine environmentalism', which has become increasingly common in the USA, where lip service masks a lack of positive actions. Wheeller (1994) goes further, criticizing the confusion caused by the sustainable tourism debate which he feels has provided no answers, 'just a never-ending series of laughable codes of ethics: codes of ethics for travellers; codes of ethics for tourists, for government, and for tourism businesses. Codes for all – or more likely, codeine for all.'

Although the above criticism may be justifiable in some cases, it is worth considering objections to these guidelines in greater detail, in order to distinguish between cynical, idealistic or simplistic codes or eco-slogans, and valuable, realistic, practical guidelines.

One of the key criticisms is that some 'green' or 'sustainable tourism' guidelines are in reality marketing documents, promoting and justifying tourism growth through 'green' products. The fact that tourism can damage the environment is ignored or glossed over, in an attempt to maintain the positive, upbeat image of the industry. For example the English Tourist Board report *The Green Light: A Guide to Sustainable Tourism* (ETB, 1991), in a section on sustainable tourism, emphasizes growth rather than limits to tourism's capacity: 'tourism will be the world's biggest industry by the year 2000'; 'tourism is racing ahead in the 1990s with a better image and better prospects'. The report plays down any negative impacts the industry may have on the environment.

An associated characteristic is the tendency, as noted by Wheeller (1991), for the industry to adopt a defensive stance, preferring to tackle the criticism levelled at it, rather than address the problems themselves. Criticisms of tourism are seen as purely an image problem, which can be overcome by promoting a counter 'green' image through sustainable guidelines. This is illustrated in the document *Sustainable Tourism* produced by The Tourism Society (which represents a wide range of UK public and private tourism interests), where they view the problems caused by increases in visitor numbers as 'a backlash against the tourist and against the industry. This backlash inspired the media horror stories and ill-informed scaremongering which haunted the industry throughout 1990' (Tourism Society, 1991). The real danger, in their view, 'is that conservationists and other pressure groups, with a vested interest in the status quo will hijack the concept (sustainable tourism) as a way of sustaining existing environments and landscapes' (Tourism Society, 1991). The implication here, it seems, is that the tourism industry should act quickly to hijack 'sustainable tourism' first, as a way of avoiding protection of environments and landscapes.

Many examples of good practice, cited in these guidelines, are designed to point out the positive role of tourism. However in many instances they illustrate the reactive nature of tourism planning, whereby the good image of tourism, and tourism growth can be maintained even where the environment has been degraded. Edinburgh is cited as an example of good (sustainable) practice by The Tourism Society:

as a major tourism destination, Edinburgh has experienced all the problems associated with a large volume of visitors. The gradual erosion of quality as a consequence of uncoordinated marketing and management, particularly of traffic, has led to the preparation of plans to improve the visitors experience (Tourism Society, 1991).

This odd example of 'good practice' seems to indicate the view that if the tourists are happy then sustainable tourism has been achieved, no matter the degraded quality of the environment. As Ashworth (1992) asked, in a critique of the ETB report *The Green Light* (ETB, 1991), 'Is this better than nothing or worse than useless? Should we praise the tourism agencies for at last waking up to some of their responsibilities or condemn them out of hand for the triviality of their response?'

The criticism of ignoring environmental consequences of tourism cannot be levelled at the 'principles for sustainable tourism' produced by the pressure group Tourism Concern in their publication *Beyond the Green Horizon* (1992). The difficulty with this document, in terms of credibility, is in the idealistic, naive, proposals suggested to tackle the negative impacts of tourism on the environment. As Ashcroft stated in his review, 'it soon became very tiresome ploughing through so many platitudinous points, which sounded like a converted and over-virtuous boyscout promise' (Ashcroft, 1993).

Some industry representatives have openly admitted that worthy statements of intent and idealistic codes will have little effect on changing industry attitudes. Noel Josephides (Director of Sunvil Holidays and Chairman of AITO until 1992) predicted that 'the WTTC would have an uphill struggle to convince the industry to act according to its slogan "the environment is our business"'. In his opinion volume operators exhibited a 'slash-and-burn' mentality, and that over-development could be prevented only by controlling and regulating all tourism sectors (Grabowski, 1994).

ECO-LABELS

Similar criticism can be made of over-optimistic predictions for new 'green' or 'ecotourism' products which often amount to no more than eco-labelling. Although some ecotourism products are genuinely more environmentally friendly than others there still remains a strong element of eco-sloganizing. Even the more genuine eco-tourism, or nature tourism, initiatives may be viewed as dangerous distractions which cater for a tiny sector of total tourism demand. The WTTERC (World Travel and Tourism Environmental Research Council) recognize this and argue that 'in fact eco-tourism can only make a marginal, though important, contribution because of the limited nature of its market . . . the true target for better performance and a globally relevant contribution must be the core 95 per cent of the world's travel and tourism' (WTTERC, 1993).

A further worrying factor relating to eco-tourism is that it tends to be located in areas with unique and fragile ecosystems, unsuited or unable to withstand the predicted growth in ecotourist numbers. The small country of Belize, often cited as the role model of ecotourism virtues (Cater, 1993), has begun to have doubts. Jose Alphuche (Second Secretary, Belize High Commission) speaking at a conference in March 1994, expressed concern over the future of specializing in this particular market segment: how to measure carrying capacity; how to cater for the local needs if 25 per cent of the land is a nature reserve; how to control foreign investments and how to avoid 'rape following foreplay' if insufficient controls are exercised (Grabowski, 1994).

It is misleading and unhelpful to categorize tourism simplistically under labels like mass tourism and ecotourism. 'Mass, as in massive, is monolithic, impersonal, depreciatory: eco, haloed in correctness, is only marginally less admirable than motherhood' (Brackenbury, 1992).

A more realistic solution but far less fashionable, is 'mass sustainable tourism', where existing tourism infrastructure (seaside resorts and urban tourism) which is robust and designed to cater for volume, is utilized to the full. This would maximize occupancy levels, could be managed in an environmentally sustainable way, and would reduce pressure on sensitive countryside or wilderness locations. Quite the opposite of ecotourism arguments.

PUBLIC POLICY WHITE WASH (OR 'GREEN WASH')

The final area of concern relating to sustainable guidelines, is that they may be used by governments to provide a 'green gloss' to their policies which often contradict what is actually implemented in relation to the environment. It is an example of the political tactic, discussed earlier in this chapter, of making changes at the 'margins' or 'fine tuning' rather than initiating fundamental policy shifts.

The debate over National Parks in Scotland in recent years may illustrate this point. National Parks have long been recognized as an appropriate mechanism for managing visitors to environmentally sensitive areas, and the attempts to gain national parks in Scotland go back to the last century. The reasons for the failure to achieve this are long and complex, the key point being that in 1990 the official conservation agency for Scotland (CCS) finally recommended 'the establishment of national parks in four areas of special importance' (CCS, 1990). This followed a lengthy consultation process, a particularly acrimonious conflict between the skiing and the conservation lobby, and recognition that development pressures had resulted in insensitive, unsightly tourist developments, commonly referred to as 'Aviemoreism'.

However, rather than implement these proposals (with the related financial costs and resistance from landowners), the government initiated another complex consultative process, created a new conservation agency structure and swamped the public with green guidelines. The documentation for these initiatives are all liberally sprinkled with sustainable terminology but there is a distinct lack of the regulatory or legislative powers which would come with national park designation.

During the 1990s the environment–tourism debate in Scotland, at the official level, has been characterized by joint initiatives, co-ordinating groups and task forces, which has resulted in a continuous flow of reports, codes, guidelines and policy statements (Scottish Tourism Co-ordinating Group, 1992; Tourism and Environment Task Force, 1993). Much of this work should be praised as there is recognition given to the adverse impacts of tourism and practical advice offered for future development. This is true of the report by the Scottish Tourism Co-ordinating Group *A Sustainable Partnership* (1992) and the 'Guidelines for the Development of Tourism Management Programmes' produced by the Scottish Tourist Board on behalf of the Tourism and Environment Task Force in 1993. *Going Green* (1993), also by the STB for TETF, outlines guidelines for the Scottish tourism industry and is a little less practical, basing its structure on questions such as 'Why go green? How green are you?' without offering enough realistic answers. What we should ask is 'Are these guidelines a substitute for conservation measures recommended by the CCS in 1990?'.

> This explosion of worthy publications must be examined in the context of an absence of government action in resolving how to adequately protect fragile mountain environments. These laudable sentiments on sustainable tourism do not offer the solutions to the problems identified in the CCS Mountain Areas report (MacLellan, 1993).

The new agency, Scottish Natural Heritage, created in 1991, places great emphasis on 'enabling enjoyment of the natural heritage in a manner which is sustainable' and prides itself in the fact that 'our founding legislation enshrines the word sustainable for the first time in UK legislation' (SNH, 1992). However, sustainable rhetoric is no substitute for national park legislation. For this new agency (and the working parties set up to consider the issue of managing tourism in fragile mountain environments), favours a new designation – 'Natural Heritage Areas' – which lack the powers and administrative (and financial) backup afforded national parks.

It seems sustainable principles, in this case, mean less control and regulation and more 'co-operation', 'voluntary' agreements and 'partnership' boards. This is ironic as the same government (albeit a different department) reiterated, in the strongest terms, its commitment to National Parks in England and Wales, viewing them as 'models for the sustainable management of the wider countryside' (Scottish Office, 1993).

It seems that 'sustainable tourism' has allowed the government to manoeuvre round the need to provide National Parks in Scotland. As in the past, the Scottish environment is compromised by a government unwilling to conflict with landowning interests and make major financial commitments (Scott, 1992). The surfeit of sustainable green guidelines cannot deflect criticism such as a World Conservation Union report which condemned Scotland for 'operating one of the weakest management arrangements for vulnerable areas in Europe' (Edwards, 1993).

CONCLUSION

There is now clearly a need to move the debate beyond codes, guidelines and sustainable platitudes. If the paradigm of sustainable tourism is to maintain credibility, the fundamental tourism truths and sustainable contradictions must be recognized. Tourism academics, public policy makers and industry experts must avoid superficial 'green smokescreens' (the public have already grown cynical through meaningless supermarket eco-labelling) and attempt to reach a consensus over terminology and eco-brands.

Micro-solutions, like ecotourism, should be welcomed but put in proportion, as they are a distraction to the core tourism–environment debate which seeks macro-solutions to this global 'mass' issue. Research and debate should concentrate on 'mass alternative' tourism or the rejuvenation of existing resorts and urban areas where infrastructure is in place for mass tourism and the environment is robust. Policies encouraging tourism in fragile, wilderness areas should be condemned as environmentally unsustainable.

Sustainable tourism principles need to be given weight (legislative powers) by supporting them with environmental regulations, and where necessary adequate finance for implementing management strategies. Voluntary codes are no substitute for statutory regulations. The path however must be trodden carefully, to avoid the pitfalls of suffocating industry or generating costly litigation (as experienced in the USA by the Environmental Protection Agency).

Industry must be convinced of the need to protect the environment by hard facts rather than idealistic philosophies. Voluntary action, led by industry, would be much more effective if they were convinced their businesses depended on it. Where possible, governments should seek market solutions but use effective regulations as a last resort. Much of the task of convincing industry lies with measurement and monitoring. Facts and figures will convince, where principles will be ignored. This seems to be one of the key challenges for tourism in the future.

TOURISM AND THE ENVIRONMENT
ORGANIZATIONAL INTERACTIONS

Tourism

WTO	–	World Tourism Organization
ETB	–	English Tourist Board
ITT	–	Institute of Travel and Tourism
TOSG	–	Tour Operators Study Group
AITO	–	Association of Independent Tour Operators
PATA	–	Pacific Area Tourist Association
BTA	–	British Tourist Authority
ABTA	–	Association of British Travel Agents
WTTC	–	World Travel and Tourism Council
GFI	–	Green Flag International
T. Soc	–	Tourism Society
ASTA	–	American Society of Travel Agents

Aviation

FAA	–	Federal Aviation Administration (USA)
IATA	–	International Air Transport Association
ATUC	–	Air Transport Users Committee
CAA	–	Civil Aviation Authority
IPCC	–	Inter-Governmental Panel on Climate Control
ECAC	–	European Civil Aviation Conference
ICAO	–	International Civil Aviation Organization
AEA	–	Association of European Airlines
ACC	–	Airport Consultative Committee

Environment

OECD	–	Orgnization for Economic Co-operation and Development
CC	–	Countryside Commission
D. Env	–	Department of the Environment
BTCV	–	British Trust for Conservation Volunteers
WWF	–	World Wide Fund for Nature
RSNC	–	Royal Society for Nature Conservation
IUCN	–	International Union for the Conservation of Nature
UNESCO	–	United Nations Educational, Scientific and Cultural Organization
NCC	–	Nature Conservency Council
CPRE	–	Council for the Preservation of Rural England
RSPB	–	Royal Society for the Protection of Birds
FOE	–	Friends of the Earth
UN	–	United Nations
FNNPE	–	Federation of Nature and National Parks of Europe
WCU	–	World Conservation Union

REFERENCES

Ashcroft, P. (1993) One Hundred and One Dull Machinations, *Journal of Sustainable Tourism* 1(2), p 346.

Ashworth, G.J. (1992) Planning for Sustainable Tourism, *Town Planning Review* 63(3), pp 325–329.

Barley, N. (1990) Tourism Herds Moving Across the World, *The Independent* 19 May.

Brackenbury, M (1992) Introduction to Ecotourism a Sustainable Option, *Tourism Society Bulletin* 76, Nov.

Bramwell, B. and Lane, B. (1993) Sustainable Tourism: An Evolving Global Approach, *Journal of Sustainable Tourism* 1(1), pp 1–5.

Budowski, G. (1976) Tourism and Environmental Conservation: Conflict, Coexistence or Symbiosis? *Environmental Conservation* 3(1), pp 27–31.

Butler, R.W. (1991) Tourism, Environment and Sustainable Development, *Environmental Conservation* 18(3), pp 201–209.

Cater, E. (1993) Ecotourism in the Third World: Problems for Sustainable Tourism Development, *Tourism Management* April.

Countryside Commission for Scotland (1990) *The Mountain Areas of Scotland* Edinburgh, CCS

CCS in S.R. Dovers and J.W. Handmer (1993) Contradictions in Sustainability, *Environmental Conservation* 20(3), pp 217–222.

Dowling, R.K. (1992) Tourism and Environmental Integration: The Journey From Idealism to Realism, *Progress in Tourism, Recreation and Hospitality Management* 4.

Edwards, R. (1993) Tourists Could Destroy Loch, Report Warns, *Scotland on Sunday* 11 July.

English Tourist Board (1991) *The Green Light: A Guide to Sustainable Tourism* London: ETB.

Grabowski, P. (1994) Working Towards Development Partnerships, *Tourism Management* 15(5), pp 393–395.

Hardin, G. (1968) The Tragedy of the Commons, *Science* 162, pp 1243–8.

Lane, B. (1994) Sustainable Rural Tourism Strategies: A Tool for Development and Conservation, *Journal of Sustainable Tourism* 2(1&2), pp 102–111.

McKercher, R. (1993a) The Unrecognized Threat to Tourism: Can Tourism Survive 'Sustainability'? *Tourism Management* April, pp 131–136.

McKercher, R. (1993b) Some Fundamental Truths about Tourism: Understanding Tourism's Social and Environmental Impacts, *Journal of Sustainable Tourism* 1(1), pp 6–16.

MacLellan, L.R. (1993) Tourism and Scottish Mountain Environments: Values and Public Policy, *Proceedings of Conference: Values and the Environment* University of Surrey, Sept. 1993.

Muller, H. (1994) The Thorny Path to Sustainable Tourism Development, *Journal of Sustainable Tourism* 2(3), pp 131–136.

Nicholson-Lord, D. (1990) Death by Tourism, *The Independent on Sunday* 5 August.

Northern Ireland Tourist Board (1993) *Tourism in Northern Ireland: A Sustainable Approach* Belfast: NITB.

Scott, M. (1992) What Future for the Cairngorms? *Ecos* 13(2).

Scottish Natural Heritage (1992) *Mission Statement and Promotional Brochure.*, Edinburgh: SNH.

Scottish Office (1993) Common Sense and Sustainability: A partnership for the Cairngorms, *The Report of the Cairngorms Working Party* March, London: HMSO.

Scottish Tourism Co-ordinating Group (1992) *Tourism and the Scottish Environment: A Sustainable Partnership* Edinburgh: STB.

Sommerville, H. (1994) Airlines, Tourism and Environment. In Seaton *et al.* (eds) *Tourism: The State of the Art* Chichester: Wiley & Sons.

Tourism and Environment Task Force (1993) *Going Green: Guidelines for the Scottish Tourism Industry* Edinburgh: STB

Tourism Concern (1992) *Beyond the Green Horizon* London: Tourism Concern and WWT

Tourism Society (1991) *Sustainable Tourism: Development in Balance with the Environment* London: Tourism Society.

Waldstein, F.A. (1991) Environmental Policy and Politics. In P.J. Davies and F.A. Waldstein (eds) *Political Issues in America* Manchester and New York: Manchester University Press.

Wheeller, B. (1991) Tourism's Troubled Times: Responsible Tourism is not the Answer, *Tourism Management* June, pp 91–96.

Wheeller, B. (1994) Egotourism, Sustainable Tourism and the Environment – A Symbiotic, Symbolic or Shambolic Relationship. In Seaton *et al*. (eds) *Tourism: The State of the Art* Chichester: Wiley & Sons.

World Commission on Environment and Development (1987) *Our Common Future* Oxford: Oxford University Press.

WTO (1991) Development of International Tourism Worldwide 1970–1990, *Industry and Environment* 15(3–4) Paris: UNEP.

WTO (1993) *Sustainable Tourism Development: Guide for Local Planners* Madrid

World Travel and Tourism Environment Research Centre (1993) *Report on Environment and Development* Annual Report, Oxford: WTTERC.

13

The Economics of Leisure Sustainability

Chris Bull

The focus of this chapter is leisure sustainability generally and the related economic aspects specifically. In addition to presenting key economic concepts and processes in the leisure context, this chapter highlights their importance in developing management strategies.

Sustainability has become one of the principal policy goals of the 1990s. Although first used in the World Conservation Strategy in 1980 (IUCN, 1980), it was the Brundtland Report in the late 1980s (WCED, 1987) which essentially developed the concept and placed it firmly on the political agenda. Since then various studies and government responses to Brundtland (Pearce *et al.*, 1989; DOE, 1994), together with the Earth Summit in Rio de Janeiro in 1992, have provided yet more weight to its importance.

When first used in the World Conservation Strategy, sustainability was expressed primarily in ecological terms with less importance being attached to economic development or the interrelationships between economics and the environment. In fact, the concept was couched in rather narrow, preservationist terms with a strong anti-development bias. By contrast, the Brundtland Report saw sustainability in much broader terms, accepting the need for economic growth and for integrating economics and environment (Pearce *et al.*, 1989). It defined sustainable development as that which 'meets the needs of the present without compromising the ability of future generations to meet their needs'. Sustainability was thus not inconsistent with economic growth; in fact Brundtland saw no limits to growth and development as long as this could be achieved in ways that would be environmentally, economically and socially acceptable. The principal concern was with the management of the political and economic systems that were responsible for development. Since the Brundtland Report and especially since the Rio Conference and associated Agenda 21 document, the concept has been applied to a wide range of situations. While initial applications of sustainability were focused on development impacts in the developing world, the concept has subsequently been applied with equal vigour to the developed world at both national and local level and in both rural and urban contexts (Pearce *et al.*, 1989; Breheny, 1992; Countryside Commission, 1993 and 1995; LGMB, 1994a, b; Selman, 1996).

One activity which has attracted significant comment in terms of sustainability is that of tourism. In many countries and regions tourism has been an important part of economic development and may account for well over 50 per cent of export earnings in some small island economies. The rush to develop tourism, often with little planning, has sometimes produced significant negative environmental, economic and social impacts (Matthieson and Wall, 1982; Ryan, 1991). Thus, tourism is a classic target for sustainable policies. One significant aspect of tourism is, of course, leisure but, while much has been written about sustainable tourism and it now also has its own quarterly journal (*Journal of Sustainable Tourism*), little has been written specifically on leisure sustainability. It is, therefore, the intention of this chapter to focus on this issue and, in particular, its economic aspects.

SUSTAINABLE LEISURE

Although most leisure takes place in or near the home, the amount of leisure activity involving a journey to other locations is still significant. There are substantial numbers of people who make trips to the countryside, to the coast, to cultural and entertainment centres, and to shop. While not strictly classed as tourism according to some established definitions, in that such activity does not involve an overnight stay, it does, nevertheless, possess some of the key attributes of tourism. Thus, in identifying the conditions for sustainable leisure, a useful starting point would be to consider those that have been listed for sustainable tourism. Cater and Goodall (1992), in their work on sustainable tourism, suggest that it is dependent on the following:

- meeting the needs of the host population in terms of improved standards of living in the short and long term;
- satisfying the demands of increasing tourist numbers and continuing to attract them to achieve this;
- safeguarding the environment to achieve the two foregoing aims.

In the context of this discussion, apart from replacing 'tourist' by 'leisure seeker', the other modification would be a change of emphasis in terms of the needs of the 'host' community. Although leisure activities may be of considerable economic significance in some locations, and a greater emphasis is being placed on the economic importance of leisure, especially in restructured rural economies, most leisure has not developed as part of an explicit strategy for economic growth. As a result, the first of the conditions listed above might be to ensure that those who live in leisure locations are not adversely affected by leisure activity and that leisure industries are able to remain economically viable.

As with tourism, the essential problem is one of managing impacts on the resource base. Large numbers of visitors to a place may produce both environmental damage, such as destruction of wildlife habitats and erosion of footpaths and other physical resources, and social problems in the form of crowding, congestion, noise and cultural impacts. Not only do such problems affect local populations producing various costs but, ultimately, such impacts could lead to a significant reduction in the leisure experience of the visitor. A degraded physical environment, crowded locations and/or overt local resentment may result in a decline in visitor numbers, possibly with economic consequences for such places.

Concerns about such impacts and how to manage them have been well documented in the leisure literature for several decades (Patmore, 1972, 1983; Pigram, 1983; Glyptis, 1991; Harrison, 1991; Curry, 1994). Much of this discussion has centred around the concept of recreation carrying capacity, which describes the level of recreation use an area can sustain without an unacceptable degree of deterioration of the character and quality of the resource or of the recreation experience. In that it suggests maximum limits beyond which unacceptable environmental damage will occur or the recreational experience will deteriorate, it is very similar to the concept of sustainability. However, there are some important differences. The concept of carrying capacity stresses fixed limits whereas sustainability accepts that, with appropriate management, limits can be changed (Ryan, 1991). Also, the underlying rationale of recreation carrying capacity was essentially negative. It came into vogue as a result of misguided 1960s concerns about leisure impacts on the rural environment and was seen primarily as a means of control. Its underlying assumptions were also highly dubious for its notion of what was unacceptable damage was entirely subjective. What might be unacceptable to the naturalist or planner may be very different to what is unacceptable to the 'ordinary' recreating public. Finally, the concept was also based on limited and partial research into the environmental affects of recreation (for a useful summary of these issues (see Curry, 1994). In contrast, sustainability is a much more positive approach which, as already mentioned, does not seek to control growth *per se*. It also advocates a much more pronounced role for economics.

If sustainable policies with more precise management strategies are to be developed in relation to leisure, it is, therefore, necessary to understand the role that economics plays in the process. Leisure economics is concerned with the use of scarce resources and their allocation among different consumers. It is concerned with the demand for and supply of leisure resources, the values people place on those resources and the related prices they are willing to pay to utilize them. Classical economic theory would suggest that there is an equilibrium situation at which both suppliers and consumers can agree on a price (the market price). In simple terms, this price would reflect both the benefit or utility which the consumer expects to obtain and a satisfactory remuneration to the supplier to cover the cost incurred in providing the good and provide a certain amount of profit. Although this concept can be applied to most goods, with many forms of leisure it is problematical. These problems have been well documented (see e.g. Vickerman, 1983; Gratton and Taylor, 1988), the principal ones being that much leisure involves a composite price (cost of travel, entrance charge, costs of time, cost of equipment); the benefits may not be immediate (the health investment aspect); some leisure goods are intangible (fresh air; relaxation); and some leisure resources have traditionally been provided free. Unfortunately, many of these problems are often most applicable to those types of leisure for which sustainability is most appropriate, namely many forms of countryside recreation. Nevertheless, the problems are not insurmountable and an economic approach may well help achieve practical sustainable policies.

A number of economic aspects are thus relevant in the context of leisure sustainability. They include pricing policies related to the economic viability of leisure enterprises, revenue for resource management, and visitor control strategies; the value that both local people and visitors place on a resource or environment which will reflect the cost of its protection; the economic benefits of leisure activities and the costs to local people from such pursuits in the form of congestion and various forms of pollution (e.g. litter, vehicle fumes and noise); and the economic value of community involvement. The following pages will deal with each of these aspects in turn.

PRICING POLICIES

The essential economic argument for the price mechanism is that it is a very efficient means of allocating scarce resources and, therefore, may be a more suitable means of achieving sustainable leisure development than the use of regulation. As Sinclair (1992) argues:

> Fees or taxes on the use of environmental resources can be imposed such
> that the price takes account not only of the marginal private cost of the use
> of the resources, but also the marginal external cost incurred by their use,
> and of the marginal user-cost which results from the depletion of resources.

Suppliers themselves may include such fee elements in their own charges or they may be imposed by government on the supplier or on the visitor depending on the nature of price elasticities and on administrative arrangements for collecting such revenues.

While in most situations prices are automatically levied where goods or resources are consumed, in the case of the leisure use of many environmental resources their consumption has traditionally been 'free'. In Britain, for example, the recreational use of much open countryside (especially upland areas), parts of the coastline and all beaches, certain areas of common land, the rights of way network, and even many specifically developed recreational resources, such as country parks and picnic sites, has not required a direct payment. Apart from the difficulties in some cases of establishing a market and collecting money, there have also been powerful arguments against charging on social, health and equity grounds (Blacksell, 1981; Gratton and Taylor, 1985). Nevertheless, in recent years a growing interest in pricing policies for countryside recreation has emerged (McCallum and Adams, 1980; Bovaird *et al.*, 1984; Schroeder and Fessenmaier, 1983; Stevens *et al.*, 1989; Gilg, 1991; Curry, 1994; Knapman and Stoeckl, 1995). In fact, Gilg (1991) has suggested this to be one of two key issues related to countryside recreation in Britain in the 1990s, the other being that of access.

There are a number of reasons for this growth of interest. One is the influence of 'new right' thinking and the shift away from policies of social provision towards a greater concern with market values. In addition, there is a strong environmentalist argument linked to sustainability for, as Pearce *et al.* (1989) argue, the simple theory of supply and demand would suggest that zero-priced resources are at serious risk of overuse. A further reason involves the restructuring of the countryside and the need to develop alternative economic activities such as leisure and tourism. This is also directly linked to the question of sustainability, for the maintenance of countryside recreation may well be essential for the economic viability of the countryside as a whole. In addition to providing valuable revenue to resource providers, charging is thus seen as fulfilling several other purposes in the context of sustainable leisure. It can provide important funds for protecting and/or repairing environmental resources; it can help protect more fragile sites through a policy of differential pricing; and it can be part of a process of education which stresses the value and fragility of resources.

While those who argue against pricing, especially in relation to the more passive forms of countryside recreation, are still very numerous and influential, there are signs that attitudes are shifting. The environment continues to be a major public concern and it is likely that people will be more willing to pay for access if it is made clear that the charge is for environmental improvements. In addition to support for this principle, however, there is also evidence that people are more likely to see outdoor recreation as just another leisure good which they would expect to pay for. People are willing to pay to walk round the grounds of stately homes and ancient monuments and paying to walk or relax in other designated areas of countryside may not be that different. In a survey of 700 residents in Bedfordshire who were questioned about their likely use of the Marston Vale Community Forest, 63 per cent thought there should be some direct payment for certain leisure activities and over half (56 per cent) thought there should be some payment even for simple access (CRRU/MVA, 1992).

One specific example where pricing and management works to produce an overall sustainable leisure environment is in the area of nature conservation. For example, at many reserves run by the Royal Society for the Protection of Birds (RSPB), visitors are charged an entrance fee (or car park charge) with society members having free access, although in reality they have already paid through their membership subscription. Although the price itself may not have much effect in rationing numbers of visitors, as the charges are relatively modest and numbers are controlled more through physical capacity and remote locations, it does provide valuable income for management purposes which benefit visitors and wildlife alike. By means of carefully managed walkways, screens and hides, visitors are able to watch the birds and other wildlife at close quarters. In fact, at the RSPB Minsmere reserve on the Suffolk coast, the number of breeding species actually rose at the same time that visitor numbers increased from a mere handful in the early 1960s to over 30,000 in the late 1970s. Of course, with many nature reserves the problems of collecting money are relatively simple as funds are either provided by society members through their subscriptions or are collected at obvious entrance/collecting points. In some situations, however, it may be difficult or even impossible to collect charges, or the costs of doing so may exceed the revenue collected. In such circumstances it may be possible to collect money through some form of indirect taxation (eg a tax on walking boots) or through donations and honesty boxes.

Although it is possible to say that people will be prepared to pay for various types of leisure resource and to demonstrate that the extra income generated in this way can be used to sustain both the environment and the leisure experience, the precise effect pricing will have on demand is more difficult to determine. While some have suggested that charging can be used as a means of visitor control (Bovaird *et al.*, 1984), others have argued that many leisure activities are relatively price inelastic and thus prices would need to be very high to achieve such an objective (Knapman and Stoeckl, 1995). Clearly there needs to be more research on this issue.

VALUING LEISURE RESOURCES

While the previous section has suggested that an extension of the price mechanism could help achieve leisure sustainability, there will be many situations, as already indicated, where this may not be possible. Charging for certain activities such as the use of areas of countryside already enjoying free access may also be politically unacceptable as a result of merit good and equity arguments. Nevertheless, policies for sustainable leisure will still be required and there will be costs and benefits associated with such policies which may need to be expressed in monetary values. If practical management and environmental protection are to be achieved and the cost of this is to be paid for out of general taxation, it is likely that priorities will need to be established given limited public funds. If people are not going to pay directly to use a particular piece of countryside or stretch of coastline then other means are needed to establish which areas or sites are the most highly valued.

While some would argue that it is difficult to quantify the benefits of leisure activity, Pearce (Pearce *et al.*, 1989) has provided a sound rationale for such procedures in relation to the environment in general which is equally applicable to leisure. Monetary values show an intensity of preference and provide a more meaningful expression of the level of support than other methods such as the subjective views of so-called experts. They also permit comparisons to be made. A clearer understanding of the economic costs and benefits of utilizing various leisure resources should enable a more efficient and equitable allocation of public funds to be devoted towards the management of such resources, either from general taxation or specific user taxes. They also enable leisure interests to compete with other land users. Without such data it would be very difficult to make decisions about protecting and managing areas for passive recreation against the claims of those wishing to develop the land for agriculture, industrial, commercial or residential use.

A number of methods are available which allow estimates of recreation benefits to be made in the absence of markets and price regimes. These are either based on invented markets using questionnaire data concerning respondents' willingness to pay (WTP), or involve establishing surrogate markets which provide information about the recreation experience by looking at other markets where goods are traded (Pearce, 1989; Stephens and Wallace, 1993). A well-known example of the latter is the travel cost method pioneered by Clawson and Knetsch (1966). This produces a proxy demand curve for a recreation site based on travel and time costs. The area under the demand curve is known as 'consumer's surplus' and represents the benefits arising from the recreational experience. The value of such benefits can then be compared against the value of benefits derived for other sites or from alternative uses for the same site. The leisure literature contains many examples of the explanation and use of this method, including its limitations based mainly on its underlying assumptions (e.g. Vickerman, 1974; Smith, 1983).

Another method which involves the use of a proxy market is hedonic pricing. This approach often uses the property market as a surrogate and is based on the assumption that differences in the quality of environmental amenity and leisure resources will be reflected in differential house prices, assuming that the other variables influencing house price variation can be accounted for. From such differences it is then possible to infer how much people are willing to pay for such resources and thus a value can be established (for a detailed discussion of the hedonic price method *see* Brookshire *et al.*, 1983; Pearce *et al.*, 1989; Garrod and Willis, 1991; and also Sinclair *et al.*, 1990 and Clewer *et al.*, 1992 where the hedonic price method has been used to estimate the price differentials of the various goods and services included in the overall tourism product such as package tours).

Contingent valuation is a further method which has received considerable attention in recent times (Bishop and Heberlein, 1986; Cummings *et al.*, 1986; Pearce *et al.*, 1989; Garrod and Willis, 1990; Willis and Garrod, 1991a, b; Bateman *et al.*, 1993; Willis *et al.*, 1993). The method is based on asking people directly what they are willing to pay for a benefit and/or what they are willing to receive by way of compensation to tolerate a cost (Pearce *et al.*, 1989). People are asked to respond on the assumption that a market does exist for the good and that arrangements could be made to collect such amounts. Several recent studies by the Countryside Change Unit at the University of Newcastle have utilized this method to assess the value of various resources ranging from National Parks (Willis and Garrod, 1991a; Bateman *et al.*, 1993) to cathedrals (Willis *et al.*, 1993). For example, the study by Willis and Garrod (1991a) of landscape values in the Yorkshire Dales National Park concluded, among other things, that the willingness of visitors and residents to pay to preserve today's landscape amounted to £42 million per year and that the benefits would clearly justify further public expenditure on its maintenance.

COSTS AND BENEFITS OF LEISURE TO HOST COMMUNITIES

As indicated earlier, many forms of leisure involve people travelling to other places to participate in their chosen activities and they inevitably produce impacts on the places they visit. There is a voluminous literature on the impacts of tourists on host populations, but short stay visitors who may not necessarily be regarded as tourists may also produce significant impacts. The impacts may be positive and beneficial to the local communities or they may be negative involving costs. However, in order for leisure to be sustainable, given our original definition, the benefits must clearly outweigh the costs.

Assessing the 'sustainability' of an individual enterprise such as a camp site or fishing lake may be relatively simple, involving a comparison of operating costs against revenue. The resulting assessment may be expressed in terms of profit or loss and some measure of the return on investment. Assessing the costs and benefits of leisure activity on the wider community, however, is clearly more difficult, especially where the principal reason for visiting an area is to use a 'free', public good, such as a beach or national park. Nevertheless, in such situations there are measurable economic benefits for the local community. Local people may be employed as park rangers or in various management tasks. They may also work in various service industries where visitors may buy meals, refreshments and souvenirs. The value of such employment and income can be expressed in terms of numbers of jobs, value of wages and total expenditure. For example, it has been calculated that the 15 million people who visited the Lake District area in 1994 spent £446 million and kept one in six of the local population employed (*Times*, 15 April 1995).

The broader economic significance of these effects can also be expressed in terms of 'multipliers' which calculate the additional or indirect income or employment produced by the primary expenditure or job creation. However, while it is relatively simple to estimate the level of visitor expenditure through questionnaire surveys and establish the number of people in leisure-related jobs, calculating the amount of money that is re-spent in the local economy or the indirect employment is a far more complicated process (for a detailed discussion of 'multipliers' see Archer, 1973, 1982; Ryan, 1991). Furthermore, even though it is essential to know this in order to assess sustainability on one level, there is no guarantee that host populations will appreciate its significance and, in any case, residents are likely to differ in their evaluation of the economic gains depending on whether or not they themselves are direct beneficiaries.

The costs of leisure developments on local communities can be seen in the form of noise, litter, crowds, vandalism, congested roads and traffic fumes. Although it may be possible to estimate some of these costs, or externalities, by assessing the level of local services required to deal with them (e.g. street cleaning, policing, road maintenance), with some key impacts such as congestion and noise pollution the costs are personal and thus more difficult to determine. As with the benefits, not everyone will be affected in the same way. People will differ in their tolerance of the various problems, and those who do derive some economic gain from leisure developments may see this as adequate compensation for any adverse effects.

Leisure facilities such as football stadia or theme parks such as Alton Towers will clearly produce negative externalities which may well be reflected in local house prices. In other areas, however, house price data may not be a useful measure as the very features that attract visitors may also make such areas residentially attractive and thus interpreting the data may be difficult.

It should be noted, however, that while some areas clearly experience significant negative impacts arising from leisure activity, most of this is very localized. As Curry (1994) points out, recreation damage in the British countryside is almost insignificant compared with the impacts of intensive agriculture and forestry. In fact, the development of leisure and tourism in rural areas is seen as part of a diversification programme for achieving economic viability and overall sustainability.

THE ECONOMIC VALUE OF COMMUNITY INVOLVEMENT

Much of the previous discussion may have implied that local people are powerless bystanders in relation to the impacts that derive from the broader process of leisure activity. However, not only may local people indulge in leisure activities themselves and be part of that process, they may also influence its nature. In fact, one of the key aspects of the 1992 Agenda 21 agreement was the important role envisaged for local communities in achieving sustainability. Local people would need to become involved in both the planning and decision-making process and also in more practical aspects of conservation and environmental management.

In Britain there is a well-established tradition of voluntary and community involvement in such matters and this has become even greater in recent times. Voluntary organizations like the National Trust and Royal Society for the Protection of Birds (RSPB) which date from the end of the last century own and/or manage substantial tracts of amenity land. The National Trust owns over 1 per cent of the total land area of Britain, much of it concentrated in National Parks and other scenic areas, while the RSPB possesses over 200 nature reserves. The county nature conservation trusts also own and/or manage 2,000 reserves. While some acquisitions and management is aided by government grants, much of the effort is supported by public subscription and voluntary labour. The National Trust, for example, has over two million members, while the RSPB has 950,000 and the county trusts collectively 250,000. With membership subscriptions averaging about £20 per person, the overall income such bodies obtain in this way is not insignificant and further income is obtained through various fund raising activities. In addition, members also provide voluntary labour for a wide array of activities ranging from office work to practical site management, the British Trust for Conservation Volunteers being especially important in this respect. The true economic value of all this effort must also be substantial.

While much of the work of these voluntary organizations involves acquiring and managing sites for the benefit of the organization and its members, such sites often have much wider significance, with some being regarded as public goods providing amenities for the wider general population. Members of voluntary groups together with many other people are also involved in a range of public amenity projects with recreational significance. For example, throughout the 1980s and 1990s a range of initiatives in Britain have attempted to bring together government agencies, local authorities, local businesses and local people and voluntary groups in an attempt both to formulate plans and to provide the relevant resources. These have ranged from the Countryside Commission's Countryside Management projects and Groundwork Schemes to more recent initiatives such as the Parish Paths Partnership and Community Forests. Whether such developments have involved people attending meetings to try to resolve conflicts, commenting on various plans or proposals, or undertaking more physical tasks such as scrub clearance or footpath maintenance, they all require local people to invest their time. While it may be difficult to quantify precisely, such time represents a substantial economic contribution to sustainability.

CONCLUSION

The last few years have witnessed a new perspective on leisure and the environment. The desire to control and curtail leisure is much weaker and greater emphasis is now placed on promoting and expanding it. Such thinking results from a wider acceptance of the social, psychological and economic benefits of leisure and from a recognition that the impacts of leisure are perhaps not as serious or widespread as once thought. Such views are also the result, however, of a more positive attitude towards leisure planning and management linked to ideas about sustainability. One of the key aspects of sustainability is that of economics and the preceding pages have summarized various ways in which it is relevant in the context of sustainable leisure. Sections have included the role of the price mechanism both for valuing leisure resources and as a management tool, alternative methods of valuing resources where normal markets are not present, the economic impacts on local communities of leisure activity and, finally, the economic value of community involvement. While it would be wrong to be complacent, for there is still a long way to go before the principles of sustainability are fully developed into a coherent set of management actions, there is, nevertheless, cause for optimism. A deeper understanding of some of the key issues is clearly emerging and associated management initiatives are being tried and tested.

REFERENCES

Archer, B.H. (1973) *The Use and Abuses of Multipliers* Tourism Research Paper 1, Bangor: Economics Research Unit.

Archer, B.H. (1982) The Value of Multipliers and their Policy Implications, *Tourism Management* 3.

Bateman, I., Willis, K. and Garrod, G. (1993) *Consistency Between Contingent Valuation Estimates: A Comparison of Two Studies of UK National Parks,* Countryside Change Working Paper No. 40, University of Newcastle.

Bishop, R.C. and Heberlein, T. A. (1986) Does Contingent Valuation Work? In Cummings *et al.* (eds) *Valuing Environmental Goods: An Assessment of the Contingent Valuation Method* Totowa, NJ: Rowman and Allanfield.

Blacksell, M. (1981) A Comment on 'Charging for Countryside Recreation: A Review with Implications for Scotland', *Transactions of the Institute of British Geographers.* NS 6(4).

Bovaird, T., Tricker, M. and Stoakes, R. (1984) *Recreation Management and Pricing* Aldershot: Gower.

Breheny, M.J. (1992) Towards Sustainable Urban Development. In A.M. Mannion and S.R. Bowlby (eds) *Environmental Issues in the 1990s* Chichester: John Wiley & Sons.

Brookshire, D.S., Schulze, W.D., Thayer, M.A., d'Arge, R.C. *et al.*, (1982) Valuing Public Goods: A Comparison of Survey and Hedonic Approaches, *American Economic Review* 72(1).

Cater, E. and Goodall, B. (1992) Must Tourism Destroy its Resource Base. In A.M. Mannion and S.R. Bowlby (eds) *Environmental Issues in the 1990s* Chichester: John Wiley & Sons.

Clawson, M. and Knetsch, J. (1966) *Economics of Outdoor Recreation* Baltimore: Johns Hopkins.

Clewer, A., Pack, A. and Sinclair, T. (1992) Price Competitiveness and Inclusive Tour Holidays in European Cities. In P. Johnson and B. Thomas (eds) *Choice and Demand in Tourism* London: Mansell.

Countryside Commission (1993) *Position Statement on Sustainability and the English Countryside* Cheltenham: The Commission.

Countryside Commission (1995) *Sustainable Rural Tourism: Opportunities for Local Action* Cheltenham: The Commission.

CRRU/MVA (1992) *The Marston Vale Community Forest: Community Survey.* A report for the Marston Vale Community Forest Project, Conservation and Recreation Research Unit, Bedford College of Higher Education.

Cummings, R., Brookshire, D.S., Shultze, W.D. *et al.* (eds) (1986) *Valuing Environmental Goods: An Assessment of the Contingent Valuation Method* Totowa, NJ: Rowman & Allenfield.

Curry, N. (1994) *Countryside Recreation, Access and Land Use Planning* London: E & F Spon.

Department of the Environment (1994) *Sustainable Development: The UK Strategy* HMSO.

Garrod, G. and Willis, K. (1990) *Contingent Valuation Techniques: A Review of their Unbiasedness, Efficiency and Consistency* Countryside Change Working Paper No. 10, University of Newcastle.

Garrod, G and Willis, K. (1991) *The Hedonic Price Method and the Valuation of Countryside Characteristics* Countryside Change Working Paper No. 14, University of Newcastle.

Gilg, A. (1991) *Countryside Planning Policies for the 1990s* Oxford: CAB International.

Glyptis, S. (1991) *Countryside Recreation* Harlow: Longman.

Gratton, C. and Taylor, P. (1988) *Economics of Leisure Services Management* Harlow: Longman.

Gratton, C. and Taylor, P. (1992) *Sport and Recreation: An Economic Analysis* London: E & F Spon.

Harrison, P. (1991) *Countryside Recreation in a Changing Society* London: TMS Partnership Ltd.

International Union for the Conservation of Nature (1980) *The World Conservation Strategy* Gland, Switzerland: IUCN.

Knapman, B. and Stoeckl, N. (1995) Recreational User Fees: An Australian Empirical Investigation, *Tourism Economics* 1(1), pp 5–15.

The Local Government Management Board (1994a) *Local Agenda 21 Principle and Process: A Step by Step Guide* Luton: LGMB.

The Local Government Management Board (1994b) *Local Agenda 21 Roundtable Guidance: Sustainable Development in Rural Areas* Luton: LGMB.

Matthieson, A. and Wall, G. (1982) *Tourism: Economic, Physical and Social Impacts* Harlow: Longman.

McCallum, J.D. and Adams, J.G.L. (1980) Charging for Countryside Recreation, *Transaction of the Institute of British Geographers*. 5, pp 350–68.

Patmore, A. (1972) *Land and Leisure* Harmondsworth: Penguin.

Patmore, A. (1983) *Recreation and Resources* Oxford: Blackwell.

Pearce, D., Markandya, A. and Barbier, E.B. (1989) *Blueprint for a Green Economy* London: Earthscan Publications Ltd.

Pigram, J. (1983) *Outdoor Recreation Resource Management* London: Croom Helm.

Ryan, C. (1991) *Recreational Tourism: A Social Science Perspective* London: Routledge.

Schroeder, T. and Fessenmaier, D. (1983) Pricing Policies in Outdoor Recreation: A Study of State Park Financing in Oklahoma. In R. Lieber and D. Fessenmaier (eds) *Recreation Planning Management* London: E. & F.N. Spon.

Selman, P. (1996) *Local Sustainability* London: Paul Chapman Publishing.

Sinclair, T., Clewer, A. and Pack, A. (1990) Hedonic Prices and the Marketing of Package Holidays: The Case of Tourism Resorts in Malaga. In G. Ashworth and B. Goodall (eds) *Marketing Tourism Places* London: Routledge.

Sinclair, T. (1992) Tourism, Economic Development and the Environment: Problems and Policies. In C.P. Cooper and A. Lockwood (eds) *Progress in Tourism, Recreation and Hospitality Management* 4, London: Belhaven Press.

Smith, S.L.J. (1983) *Recreation Geography* Harlow: Longman.

Stephens, B. and Wallace, C. (1993) Recreation, Tourism and Leisure through the Lens of Economics. In H.C. Perkins and G. Cushman (eds) *Leisure, Recreation and Tourism* Aukland: Longman Paul.

Stevens, T. *et al.*, (1989) Pricing Policies for Public Day Use of Outdoor Recreation Facilities, *Journal of Environmental Management* 28, pp 43–52.

Vickerman, R.W. (1974) The Evaluation of Benefits from Recreational Projects, *Urban Studies* 11, pp 277–288.

Vickerman, R.W. (1983) The Contribution of Economics to the Study of Leisure: a Review, *Leisure Studies* 2, pp 345–364.

World Commission on Environment and Development (1987) *Our Common Future* Oxford: Oxford University Press.

Willis, K. and Garrod, G. (1991a) *Landscape Values: A Contingent Valuation Approach and Case Study of the Yorkshire Dales National Park* Countryside Change Working Paper No. 21, University of Newcastle.

Willis, K. and Garrod, G. (1991b) *Valuing Wildlife: the Benefits of Wildlife Trusts* Countryside Change Working Paper No. 46, University of Newcastle.

Willis, K., Beale, N., Calder, N. and Freer, D. (1993) *Paying for Heritage: What Price for Durham Cathedral?* Countryside Change Working Paper No. 43, University of Newcastle.

SECTION SIX
INTERNATIONALIZATION

14

Continuity or Change in the International Hotel Industry?

Dennis Nickson

This chapter offers insights into understanding how the international hotel industry has developed, and the prominent role ascribed to American hotel organizations within this development. Such understanding, it is argued, may underpin attempts to add to the theoretical knowledge base of hotel internationalization, an area which has been described as undertheorized.

INTRODUCTION

A key feature of much of the work on hotel internationalization is the description of the rise and fall of an American model of internationalization, which initially dominated the international hotel industry, but is now seemingly in decline. As Barge (1993) notes, 'the industry is currently in transition from the present era (that of management efficiency, practised and dominated by American companies) to one as yet still indistinct'. What has been identified is a rise and perceived fall in American influence of the international hotel industry. Understanding what this American model is and the implications of its supposed decline are essential to an appreciation of current trends in the management and organization of the international hospitality industry.

As Litteljohn and Roper (1991) note:

> The past 30 years have been a dynamic period in the internationalization of the hotel industry. This internationalization has been characterized by a growth of *American-type brands* (emphasis added), albeit that there has often been a change in the ownership of the parent company. These changes in ownership have given the industry a more truly international flavour, with Japanese, British, Scandinavian, Hong Kong and French operators.

This shift to a 'more truly international flavour' has led many to argue that the American influence in the international hotel industry has become increasingly marginalized (see, for example, Barge 1993; Go and Welch 1991; Guerrier 1993). Recently, Paul Slattery, Director of Research at Kleinwort Benson Securities, has argued that the US hotel companies play a minor role on the international hotel scene (Gordon, 1994). Moreover this marginalization has occurred at two levels. First, in terms of the dilution of American ownership of the major world players (Litteljohn and Roper, 1991; Roper *et al.*, 1995; Go and Pine, 1995); and second, and more importantly, it is also argued that there has been a decline in the American approach to hotel management, which had previously been thought of as supplying a 'best practice' model (Barge, 1993).

The key question is whether this marginalization is characterized by a complete shift away from this 'best practice' model, or whether it has been more concerned with mediating and reconfiguring it. In this sense Go and Welch (1991) recognize that the American multinationals did initially dominate the international hotel industry, and provide a 'best practice' hotel management model. This transfer of management practices, standardized hotel formulas and modern marketing expertise was achieved as US multinationals followed the flow of American businessmen and tourists to Europe in the post-war period (Go and Pine, 1995). Go and Welch (1991) argue though that over time European multinationals first adopted and then subsequently adapted these management techniques and in doing this added a 'European flavour', which has subsequently been re-exported back to the USA and elsewhere. There is also an increasing awareness of a distinctive style emerging from Asia Pacific, as exemplified by a more long-term orientation in the strategic approaches adopted by Asian multinational hospitality companies (Go and Pine, 1995). Such approaches are set to become increasingly important as foreign direct investment (FDI) from Asian multinationals continues to grow and indeed Parker (1995) speculates that by the year 2019 half of the top ten hotel chains will be Asian owned.

This mediation by host countries (and regions) of 'best practice' models is not new and is, for example, also recognized by Elger and Smith (1994) discussing the automobile industry. They recognize that FDI often meant that American and Japanese companies were 'carriers of new standards and repertories which shape, but also are reshaped by, the particular conditions within their host environment'. This notion of the export and re-export of management models would seem to be the key in assessing the American model of hotel internationalization. To do this, we need to ask what exactly was this influential American model? Why and to what extent has it declined? What has been the effect of such a decline? And finally, if there is a recently emergent 'new approach', is it significantly different and in what ways?

THE EARLY YEARS OF THE AMERICAN HOSPITALITY INDUSTRY

Barge (1993) argues that 'the international hotel industry has gone through at least two management eras in the last one hundred years, during which operating philosophies and values have been clearly shifted'. The first of those eras, which Barge characterizes as 'the European hotelier', saw the development of 'modern' hotel management beginning in Europe around the mid-1800s. This development was driven by the increased travel opportunities offered by the industrial revolution, which allowed the landed gentry to stay in the 'grand' hotels of Europe. These 'grand' hotels were independent and family-run and in time produced hoteliers like Caesar Ritz, a name synonymous with luxury (Guerrier, 1993). Soon these pleasures became available to the burgeoning middle class, who took advantage of the coming of mass tourism (Urry, 1990).

At the centre of this emerging hotel industry was Interlaken in Switzerland, which later allowed for the development of the Swiss paradigm of hotel management education, embodied most obviously at the Lausanne Hotel School (Guerrier, 1993). This Swiss system placed a greater emphasis on the operational side of the hotel as opposed to the business issues, which were likely to be the responsibility of a separate person, or the owner of the hotel. The operations manager was concerned wholly with the guests, and this style of management was personified in the label of 'hotelier' (Barge, 1993).

Barge (1993) asserts that in many respects the pattern of development of accommodation in North America was similar. The major difference lay in the rise of hotels which were much more commercially driven, and had less of a tradition of family ownership. Woods (1991) argues that there has been no real scholarly historical analysis of the American hospitality industry, and in that sense 'preferred management styles of the past remain a conundrum'. However he does suggest that Taylorism in particular might have influenced the industry, as hotels were expanding around the time scientific management was in vogue. Thus although there is no accepted definitive view on the nature of the early American hotel industry and preferred management styles, the sources which are available seem to describe a very particular approach.

Consequently the men who Barge (1993) calls the 'early hotel magnates' developed an approach of 'systematized management efficiency'. This was later further developed by the 'giants' such as Conrad Hilton and Kemmons Wilson (the founder of Holiday Inn), names synonymous with what Go and Pine (1995) call the 'hotel chain phenomenon'. Nickson (1996) in reviewing the auto/biographies of several famous hospitality entrepreneurs offers some interesting insights into the early years of the incipient American corporate hospitality sector which emerged with the success of the likes of Hilton, Holiday Inn and Marriott. Thus Conrad Hilton bought his first hotel, the Mobley, in 1919, describing it as 'a cross between a flophouse and a gold mine' (Hilton, 1957). In this hotel Hilton established many of the practices which would make him successful in later years, such as the maximization of space and the need to engender 'Esprit de Corps' in each of his hotels. These being the 'two principles that [were] basic in every one of [Hilton's] subsequent operations from Waco to Istanbul' (Hilton, 1957).

Kemmons Wilson developed the idea for Holiday Inns (the first one opened in 1952) after the experience of what he called 'the most miserable vacation of my life' (Lee, 1985). This was a result of the unpredictable quality and price of motels which Wilson had experienced. As a result of this Holiday Inn was based and developed on the notion of concept standardization, to ensure operational control and guest consistency. Wilson soon enjoyed success with his concept, and began selling franchises in 1955, which made rapid expansion possible and indeed Go and Pine (1995) suggest that the franchise strategy pursued by Holiday Inn 'is among the greatest success stories in US business'. In operating franchises Holiday Inn ensured that they applied strict operating standards and supplied franchisees with almost everything, apart from the land upon which the hotel would be built, in order to ensure there were 'No Surprises' (Luxenberg, 1985). This was the beginning of a chain then that was to make its reputation on universality, quality and consistency (Lundberg, 1969), and as Teare (1993) notes, 'the original Holiday Inn concept or "core brand" gained international recognition for setting and achieving consistently high standards in product design and service'.

A further sense of what this high degree of standardization meant can also be found in the biography of J. Willard Marriott, founder of the Marriott Corporation, which was initially built around fast food outlets. Although Woods (1991) rightly believes this essentially hagiographic 'official' biography and other auto/biographies on Kemmons Wilson and Conrad Hilton seek more to 'glorify their subjects than to provide their readers with a good understanding of their roles in the history of the industry', they do provide some useful and important insights (Nickson, 1996). In Marriott's case this can be seen in the descriptions of how the company expanded in its early years, and how such expansion was facilitated via strict standardization and recognizably Tayloristic principles.

O'Brien (1977), Marriott's biographer, describes how the early years of the company were characterized by rigid standardization and strict insistence on universal operating procedures via a small book 'setting forth company policies and the way he wanted things done with regard to operations, employee relations and customer relations, accounting practices and all other administrative procedures'.

This strict control survived as the company grew bigger and branched out into the hotel business and as Lee (1985) notes:

> Although he differed with his father on the speed of expansion, Bill Marriott (jnr) did not abandon his father's principle of central control of operations. As a result virtually every operating detail is specified in large manuals, and decision-making is centralized at the regional or corporate level.

One final description of the emergent management model of the American hospitality industry is outlined by Vallen *et al.* (1978), who elucidate very clearly how Ernest Henderson (the founder of Sheraton) meshed management efficiency with scientific management in the 1950s:

As recently as two or three decades ago the stature of a hotel man (sic) was often measured by the extent of his personal charm, the degree of his individual popularity and by the number of people he could greet by name. Today the axis is shifting. Maybe we are sacrificing some of the industry's picturesque glamour on the altar of hard facts, know-how and a familiarity with the tools of scientific management. But it is these latter that pay off when the monthly system or annual report is issued. A hunch sometimes pays off, but facts and knowledge pay bigger dividends. Modern competitive conditions demand a scientific approach' (Vallen *et al*, 1978, cited in Guerrier, 1993).

What has seemingly been described, albeit within the scope of relatively limited available evidence, is an emergent model of hotel management in the United States, based on management efficiency, standardization, consistency, and the systematic rigidities of scientific management. It was such a model which was to be exported by the newly internationalizing American companies.

THE AMERICAN MODEL OF HOTEL INTERNATIONALIZATION

Go and Welch (1991), Go *et al.* (1992), Go and Pine (1995), Guerrier (1993), and Litteljohn and Roper (1991), all describe (although usually briefly) an internationalization process which drew heavily on the certainties offered to the American hotel chains in their home country. Thus as these firms began to serve markets outside of their home country, they did so in a resolutely 'American way'. Go and Welch (1991) believe that international hotel operations began in the 1940s with the creation of Intercontinental by Pan American Airways in 1946. This was the start of the internationalization process, with American-branded organizations, which 'saw the potential of catering for international travelling markets, although inevitably they placed a heavy emphasis on their American parentage in the style of their operations and management' (Go *et al.*, 1992).

Essentially then, companies like Hilton, Holiday Inn, Intercontinental and Sheraton were concerned with creating a, usually up-market, home away from home for American travellers, particularly business travellers.[1] (Go and Pine, 1995; Nickson, 1996) This is clearly illustrated by a passage from Boorstin (1963) who cites Conrad Hilton describing the opening of the Istanbul Hilton in 1955:

When we flew into Istanbul for the opening with our guests from America, Carol Channing, Irene Dunne and her husband, Dr. Francis Griffin, Mona Freeman, Sonja Henie, Diana Lynn, Merle Oberon, Ann Miller, representatives of the American press . . . there is no question that we all felt the antiquity, romance and mystery of this ancient city . . . I felt this 'City of the Golden Horn' was a tremendous place to plant a little bit of America. Each of our hotels [Hilton announced at the opening] is a 'little America'.

As Boorstin (1963) wryly observes this nicely reflects 'the spirit of these ne⟨ hotels'. He also goes on to offer his own criticism of the hotels, which he staye⟨ in:

> the Caribe Hilton and Istanbul Hilton . . . are both models of American modernity and antisepsis. They are as indistinguishable in interior feelings and design as two planes of the American Airlines. Except for the views from the picture windows, you do not know where you are. You have the comforting feeling of not really being there. Even the measured admixture of carefully filtered local atmosphere proves that you are still in the USA (Boorstin, 1963).

This seemingly, though, was what the majority of American travellers were (an⟨ arguably still are) comfortable with in their search for the 'pseudo-even⟨ (Boorstin, 1963), where they can disregard the 'real' world outside. Urry (199⟨ describes this as the familiar American-style hotels providing an 'enviror⟨ mental bubble' which 'insulates the tourist from the strangeness of the hos⟨ environment', or more prosaically *'Instant America'* (Comfort, 1964, emphasis i⟨ original).

Similar criticisms, as those suggested by Boorstin (1963), can also be foun⟨ in the wittily acerbic travel writing of Irma Kurtz and Bill Bryson. Firstly Kurt⟨ (1994) nicely captures the typical Hilton customer in *The Great American Bu⟨ Ride*:

> When I was young and learning to survive on the roads of Europe, Hilton was anathema to me and other wanderers of my ilk. Hilton was the home away from home for all bourgeois American tourists; Hiltonites were be-cameraed and wore Bermuda shorts on the Champs-Elysèes. Our parents stayed at the Hilton when they came to check up on us.

Bryson (1992) also despairs at what can be considered the 'American chai⟨ phenomenon':

> as I reached the far end of Nieuwezijds Voorburgwal, there, where once a fine gabled house must have stood, squatted a new Holiday Inn. A building so ugly, so characterless, so *squat* (emphasis in original) that it stopped me in my tracks. Everything about it was cheap and unimaginative – the cardboard-box shape, the empty, staring windows, the acrylic canopy over the entrance, the green plastic signs, the wall-mounted video cameras peering at every passer-by. It looked like a parking ramp. *Not the tiniest effort had been made to give it any distinction* (emphasis added).[2]

As Segal-Horn (1994) argues though, this was apparently what the busines⟨ traveller and tourist valued and expected, and as a consequence 'internationa⟨ hotel chains (Hilton, Sheraton, Intercontinental) undertook to make the trav⟨ eller's experience of Tokyo, London, Milan or Sydney as similar as possible'.

This description of American hegemony, in both ownership and operating terms, in many respects should not be surprising given the economic strength, and political and cultural influence of America at that time (Waters, 1995). This substantiates Ferner's (1994) view that the capitalist economy in the hegemonic position will often provide 'methods of organizing production and work organization which establish standards of "best practice",' within which 'the MNC is itself the key mode of diffusion of such practices'. This view of America as the global leader was also articulated by Servan-Schrieber (1968) in the *American Challenge*. Citing that work, Peterson (1993) believes it demonstrated that 'America was at the leading edge', so consequently, 'countries hoping to compete with the United States would have to accommodate American ways of managing and American technology'. It is hardly surprising then that Dunning (1993) outlines an 'Imperialist' approach to internationalization undertaken generally by American business in the post-war period:

> The achievement of business goals was perceived to be a culture-free phenomenon. Such a perception led to ill-concealed attitudes and inappropriate behaviour. For example, it encouraged a parochial and ethnocentric approach by both American business and government. The argument in the 1950s and early 1960s seemed to run something like this. US industry in the US is efficient; its technology, management and marketing skills are the best in the world. Therefore when a US industry goes abroad, US products, skills and production methods should follow . . .From the perspective of a hegemonic power, any reaction of other firms or governments to what US firms or the US government did or did not do was assumed to be of negligible significance.

Similarly Barham and Rassam (1989) describe the 'American Way' as a role model which was based 'on strong central control from the USA'. The approach then to internationalization followed by the American companies in the hotel industry can be seen as an exemplar of this 'Amerocentric' approach. The 1950s and 1960s continued to see the success of a model which promised certainty and consistency for the guest, built around the exporting of a standardized product (Teare, 1991; Go and Pine, 1995), within the strict control of strong centralized management systems, usually via the 'manuals'. The 'manuals', as has already been noted, played an important part in ensuring consistency and common procedures, usually being characterized as Standard Operating Procedures, (SOPs).

Guerrier (1993) offers some interesting insights as to the nature of such SOPs by citing discussions from the participants of focus groups who were attempting to draw up a 'Corpus of Professional Knowledge' for the Hotel, Catering and Institutional Management Association (HCIMA) in 1977. These describe the American approach in more detail and suggest a recognition of the 'uniqueness' of the American approach by those working in the industry. For example, British managers recognized the influence of the tight control via systems and the 'manuals': 'the Americans seemed to have more business-like systems and revolutions occurred when they became involved in business. They

were brash and new and they had a lot more systems, the manuals'. There was
also a recognition of the more business oriented approach which seemed to
delineate a qualitatively different style to that characterized as the 'hotelier':

> the Americans were into profit accountability and it was earth shattering
> at the time. (American companies made us realize) that where you were
> making money was the rooms.

A NEW APPROACH?

This approach and its implications was also seemingly recognized by other companies explicitly seeking to delineate alternative styles to organization and
management. For example, Barham and Rassam (1989) cite an executive from
the French hospitality company Accor, who felt that:

> In the 1960s American companies came in very strongly and emphasized
> common procedures for overseas operations. We don't do that. Our flexibil-
> ity and ability to adapt to the local environment is the big difference that
> we have with the Americans. We are not imperialist.

Nonetheless by the 1970s American companies largely dominated the international hotel industry, both in ownership and operating terms. Dunning and
McQueen (1982) found that in 1978, eight of the top ten international hotel companies were owned by American based companies. They also revealed that of 81
transnational corporations operating 1,025 hotels and 270,646 rooms, 22 were
American operating 508 hotels and 56 per cent of internationally held rooms.
However the same survey also revealed that at least in ownership terms there
was some diversity, with French and UK domiciled companies accounting for
respectively 13 and 12 per cent of internationally held rooms. On the question
of the operating procedures, if anything there appears to have been even greater
standardization (Watson and Litteljohn, 1992). Certainly Crawford-Welch
(1992) is able to note:

> The 1970s saw the international hospitality industry passing through a
> period of intense standardization, whereby the provision of a single stan-
> dard product, operated almost independent of unique locational influences,
> was the norm.

This would seem to exemplify Ritzer's (1996) Weberian critique of an increasingly 'McDonaldized' society, which is based on efficiency, calculability, pre-
dictability and control. Indeed it may well have been the 'efficiency, speed, pre-
dictability and impersonality of McDonaldized systems and services' (Ritzer,
1996), which was so attractive to the American traveller. Ritzer cites the hotel
industry to argue that the emergence of highly standardized accommodation

developed by the Best Western Motel chain, the Holiday Inn chain and the Howard Johnson chain was the inevitable result of rationalization, scientific management and mass production assembly lines.

The 1980s, though, saw a 'significant growth in the international nature of the hotel industry' (Litteljohn and Roper, 1991), with the arrival of newer non-American companies, and the dilution of US ownership. Most obviously and spectacularly this is illustrated by the growth of the French-owned Accor group, which grew from 45 hotels in 1978 to 263 in 1989, a rise of 484 per cent, and in 1994 had 2,265 hotels all over the world (Accor Company Report, 1994). Equally three of the major American players were sold to British companies, thus the Holiday Corporation sold its interests in Holiday Inn to Bass, Hilton International is now controlled by Ladbrokes,[3] and Intercontinental was sold to Grand Metropolitan, who subsequently sold it on to Seibu Saison of Japan. The American-owned Ramada chain was also sold to the Hong Kong-based New World group.

The decline of American business hegemony is also recognized more generally with Rhinesmith (1993) offering a *Managers Guide to Globalization* to American managers, in order that they can compete in a changing world. For example, Marriott have utilized Rhinesmith in a consultancy role to advise them on how best to follow a 'globalization agenda' (Rhinesmith, 1991). The 'manifesto' contained in a *Manager's Guide to Globalization* puts forward his prescriptions for international organizations to act upon, in order to create managers with a 'global mindset'. This notion is underpinned by the recognition that 'we will need to realize that the new game will not be played or driven by the US business model' (Rhinesmith, 1993). Relinquishing their hegemonic position may be difficult to accept, though, for American organizations. Thus 'this shift in thinking will be particularly difficult for those American enterprises that have done little in the last 30 or 40 years to educate and train their managers to organize and manage the firms resources from a multi-cultural or international perspective' (Rhinesmith, 1993). Such a description would seem to be applicable very much to the approach adopted by American organizations in the international hotel industry prior to the 1980s.

Such a shift would however evidently be inevitable, and would appear to be occurring in the international hotel industry, given the rise of a more flexible European approach (Barham and Rassam, 1989), which increasingly would seem to be less concerned with such rigidity and standardization, and the aforementioned influence of groups emanating from Asia Pacific. A substantial number of writers have also argued that increasingly companies are beginning to recognize the limits of strict standardization (Barge, 1993; Go and Welch, 1991; Jones *et al.*, 1994; Roper and Brooks, 1996; Watson and Litteljohn, 1992). Thus it is claimed that the American model has reached the end of its effectiveness in the international hotel industry and as Barge (1993) concludes, 'The management systems which were so successful in providing consistency of experience and efficiency all over the world have contributed as much as they will be able', and thus he goes on to ask, 'What management philosophy will be necessary to succeed into the next century?' As a consequence 'the race for hegemony in the international market place is now on' (Go and Welch, 1991).[4]

CONCLUSIONS AND DISCUSSION

This chapter has endeavoured to address the largely historical nature of the work which has emerged on hotel internationalization, by attempting to describe the rise and fall of an American model of hotel internationalization. In this sense it can be seen to have some utility in offering a historical perspective to begin to understand current trends in the management and organization of the international hotel industry. Arguably then, the perceived rise and fall of an American model of internationalization has implications for a wide range of emergent work which seeks to broaden the theoretical and conceptual understanding of the international hotel industry. Thus the work of Burgess *et al.* (1995) on what makes international hotel groups 'successful'; Clifton and Gannon (1995) on deciphering the international orientation of the hospitality firm; Gannon and Jameson (1995) on international managers in hotel companies; Jones *et al.* (1994) on the transfer of corporate knowledge and culture across national boundaries; and Roper and Brooks (1996) on whether international hotel chains should standardize or differentiate their product either implicitly or explicitly, is reliant on a recognition of the dominance of American organizations of the early years of hotel internationalization. These works also rely on the effect of the suggested decline in such dominance as the industry becomes 'truly international'. In this way researchers can begin to address the question of whether this American model is totally redundant with the relative decline in American ownership and hegemony or whether – and in what ways – it may have been reconfigured in the management and organization of present day international hotel companies.

REFERENCES

Accor Annual Report (1994) *Accor – A World of Travel, Tourism and Services* Paris: Accor Corporate Communications.

Barge, P. (1993) International Management Contracts. In P. Jones and A. Pizam (eds) *The International Hospitality Industry – Organizational and Operational Issues* pp 117, 118, 125 London: Pitman.

Barham, K. and Rassam, C. (1989) *Shaping the Corporate Future – Leading Executives Share Their Vision and Strategies* pp 39, 43 London: Unwin Hyman.

Boorstin, D. (1963) *The Image or What Happened to the American Dream* p 106 London: Penguin.

Bryson, B. (1992) *Neither Here Nor There – Travels in Europe* p 90 New York: Avon Books.

Burgess, C., Hampton, A., Price, L. and Roper, A. (1995) International Hotel Groups: What Makes Them Successful? *International Journal of Contemporary Hospitality Management* 7(2/3) pp 74–80.

Clifton, W. and Gannon, J. (1995) Deciphering the International Orientation of the Hospitality Firm. Paper presented to the *Fourth Annual Council for Hospitality Management Education (CHME) Research Conference* Norwich.

Comfort, M. (1964) *Conrad N. Hilton – Hotelier* p 231 Minneapolis: T.S. Dennison and Company.

Crawford-Welch, S. (1992) Competitive Marketing Strategies in the International Hospitality Industry. In R. Teare and M. Olsen (eds) *International Hospitality Management – Corporate Strategy in Practice* p 98 London: Pitman.

Dunning, J. (1993) *The Globalization of Business* pp 9–10 London: Routledge.

Dunning, J. and McQueen, M. (1982) Multinational Corporations in the International Hotel Industry, *Annals of Tourism Research* 9, pp 69–90.

Elger, T. and Smith, C. (1994) Global Japanization? Convergence and Competition in the Organization of the Labour Process,. In T. Elger and C. Smith (eds) *Global Japanization? The Transnational Transformation of the Labour Process* p 45 London: Routledge.

Ferner, A. (1994) Multinational Companies and Human Resource Management: An overview of research issues, *Human Resource Management Journal* 4(2), pp 79–102.

Gannon, J. and Jameson, S. (1995) Identifying Patterns in the Human Resource Policies of Global Hotel Companies. Paper presented to *Human Resource Management in the Hospitality Industry Conference* London.

Gilpin, R. (1987) *The Political Economy of International Relations* p 256 Princeton: Princeton University Press.

Go, F. and Welch, P. (1991) *Competitive Strategies for the International Hotel Industry* p 81 London: Economist Intelligence Unit (Special Report no. 1180 March).

Go, F., Goulding, P. and Litteljohn, D. (1992) The International Hospitality Industry and Public Policy. In R. Teare and M. Olsen (eds) *International Hospitality Management – Corporate Strategy in Practice* p 53 London: Pitman

Go, F. and Pine, R. (1995) *Globalization Strategy in the Hotel Industry* pp 150 276, 278–81, 331–3 London: Routledge.

Gordon, R. (1994) US Hotels Losing the Global Race, *Caterer and Hotelkeeper* 30 June.

Guerrier, Y. (1993) The Development of a 'Corpus of Knowledge' for Hotel and Catering Managers. Paper presented to the *11th European Group of Organization Studies (EGOS) Colloquium* pp 5, 7 Paris.

Harzing, A. and Van Russeyveldt, H. (1995) *International Human Resource Management* London: Sage.

Hilton, C. (1957) *Be My Guest* pp 109, 113 Englewood Cliffs NJ: Prentice-Hall.

Hirst, M. (1992) Creating a Service Driven Culture Globally, *International Journal of Contemporary Hospitality Management* 4(1), pp i–iv.

Jones, C., Nickson, D. and Taylor, G. (1994) Ways of the World: Managing Culture in International Hotel Chains. In A. Seaton, C. Jenkins, R. Wood P. Dieke, M. Bennett, R. MacLellan, and R. Smith (eds) *Tourism: The State of the Art* Chichester: John Wiley and Sons.

Jones, P. and Pizam, A. (eds) (1993) *The International Hospitality Industry Organizational and Operational Issues* London: Pitman Publishing.

King, I. (1996) Room for a Hotel Deal as Ladbroke and Hilton Talk, *Guardian Newspaper* 30 April, p 18.

Kurtz, I. (1994) *The Great American Bus Ride* pp 153–4 London: Fourth Estate

Lee, D. (1985) How They Started: The Growth of Four Hotel Giants, *Cornell Hotel and Restaurant Administration Quarterly* May, pp 22–32.

Litteljohn, D. and Roper, A. (1991) Changes in International Hotel Companies

Strategies. In R. Teare and A. Boer (eds) *Strategic Hospitality Management – Theory and Practice for the 1990s* pp 200, 210 London: Cassell.

Lundberg, D. (1969) The Key to Marketing Success Might Well be Defined as Holiday Inns of America, *Cornell Hotel and Restaurant Administration Quarterly* 9(4), pp 100–103.

Luxenberg, S. (1985) *Roadside Empires – How the Chains Franchised America* New York: Viking Penguin.

Nickson, D. (1996) Colourful Stories or Historical Insight? A Review of the Auto/Biographies of Charles Forte, Conrad Hilton, J.W. Marriott and Kemmons Wilson, *Fifth Annual Council for Hospitality Management Education (CHME) Hospitality Research Conference Papers* pp 182–5 Nottingham: The Commercial Centre, Nottingham Trent University.

O'Brien, R. (1977) *Marriott: The J Willard Marriott Story* pp 168–9 Salt Lake City: Desert Book Company.

Parker, A. (1995) Times of Change, *Hospitality* February/March, pp 25–27.

Peterson, R. (1993) Future Directions in International Comparative Management Research. In D. Wong-Reiger and F. Reiger (eds) *International Management Research – Looking to the Future* p 14 Berlin: De Gruyter.

Rhinesmith, S. (1991) Going Global From the Inside Out, *Training and Development* 45, pp 42–47.

Rhinesmith, S. (1993) *A Managers Guide to Globalization – Six Keys to Success in a Changing World* pp 4, 6 American Society for Training and Development.

Ritzer, G. (1996) *The McDonaldization of Society: An Investigation into the Changing Character of Contemporary Social Life – Revised Edition* p 178 London: Pine Forge Press.

Roper, A., Burgess, C., Hampton, A. and Price, L. (1995) Successful International Hotel Groups: Measuring Them and Making Them. Paper presented to the *1995 Annual CHRIE Conference* p 4 Nashville.

Roper, A. and Brooks, M. (1996) 'To Standardize or not to Standardize? Marketing International Hotel Groups'. *Fifth Annual Council for Hospitality Management Education (CHME) Hospitality Research Conference Papers*. Nottingham: The Commercial Centre, Nottingham Trent University.

Segal-Horn, S. (1994) Are Services Industries Going Global?. In C. Armistead (ed.) *The Future of Service Management* p 53 London: Kogan Page.

Servan-Schreiber, J-J. (1968) *The American Challenge* London: Hamish Hamilton.

Teare, R. (1991) Developing Hotels in Europe: Some Reflections on Progress and Prospects, *International Journal of Contemporary Hospitality Management* 3(4), pp 55–59.

Teare, R. (1993) Designing a Contemporary Hotel Service Culture, *International Journal of Service Industry Management* 4(2), pp 63–73.

Urry, J. (1990) *The Tourist Gaze* p 7 London: Sage

Vallen, J., Abbey, J. and Sapienza, D. (1978) *The Art and Science of Managing Hotels / Restaurants / Institutions* (2nd edn) p 30 New Jersey: Hayden.

Waters, M. (1995) *Globalization* p 78 London: Routledge.

Watson, S. and Litteljohn, D. (1992) Multi-and Transnational Firms: The Impact of Expansion on Corporate Strategies. In R. Teare and M. Olsen (eds) *International Hospitality Management – Corporate Strategy in Practice* London: Pitman.

Woods, R. (1991) Hospitality History: Who Wrote What About When, *Cornell Hotel and Restaurant Administration Quarterly* August, pp 89–95.

NOTES

Indeed this is something which was noted by Michael Hirst, then the chairman and chief Executive Officer of Hilton International, in his recognition that, 'once, the image of a global hotel chain was one that offered a standardized ideal of American service (principally for American travellers) – a home away from home' (1992). It was the recognition of the limits of standardization, which is seen as being no longer appropriate, which lies at the heart of Hilton International's attempts to create 'a Service-driven culture Globally'. An example of this is Hilton International's pioneering Japanese service brand, Wa No Kutsurogi (see Teare, 1993).

The insistence on rigid standardization by Holiday Inn did have its limits. Thus despite the success of the brand in pursuing such a policy, Go and Pine (1995) note how the company's obsession with standardization, combined with the psychological momentum of the founder, stifled change'. For example, Luxenberg (1985) suggests that 'the standard American brick facades seemed drab to French and Belgian customers used to variety and regional nuances' and consequently Holiday Inn lost $28 million between 1971 to 1975 as a result of their failure to make any concessions to local tastes or ways of operating.

Interestingly, there has been some recent speculation as to whether Ladbroke will complete the acquisition of the Hilton name by purchasing, or at least doing a deal with Hilton Hotels Corporation (HHC), which owns the Hilton Hotel brand within the United States. King (1996) suggests that if this were to occur 'there is little doubt that a combined Hilton brand, operating globally, would be one of the mightiest in the world'.

The 'race for hegemony' in the international hotel industry is also one which is being conducted more generally in the wider global business environment (Waters, 1995; Harzing and Van Russeyveldt, 1995). In part this also demonstrates the greater internationalization of multinational companies generally and in particular the rise of multinational enterprises originating in developing societies such as the 'Asian Dragons'. This reflects the recognition that 'the day is passed when corporations of the United States and a few other developed countries could operate freely in and even dominate the host economies and when foreign direct investment meant the ownership of wholly owned subsidiaries' (Gilpin, 1987 cited in Waters, 1995).

15

Hotels Chains and their Strategic Appraisal

David Litteljohn

In reviewing the changes faced by hotel chains in the next ten years, the importance of taking a resource-based view, which emphasizes the importance of core functions and core competencies, is argued. The need to apply these sensitively to both hard and soft areas of hotel chain operations is argued, while at the same time recognizing fully the nature of the chain – its methods of ownership / operation and the type of areas in which it locates.

INTRODUCTION

Hospitality operations and their managers must address changes in their environments. This discussion concentrates on the development of methods for the strategic analysis of hotel chains. For the purpose of this chapter a hotel chain is a group of hotels operating in different locations. Units may or may not be branded and chain units may be operating at several different market levels/operation specifications. Attention is given to chains where there is a bond of ownership and operation rather than those which may be a essentially an aid to joint marketing and/or purchasing arrangements.

It is here assumed that the analysis of competitive advantage of chains will become more important. It is held that hotel chain characteristics, including the multi-site nature of their organization, inject a high element of complexity into hotel operations and analysis. By drawing on the work of researchers and by highlighting the nature of challenges which will emerge in the medium term, factors to help in this type of analysis are identified.

BACKGROUND

The period of the early 1990s has seen changes in the structure of the global hotel industry. Take-overs, for example Accor/Wagon Lit in France and Belgium and Granada/Forte in Europe, have provided changes in attitudes to running hotel chains; 'fire sales' of properties caused by tourism down-turns in the early part of the decade play an influence on the property market even after 1995 – for example, Queens Moat House Hotels in the UK were still rationalizing their portfolio in 1996.

Reorganization by de-layering hierarchies and by a sharpening of market focus has occurred concurrently with a need to deal with the opportunities and threats posed by the development of new information technologies. These have the potential to increase both organizational efficiency (e.g. property management systems) and organizational effectiveness (e.g. to increase occupancies and room rates achieved by the use of reservation/global distribution systems and yield management).

All these trends have coincided with a search for growth in size and market share by chains, causing some commentators to question whether a role for the independent hotel remains a real option for the future (Slattery, 1992).

THE HOTEL CHAIN AS A SYSTEM

Any strategic analysis must start with an adequate understanding of the type of organization being researched. In order to analyse a hotel chain holistically it is useful to visualize it as a system of interlocking resources and processes. A relatively simple approach in achieving this is through the application of general systems theory which sees an organization as having three main levels of activity: core functions; a co-ordination level; and an institutional level which co-aligns the organization with the changes in its environments. As applied to hotels the model below puts four basic functions at the core level of the organization. Particular functions chosen reflect the nature of hotel chain operations.

At any one time managers will have to ensure that resources within the organization are harnessed effectively so that the core functions are co-ordinated effectively: e.g. that customers are satisfied and that the operation is financially sound. Managers also have to ensure that the organization is best placed to take into account future developments which cover a spectrum of activities from staffing to customer issues. In other words, management must sustain current effectiveness and plan for future success. The four core functions shown in Figure 15.1 are market skills, operations skills, inventory skills and capital management.

Market skills spring from dealing with complex demand patterns. While at a general level all hotels must ensure that they respond to social and economic changes which occur at national and, in the case of international travel markets, at global levels, other factors require attention. A hotel room is often part of a larger purchase which at its simplest could be differentiated as business or leisure tourism. Different market segments may react differently to any given

change in the general environment. Making strategic sense of these characteristics in a chain where locations have diverse 'micro-environments' and
contrasting market mixes creates both problems and opportunities in chain
management.

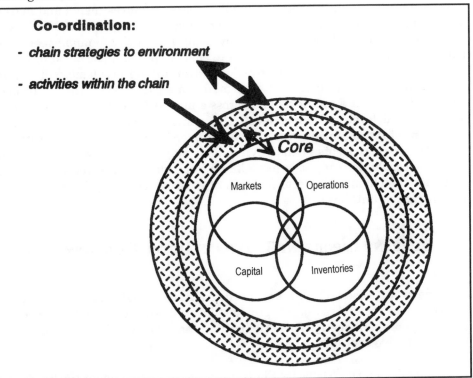

Figure 15.1: The management mix in hotel chain operations

Operation skills come from the need to manage service provision consistently and efficiently achieved throughout a multi-site organization. Chains
have to ensure that an optimum mix of services are provided by market and performance criteria. While an operational focus acknowledges units as the front
line in the delivery of labour intensive service, it includes attention to recruitment, staff development, product testing, operations planning and monitoring,
communication and reporting systems and other functional areas.

Complexities arising in the management of inventories spring from the need
to sell a perishable inventory (rooms per night) from the present well into the
future. Market mix and room rate planning may cover a time span for up to two
or three years. Effects of poor decisions may be drastic, yet the forecasting problem is formidable. Chains may also face internal tensions in yield decisions. For
example, while there are strong reasons for instituting firm-wide policies (e.g.
prices for some market segments), units may feel that their micro-environments
require a different approach for success.

Capital management complexities derive from the need to ensure an effec‑
ive distribution of a chain's capital assets. Hotel operations are often seen
capital intensive, yet present distinctive investment features which create pro
lems of identity for investors. For example, a fund manager may experience d
ficulties in differentiating between hotels as property investments and mark
operations (see, for example, Pannel Kerr Forster Associates, 1989). Chaiı
may respond to this type of problem by using franchising, management co
tracting, leasehold and other strategies to ensure optimum use of capital.

The four areas as described invariably overlap and problems will requi
solutions which take into account aspects from more than one of them. The nec
for co‑ordination at a unit level and across a multi-site organization is handlc
at the second level and upper level. The systems approach also stresses c
alignment of the organization to the environment at the third, or institutiona
level. However, concepts of the environment may well differ according to tł
locus of decision making: it is more likely to be global if the decision is beiı
made for the chain while local features of environments may be given high
prominence at unit levels.

CURRENT IMPORTANT TRENDS IN HOTEL ENVIRONMENTS

The views of Olsen (1995) are used as a base. His position with th
International Hotel Association provides an authority which reflects a broa
knowledge of the industry. This brief outline can in no way, however, be held t
be a exhaustive exposition of his views:

(1):What Olsen terms 'Capacity Control' (earlier discussed under the heading c
inventories) will be significantly affected through availability and use of infor
mation super-highways. It is evident that because of increasing costs in infor
mation technology software development scale of provision will play an impor
tant part in their future characteristics and operating costs/charges. Impact
here are likely lead to changes in the structure of travel distribution networks
Future roles of members of the distribution system will evolve as communica
tions technology moves forward – e.g. several US airlines have already limite
the amount of commission on domestic travel that travel agents can make.

The same electronic and telecommunications technology will directly impac
on the internal workings of the organization. 'As hotel chains adjust to highe
costs of labour and higher costs of capital, the developing technologies wil
become more central to successful performance' (Olsen, 1995). Decision suppor
systems – property management, yield management, database marketing an
management accounting systems will become more integral to day-to-day man
agement.

Technology also has great potential in customer service support. Foı
example, there are already examples of the 'electronic concierge' (Olsen's term

or destination information systems. With developments of existing digital systems and enhancements in newer applications like virtual reality, systems will become more user-friendly and customized to individual needs.

(2):Levels of capital available for investment in hotels will remain low. Thus, it can be assumed that there will be intense competition for whatever capital is available. This will result in higher demands on business to obtain the most productive use of assets. In addition, the international mobility of capital allows flows of capital to develop in response to perceived investment attractiveness. Thus quality projects in developing countries may not necessarily be at a disadvantage in gaining capital. Indeed, with economic policies in many developed economies aimed at keeping inflation low, investment gains based on increasing property values will be lowered, possibly placing these regions at a competitive disadvantage.

Governments, traditionally a source of hotel development capital in emerging tourism destinations in the 1960s to 1980s may well deploy cash from hotel support to fund competing projects. An example of this is the decision reported in July 1996 of Moscow's city government to put 200 hotels on the market with a price of at least \$1 billion (Daneshkhu and Thornhill, 1996). Within this competitive investment scenario it is not difficult to foresee a more influential role for professional investors with demands for returns to those comparable in other industries. However, the appeal of the industry will still be a powerful magnet to corporate fund holders seeking diversification and rich (possibly oil rich) individuals and organizations.

Olsen's (1995) views emphasize the importance of outside pressures in the business environment. Relating these directly to the skills needed, Olsen (1995) feels that this creates a need for 'boundary spanners' – managers whose expertize bridges over specialisms and who can provide solutions which can integrate ideas across different professional areas. Bearing in mind the pace of change in the environment, managers will increasingly have to be proactive rather than reactive to changes which will effect their markets, work force and organization.

HOTEL CHAINS AND THEIR RESOURCES: STRATEGIC APPLICATIONS

This will present a brief review of three main ways of approaching the resources and operating features of hotels: what are termed the traditional resource-based view, the contemporary resource-based view and the eclectic approach.

The Traditional Resource-based View

Much drive and hotel success is built on entrepreneurial energy and individuality. For example, Charles Forte (1987), at the time founder of the largest UK hospitality company, confirmed a need for customization and specializatio built up from his experience: 'We try to run our hotels not as a chain, bu as . . . individual units, with centralized services and individualistic manage ment . . . we must remain artisans . . . in total control at all levels of our oper ation, while making the greatest possible use of the skills of the accountant financier, lawyer and any other relevant specialist'. The role of non-operation areas is not ignored: rather Forte emphasizes the centrality of craft resource and unit management. This view also sees a very close link between unit loca tion and success: it is commonly held that this is the most important determi nant of a unit's success. Thus chain performance is viewed mainly as an aggre gation of the performance of individual hotels, with the role of th leader/founder central in setting organizational style and providing co ordination and co-alignment elements. Leadership provides not only the visio for the business, but also the entrepreneurial drive necessary to achieve satis factory performance. The role of the founder as leader is often essential; th organization frequently has his name (e.g. Forte, Hilton, Marriott) and leader ship is exercised paternalistically (see, for example, Nickson, 1996 and Forte 1987).

It is possible to conceptualize this approach as a system where established units co-ordinate resources at local levels while corporate managers concentrate on developing new operations in the 'right' locations, as well as ensuring tha aggregate unit performance meets the objectives set for the chain. Undoubtedly scale can develop some advantages (for example the use of specialists may become more cost effective) – however, potential synergistic advantages of chain operation are perceived as less important than the ability of units to meet the unique needs of their locations. The approach provides an attractive logic in analysing hotel chain strategy: firms should concentrate on quality through delivering appropriate craft standards and high levels of local market aware ness.

However, there are dangers in over-reliance of this traditional resource based approach. A strategy of decentralization of some functions to unit level combined with a centralized policy of standards control may produce a system with resource allocation and management tensions between the centre and the units. It could be further argued that this type of resource-based view ignores fundamental elements of change:

- the role of the founder-leader is limited to smaller organizations. Many hospitality organizations have outgrown the period when the founder played a pivotal role; while this type of leadership style may be important for many smaller organizations, leaders will need to ensure that top management adapts to implement new management systems and philosophies as the chain expands;
- consequences of the information society have major implications for internal management within the organization (e.g. storing, order ing and organizing data and channelling information flows) as well as communications with suppliers and customers outside the organization;

- capital markets increasingly place new demands on chains, and large chains may inevitably be substantial procurers of capital. This will often require equity. Shareholders place significant demands on the management of finance within a company. Managers will have to inspire confidence in terms of capital value through ensuring optimum share prices and confidence of future projects and operations;
- hotel markets are larger and more globally dispersed than they were twenty years ago. Many markets are now at a stage of maturity, though market stages and trends may be unlike in different regions of the world. As chains grow so competition at a corporate level will be overlaid to that of local competition.

These changes point towards the need to build on the traditional resource-based view. Essentially the strengths that can be built up around a strong vision and strict control need to accommodate factors such as anticipating market trends, being flexible to respond to unforeseen contingencies and creating teams who can co-ordinate and implement change. This does not mean that all aspects of that model should be forgotten: for example, Forte's desire for individualism at a local level can be incorporated into a view which recognizes that a service chain cannot be managed with the same philosophy and strategies as large centralized manufacturing organizations.

Contemporary Resource-based Views

Newer approaches to resource appraisal place emphasis on core competencies of an organization. Like the traditional approach the contemporary resource-based view develops an industry/organization context for appraising firm resources. Prahalad and Hamel (1990) see core competencies as the collective learning of the organization in the delivery and co-ordination of value. Over time, knowledge and skills may become diffused within the organization allowing strong bonds to develop across organizational boundaries. This process can provide the organization with a distinctive capability not necessarily shared by competitors. Two studies following contemporary resource-based approaches are examined here.

The first case involves a study of 251 managers in 44 hotel management teams (in hotels of at least 160 rooms) in Utah and north-eastern states of the USA by Roberts and Shea (1996). By concluding that core hotel (chain) competencies could be built around seven factors, this research stresses relatively 'hard' functional capabilities in hotel chains. They are:

- Intangible assets comprising: reputation; loyalty (both employee and customer); employee commitment;
- Tangible Assets: asset items such as computer systems databases; real estate; brand;

- Human Resource Management: training; recruiting; sta
  motivation;
- Sales: sales and marketing; reservation processing;
- Architectural design;
- Pricing;
- Marketing Planning: advertising; market research; financi
  planning.

This approach identifies a wider range of areas implicit in the tradition
resource-based model, while at the same time remaining remarkably faithful t
its spirit.

In addition, the authors differentiate between core *requirements* and cor
competencies. Core requirements refer to factors which are necessary for su
cessful operation but do not necessarily confer competitive advantage on th
chain. Thus (computerized) yield management systems which, at the time of th
survey, had been broadly implemented across the industry no longer provided
distinct advantage.

The notion of 'requirement' rather than 'competence' can be extended t
many other factors used in strategic analysis, though only one will be chose
here – that of location, often given such a pre-eminent status. In this way loca
tion can be viewed as a requirement rather than a competence: while not hav
ing a 'good' location does not augur well for success, having a good location doe
not, in itself, guarantee success. This is an important distinction, particularl
in the conditions of a mature industry where rivalry for market share provide
a competitive environment no matter how good the location. Roberts and She
also stress many individual unit values: thus they give as their example of cor
competencies the development of the provision of high service quality *within*
single unit rather than *across* a chain organization.

The second case uses the contemporary resource-based approach to examin
the operation of one particular organization – the Novotel chain of the Frenc
hospitality conglomerate Accor. Segal-Horn (1995) is able to show how th
transformation of organization structures and procedures allows not only for de
layering, but also for a change in organizational relationships between head
office and units in such a way as to allow information flows and collaboratior
across and between management levels throughout the organization. A com
mand and control type approach to ensuring quality was dismantled in favou
for sets of inter-functional and General Management groups among units with
similar characteristics (e.g. airport hotels) across national boundaries. The
analysis highlights the need for strategic interpretations of hotel chains to view
the organization as a series of (interlocking) networks. Thus softer areas o
organizational design, communication, innovation are seen to be able to be
'managed' and to produce direct operational benefits. The complexity of multi-
site, multi-market organizations is given full attention in this work.

Taken together, these two cases fit well with works on service chains, such
as that of Fitzsimmons and Fitzsimmons (1994), who examine growth strategies

of service organizations. They differentiate between single site and multi-site service organizations and contrast management requirements in organizations that provide a range of services (diversified organizations) as against those which provide a single service (focused organizations). Chain organizations, whether a focused or a diversified network (and it could be argued that hotel chains might possess the characteristics of either or both) require their specialist management skills or competencies. Sophisticated communication and control systems and a rationalized and consistently delivered service concept are especially important in the case of a focused service network or, in the case of diversified networks, carefully developed core and branding strategies.

The work of Olsen (1989) further supports this type of resource-based analysis. He points to three structural elements in organization design which should be analysed: formalization – the extent of procedures within the organization; centralization – the arrangements of power and control within the organization; and, third, the nature of specialization within the firm. 'For an organization to compete in a mature and competitive environment over the long range it must be able to match these structural variables with activities and trends occurring in the environment' (Olsen, 1989).

The two main studies cited here and other work mentioned point to the value of developing contemporary resource-based views in appraising strategy. Internal and external factors have been identified as being of importance in delivering success. However, developing the approach further must take into account the full range of internal and external contributors to chain success. In coming to this point one other approach of identifying key success is discussed.

The Eclectic Approach to Strategic Analysis and Competitive Advantage

This approach is broader than the resource-based view, while encompassing many similar features. It has been applied to the international hotel industry by Dunning since the early 1980s: the work used here relates to Dunning and Kundu (1995) which examined perceptions of chain executives on the significance of a range of factors to the success of their operations. Results come from a sample of 34 hotel multinational hotel chains operating in thirteen countries, with foreign holdings accounting for 57 per cent of capacity. Locations for expansion were categorized as being either developed or developing countries.

The eclectic paradigm takes into account a chain's resource base or ownership factors (O) and the characteristics of the location (L) into which expansion is planned. The approach also seeks to explain what type of expansion or investment method (I) will be used in any given location: for example, whether by direct investment or by management contracting or franchising. As greatest levels of control over the use and upgrading of resources, capabilities and markets are achieved through the ownership of a substantial equity stake, the approach assumes that this will normally be the preferred method of expansion though

outside conditions may influence the chain to adopt different strategies.
Ownership specific advantages (O) can be subdivided as follows:

(i)   Asset specific (OA) which include the size of the firm; its international experience; its trade mark and brand image; the extent and scope of training programmes; access to referral and reservation systems; and knowledge of customer tastes and requirements;

(ii) Transaction specific (OT) advantages are the competitive advantages which stem from common control of separate but interrelated assets and reflect the perceived success of the chain in co ordinating its domestic and foreign hotel operations. These include the gains which may arise from the chain's multinationality in what may be termed *sequential* advantages (Kogut, 1983). Specifically: size and structure of the home industry; economies of scope and joint supply; economies of scale.

Under location characteristics (L) are grouped the following factors: economic features of the country into which development is planned; particular characteristics of a city location in which development is taking place; opportunities in tourist markets to that location; the state of infrastructure; the proximity of the location to the chain's existing operations; the policies of the host government to foreign direct investment; the overall business stability of the location.

It is not within the scope of this chapter to make a detailed analysis of Dunning and Kundu's work; in many respects their approach is similar to the resource-based view. They do, however, bring out location specific advantages while at the same time making very explicit the mode of expansion to any strategic analysis. This latter aspect is included in the resource-based approach – however, as implemented in Roberts and Shea (1996), while reference is made to an aspect like franchising skills in its own right this type of variable is given specific treatment in the eclectic approach. As an example, variables associated with different methods of international expansion are shown in Table 15.1. Ratings are given for a list of advantages conferred by different forms of ownership/operating. In this case data refers to locations in developed economies.

The differences apparent in the ranking and the weighting of the variable by the different ownership/operation method confirms that in any strategic analysis the resource-based view of strengths and weaknesses must take the corporate structure fully into account in any appraisal of a chain, its competencies and its goals.

The resource-based view, therefore, can be applied to the development of hotel chains. Given the addition of the eclectic approach, attention should also be paid to ownership/operation variables and location differences. To illustrate the importance of this conclusion one aspect is examined below: the extent of large chains and difference in ownership/operation strategies in different regions.

Advantages	Fully Owned	Partly Owned	Franchised	Management Contract
Ensure adequate quality control (OA)	4.73	3.96	3.80	4.35
Experience in international business (OA)	3.62	3.70	3.60	3.54
Co-ordinate capabilities of parent company (OT)	4.38	4.22	3.20	3.58
Activities of parent company (OT)	4.19	3.58	3.20	3.58
Minimize negotiation and transaction costs (OT)	3.81	3.65	3.90	3.31
Exploit economies of scope (OT)	4.00	3.29	3.20	3.15
Economic and financial condition of host country (L)	4.00	3.96	3.20	3.50
Host country policy towards FDI (L)	4.15	4.04	2.80	3.50
Strength of home currency and interest rates (L)	3.62	3.61	3.40	3.08
Sample	n = 26	n = 24	n = 10	n = 26

Note: the closer to five, the more importance ascribed to the given variable: figure given refers to averaged Likert scale response.

Source: John H. Dunning and Sumot K. Kundu (1995)

Table 15.1: Ratings of international advantages perceived by parent hotels in developed countries

CURRENT TRENDS IN HOTEL CHAIN SIZE
AND EXPANSION METHODS

To obtain a view on the competitive position of the hotel industry it is useful examine industry structure. Essentially a fragmented industry, hotel cha have grown considerably, both by their size (in terms of rooms) and by the nu ber of chains. This analysis deals only with global figures on size and meth of expansion/operation. Figures come from the Kleinwort Benson Hot Database (Slattery *et al.* 1996). The database contains publicly quoted chai excluding private chains and those which are government held. In all 62 co panies which have publicly traded shares are covered; 34 of these compan have hotel holdings of over 1,000 rooms.

Table 15.2 shows those companies which have over 1000 rooms. Named a the holding companies which may or may not be the name of the chain(s) th operate. For example, Accor and Hospitality Franchise Systems each run s eral chains; Ladbroke's own Hilton International, while other companies n operate, through franchise, hotels of another company – for example Whitbre franchises Marriott hotels in the UK.

In total these 34 companies control 2.15 million rooms globally. This is s stantial, even if it represents only a small proportion of hotel operators. Cha in the sample, however, exhibit great differences in size. Eleven chains poss from 1,001 to 5,000 rooms; eight from 5,001 to 10,000 rooms; two from 10,001 15,000 rooms. Only one falls in the 15,001 to 20,000 room category and th are none at all in the 20,001 to 25,000 group. Of the remaining companies have up to 100,000 rooms, three of which reflect the earliest wave of hotel int nationalization in the early 1950s: Hilton is now split between Hilton Hot Corporation of the USA and Hilton International owned by Ladbrokes of the l and Intercontinental owned by Seibu Saison from Japan. At nearly 140,0 rooms another early USA chain to internationalize, Sheraton (now an ITT ho brand), is the next largest group. This leaves five companies: three of these i into a category of between 200,001 and 300,000 rooms – Marriott, Accor a Manor Care. The remaining two are Bass (Holiday Inn) at 377,661 rooms a Hotel Franchise Systems at 434,268 rooms. In 1995 Hotel Franchise Syste ran the following chains: Days Inn of America; Howard Johnson; Knig Franchise; Park Inns International; Ramada Inns, Limited and Plaza Hot Super 8 Motels; Villager Lodge; Wingate Inns. These examples show both t complexities inherent in large hotel chains and one strategy of dealing w complexity – that is, operating different brands at different market levels.

Geographically, the room stock operated by these chains is predominan located in the Americas – mainly USA and Canada – with 1,558,064 rooms 72.4 per cent of the total covered. On the same basis Europe has 19.0 per ce Asia and the rest of the world 4.3 per cent each. Not unnaturally most of chains have a strong American flavour: even chains now owned by UK com nies (e.g. Holiday Inn/Bass and Hilton International/Ladbroke) have a No American pedigree.

Owner	Rooms by defined regions						
Company	Total Europe	USA	Rest of Am'cas	Total Am'cas	Asia	Rest of World	Total
Accor	128501	87659	6167	93826	8099	17737	248163
Bass	22395	298555	24621	323176	18832	13258	377661
Brierley	13841						13841
Cofir	5995						5995
Commonwealth Hospitality			2271	2271			2271
Dusit Thani (1)	2151	618	634	1252	1614	323	5340
Eurodisney	5211						5211
Four Seasons	325	5673	1910	7583	3753	1583	13244
Friendly	3324						3324
Granada (2)	43985	2847	4250	7097	3272	6878	61232
Greenalls	4521	285		285			4806
HHC (3)	620	89802	302	90104	513	1369	92606
Hospitality Fran. Systems	178	408180	24876	433056	389	645	434268
ITT (4)	15995	81743	13269	95012	13513	15214	139734
Jolly	6322	246		246			6568
Jurys	1884						1884
Ladbroke (5)	19446	1213	7822	9035	11125	11142	50748
Lonrho	2278	917	3729	4646		940	7864
Manor Care	16047	223321	20796	244117	3563	3254	266981
Marriott	3751	202210	5600	207810	4356	3862	219779
Mandarin Oriental		523		523	4106		4629
Movenpick	3291				427	2788	6506
Queens Moat	19249						19249
Rank	4401	177		177			4578
Regal Hotels	1073						1073
Renaissance	10105	16338	6791	23129	10572	3737	47543
Ryan	1059						1059
Scottish and Newcastle	1466						1466
Sea Containers	346	439	223	662		399	1407
Seibu Saison (6)	17731	7314	6743	14057	7452	8660	47900
Societe du Louvre	34870						34870
Stakis	5162						5162
Vaux	4450						4450
Whitbread	9857						9857
Total	409830	1428060	130004	1558064	91586	91789	2151269

Notes
(1) This includes Kempinski holdings, which were taken over by Dusit Thani in 1995;
(2) Includes Forte (taken over early 1996);
(3) HHC = Hilton Hotels Corporation, USA;
(4) ITT own Sheraton;
(5) Ladbroke own Hilton International;
(6) Seibu Saison own Intercontinental Hotels

Source: derived from Kleinwort Benson Securities Limited, London, 1996

Table 15.2: World room holdings by quoted company, 1995
(minimum holding of 1,000 rooms)

Methods of ownership/operation are significantly different by region. Thi
illustrated in Tables 15.3 and 15.4 which show the distribution, by room st
of the holdings of all 62 companies on the Kleinwort Benson database by
categories:

- rooms owned;
- rooms leased;
- management contracts with an equity stake;
- management contracts without an equity stake;
- franchised operations.

Table 15.3 shows distribution of rooms by major region and Table 15.4 sho
in rather more geographical detail, the mix of different forms of ownership/op
ation by named country/grouping, in percentage terms.

Area	Rooms owned	Rooms Leased	Mgt Con'ct. Eq. Stake	Mgt Con'ct No Eq. Stake	Franchised	Total
Total Europe	234083	20049	2705	62889	95664	41539
USA	148320	4736	15082	353944	905978	142806
Total Americas	170148	9495	18440	383833	976484	155584
Asia	11465	687	6239	61081	12114	9158
Rest of the World	15218	7279	2388	64003	2901	9178
Overall Total	430914	37510	29772	571806	1087163	215716

Source: Kleinwort Benson Securities Limited, London, 1996

Table 15.3: Quoted hotel room stock, by area and ownership / operation type, 1995 (room

Regions exhibit different ownership profiles. It has already been establish
that the USA is the largest domestic market in terms of rooms operated by the
companies. It is further shown that, together with its neighbour Canada,
exhibits a high rate of franchise operations. On the other hand Europe in ge
eral and the UK in particular exhibit low rates of franchising. Less develop
destinations for hotel chains such as Asia and 'Rest of the World' will be me
likely to depend on Management Contracting (with no equity stake).

The data show that chains differ greatly in their size and sophistication.
addition the mix of ownership/operations methods currently used in differe
parts of the world show substantial variations. This implies that the resourc

hains have at their disposal in future will vary, and that the skills required to
e successful in different regions will also alter.

Area	Rooms owned	Rooms Leased	Mgt Con'ct Eq. Stake	Mgt Con'ct No Eq. Stake	Franchised	Total
Europe:						
France	39.1	0.6	0.5	19.0	40.8	100
Germany	46.3	7.5	0.9	16.8	28.5	100
Italy	56.5	3.0	0.4	19.4	20.7	100
Spain	90.4	0.0	1.6	4.6	3.5	100
UK	84.8	9.7	0.5	3.9	1.1	100
Rest W. Europe	46.0	4.9	1.4	23.5	24.2	100
(Total W. Europe	57.5	5.0	0.7	14.2	22.6	100)
East Europe	22.9	0.0	0.0	41.2	35.8	100
Total Europe	56.4	4.8	0.7	15.1	23.0	100
Americas:						
USA	10.4	0.3	1.1	24.8	63.4	100
Canada	9.3	0.5	3.1	18.4	68.7	100
Rest of Americas	26.0	7.5	2.0	28.5	36.0	100
Total Americas	10.9	0.6	1.2	24.6	62.7	100
Asia	12.5	0.8	6.8	66.7	13.2	100
Rest of the World	16.6	7.9	2.6	69.7	3.2	100
Overall Total	**20.0**	**1.7**	**1.4**	**26.5**	**50.4**	**100**

Note: Figure rounding leads to minor arithmetical errors in two cases. These are not
significant.

Source: Kleinwort Benson Securities Limited, London, 1996

*Table 15.4: Quoted hotel room stock, by area and ownership/operation type, 1995
rooms shown in percentage distribution by area)*

CONCLUSION

Managers in hotels, as in other businesses, face considerable challenges a
organizations adapt to fast-changing economic and social condition:
Turbulence affecting their planning arises from changes inside the organizatio
as well as from outside forces. General prescriptions for strategy in an era
change are remarkably few. While managers can inform their analysis by th
works on a broad business plane: e.g. Porter (1980), Goold and Campbell (1987
these must be adapted to their own particular circumstances – in this case, tha
of the hotel chain. As informed by the analysis in this chapter, chains then
selves vary greatly. While they share a complexity in their multi-site natur
there are great differences in their internal features as well as their enviror
ments. Solutions that deliver competitive advantage are unlikely to be off-the
shelf.

Contemporary resource-based views provide a solid foundation on which
start the analytic process. Their approach concentrates on identifying core con
petencies, promoting collective learning and through the development of link
across conventional organizational boundaries. This appears not only to provid
a framework for analysis, but also to present the beginnings of a solution as
addresses the need for 'boundary spanners' referred to in the chapter. In on
way this role can be seen as an updating of that undertaken by th
founder/leader at earlier times in smaller organizations – they were the orig
nal boundary spanners. Creating favourable conditions for this to happen with
in a much larger multi-site organization may not be a simple proces.
Traditional functional specialisms and geographic distance separating unit
from head-office and from one unit to another create significant barriers t
effective communication.

Changes in the general environment combined with hotel chains' quest fc
growth will, however, add to the need for vision and performance at a corporat
level. To achieve this managers must take careful account of the environment
in which they operate: not only the global characteristics of the business env
ronment but also the particular conditions into which they decide to expand. I
this the task of analysis becomes broader and even more complex, and bound
ary spanners must be complemented by those whose vision is clear enough fc
them to prioritize action to guarantee the chain's present and future success.

REFERENCES

Daneshkhu, S. and Thornhill, J. (1996) Moscow to Sell 200 Hotels for $1 bn, *Financial Times*, 8 July, pp 1, 18.

Dunning, J. H. and Kundu, S. K. (1995) The Internationalization of the Hotel Industry – Some New Findings from a Field Study, *Management International Review* 35(2), pp 101–133.

Fitzsimmons, J. A. and Fitzsimmons, M. J. (1994) *Service Management for Competitive Advantage* New York: McGraw Hill Inc.

Forte, C. (1987) *Forte: The Autobiography of Charles Forte* p 117, London: Pan Books.

Goold, M. and Campbell, A. (1987) *Strategies and Styles* Oxford: Blackwell.

Kogut, B. (1983) Foreign Direct Investment as a Sequential Process,. In C.P. Kindleberger and D. Ausretsch (eds) *The Multinational Corporation in the 1980s* Cambridge, MA: MIT Press.

Nickson, D. (1996) Colourful Stories or Historical Insight? – A Review of the Auto/Biographies of Charles Forte, Conrad Hilton, J W Marriott and Kemmos Wilson, *Fifth Annual Hospitality Research Conference, Council for Hospitality Management Education* Nottingham Trent University, April 1996, pp. 176–190.

Olsen, M. (1989) Issues Facing Multi-unit Hospitality Organizations in a Maturing Market, *Journal of Contemporary Hospitality Management* 1(2), pp 3–7.

Olsen, M. (1995) Events Shaping The Future Of The Hotel Industry. In P. Slattery, G. Feehely and M. Savage *Quoted Hotel Companies* pp 92–95 London: Kleinwort Benson.

Pannel Kerr Forster Associates (1989) *Institutional Investment in the Hotel Industry* London.

Porter, M. (1980) *Competitive Strategy* New York: Free Press.

Roberts, C. and Shea, L. (1996) Core Capabilities in the Hotel Industry, *Hospitality Research Journal* 19(4), pp 141–153.

Prahalad, C. K. and Hamel, G. (1990) The Core Competence of the Corporation, *Harvard Business Review* May/Jun, pp 79–91.

Segal-Horn, S. (1995) Core Competence and International Strategy in Service Multinationals. In R. Teare and C. Armistead (eds) *Services Management: New Directions, New Perspectives* Conference Proceedings, University of Bournemouth.

Slattery, P. (1992) Unaffiliated Hotels in the UK, *Travel and Tourism Analyst* 1 pp 90–102.

Slattery, P., Feehely, G., Savage, M. and Tull, Z. (1996) *Quoted Hotel Companies – The World Markets, 10th Annual Review* London: Kleinwort Benson.

Index of Names

Subject Index